T0358503

ECONOMIC HISTORY

AMERICAN BUSINESS CYCLES 1945–50

NORTH AMERICA

AMERICAN BUSINESS CYCLES 1945–50

C.A. BLYTH

LONDON AND NEW YORK

First published in 1969

Reprinted in 2006 by
Routledge
2 Park Square, Milton Park, Abingdon, Oxon, OX14 4RN

Routledge is an imprint of Taylor & Francis Group

Transferred to Digital Print 2010

© 1969 C.A. Blyth

All rights reserved. No part of this book may be reprinted or reproduced or utilized in any form or by any electronic, mechanical, or other means, now known or hereafter invented, including photocopying and recording, or in any information storage or retrieval system, without permission in writing from the publishers.

The publishers have made every effort to contact authors and copyright holders of the works reprinted in the *Economic History* series. This has not been possible in every case, however, and we would welcome correspondence from those individuals or organisations we have been unable to trace.

These reprints are taken from original copies of each book. In many cases the condition of these originals is not perfect. The publisher has gone to great lengths to ensure the quality of these reprints, but wishes to point out that certain characteristics of the original copies will, of necessity, be apparent in reprints thereof.

British Library Cataloguing in Publication Data
A CIP catalogue record for this book
is available from the British Library

American Business Cycles 1945–50
ISBN 0-415-38003-0 (volume)
ISBN 0-415-37974-1 (subset)
ISBN 0-415-28619-0 (set)

Routledge Library Editions: Economic History

AMERICAN BUSINESS CYCLES 1945–50

By the same Author

THE USE OF ECONOMIC STATISTICS

4th printing

AMERICAN BUSINESS CYCLES 1945–50

C. A. Blyth

PRAEGER PUBLISHERS
New York · Washington

has shock absorbers, and requires a more or less continuous sequence of pushes to show any sustained rocking movement. Where in the range of possible stages in the analogy should postwar business fluctuations be placed? What has been the relative importance of shocks (pushes or pulls) and structural properties such as lags, multipliers and accelerators? Is there a pronounced, systematic, cyclical fluctuation in the industrial economies or is it mainly a matter of specific, accidental happenings? Out of these questions come others more specifically designed for statesmen and their advisers: What has been the effect of government intervention (whether it has been intended to be stabilizing or otherwise)? Has the growth since 1945 been inescapably unstable, and if so, to what extent and why?

The research on which this book is based was started as part of a study of business fluctuations since 1945 in the industrial economies and their effect on the primary exporting economies. Because of an earlier interest in the 1948–49 American recession I began the study by reviewing the early postwar American business fluctuations. It quickly became apparent to me that not only was a detailed case study of business fluctuations between the end of World War II and the beginning of the Korean War needed to understand the 1948–49 recession, but such a study would go a long way to giving answers to the more general questions about business cycles and instability since 1945. This book is my report on that case study. The core of it is a description and analysis of the changes in economic activity between 1945 and 1950, covering demobilization and reconversion, inflation, the 1948 downturn, the recession and the recovery. This case study is prefaced by a survey of American business fluctuations from 1945 to 1967, intended to put the early postwar changes in perspective and provide a basis for comparison.

The progress of knowledge depends upon the separation of regular from unusual features of change. The model which seems to me to be most useful in explaining the modern business cycle in the United States makes this separation quite explicitly (it is set out in both the first and last chapters). I have relied extensively on the published econometric results of others to provide, where it seems appropriate, the means of isolating regularities in economic behaviour. I think my use of the econometric results, while I may have committed some errors and made omissions, reflects the strengths and weaknesses of present econometric research, in particular its modest success in unravelling the strands in private consumption and investment behaviour, and its failure to quantify the inflationary process in an unambiguous way. The notes at the end of the book provide a selective review of the econometric research used as well as material to supplement the statements in the chapters.

Not only has the writing of this book depended on the published research of others, but it has also depended on the comments and criticism of many friends. Harry Johnson and Nicholas Kaldor in Cambridge in 1954 first encouraged me to explore what seemed then to be some odd features of the 1948–49 recession, thus starting an interest which has continued ever since. Max Corden and David Butt in Canberra have challenged me to make clear what I thought econometrics was saying. Heinz Arndt constructively criticized early drafts of the book. Sir John Hicks commented on an early version of Chapter 7. But most of all I have been fortunate in Rendigs Fels giving his time to provide me with detailed comments on the penultimate draft.[1] Professor Fels has acted most generously in giving me the benefit of his knowledge and scholarship, and while he is in no way responsible for my errors and omissions, his assistance has enormously improved the content and presentation of my work: in particular his comments on my original analysis of inflation in 1946 and on the 1948 fiscal and monetary changes forced me to rethink and alter my approach to those problems. I have indicated in some places my indebtedness to particular suggestions, but in fact the whole book as it now stands is a response to Professor Fels' comments and criticism. If all authors could rely on such help, fewer books would be written and those that were written would be better.

I have been fortunate in having in Mrs Beverly Gothe a research assistant who has taken a personal interest in this study from its beginnings, and who has helped efficiently and cheerfully in all its stages from reading the *New York Times* to

[1] Professor Fels has asked me to record that during the time he read my manuscript he was the beneficiary of a grant from the National Science Foundation, without which he could not have devoted so much time to it.

compiling the index. The typing of the final draft has been done with speed and care by Mrs Helena Michel, and Miss Sue Haeney skilfully drew the figures ready for printing.

Canberra,
April, 1968. C. A. Blyth

NOTE ON REFERENCES, ABBREVIATIONS AND STATISTICAL SOURCES AND CONVENTIONS

1. First references to books and articles in the text are given in full; subsequent references are given by author and date of publication; the full reference is repeated in the List of References on p. 289.

Abbreviations of titles of journals used are as follows:

Amer. econ. R.	*American Economic Review*
Econ. J.	*Economic Journal*
FRB	*Federal Reserve Bulletin*, including its occasional industrial production supplements
J. polit. Econ.	*Journal of Political Economy*
Manchester Sch.	*Manchester School*
National Tax J.	*National Tax Journal*
NYT	*New York Times*
R. Econ. Statist.	*Review of Economics and Statistics*
SCB	*Survey of Current Business*, including its biennial supplement Business Statistics and occasional national income supplements.

2. Detailed references to standard official statistical sources are not normally given. The basic statistical sources that have been used unless the contrary is indicated are:

National income, expenditure and output: 1966 Supplement to the *Survey of Current Business, National Income and Product Accounts of the United States*, 1929–1965. Balance of payments: 1962 Supplement to the *Survey of Current Business, Balance of Payments Statistical Supplement Revised Edition.*

Indexes of industrial production: *Industrial Production*—1957–59 *Base* (Washington: Board of Governors of the Federal Reserve System, 1962).

Other statistics: biennial supplement *Business Statistics* to the *Survey of Current Business.*

3. All references to GNP, output or expenditure are to quantities measured at constant 1958 prices (i.e. as volume indexes), adjusted to remove regular seasonal influences, and expressed as annual rates, unless the contrary is indicated explicitly or by the context. References to income are to undeflated money income unless the contrary is indicated.

4. One billion means one thousand million.

5. I, II, III and IV are used to indicate quarters of the calendar year. Thus 1946 I means January, February and March of 1946.

6. The words 'output' and 'production' are used, whenever the context is clear, as alternatives to the more cumbersome 'gross national product' and the infelicitous 'GNP'. Similarly 'volume of consumption' is used as a synonym for 'PCE at 1958 prices'.

7. *Other abbreviations:*

BLS	Bureau of Labor Statistics
CBI	Change in business inventories
CCC	Commodity Credit Corporation
CPI	Consumer price index
DPI	Disposable personal income
FHA	Federal Housing Administration
FNMA	Federal National Mortgage Association
FR	Federal Reserve System
GNP	Gross national product
NBER	National Bureau of Economic Research
OBE	Office of Business Economics, U.S. Department of Commerce
PCE	Personal consumption expenditures
PFI	Private fixed investment
VA	Veteran's Administration.

8. In the econometric notes, $\bar{R}^2$ is the correlation coefficient adjusted for degrees of freedom, brackets indicate the standard error of a regression coefficient, and the statistic used for testing serial correlation in residuals is shown where available.

CONTENTS

TABLES

CHAPTER I

The American Business Cycle, 1945 to 1967

Since 1945 the United States economy has continued to experience alternating recessions and expansions in business activity. Leaving aside the fall in output following the end of the Second World War, there have been serious recessions in 1948–49, 1953–54, 1957–58 and 1960–61 when industrial production and employment fell sharply and for several months. Each was followed by an equally rapid, though short-lived (except in 1950), rise in output. In 1950 the expansion was prolonged by the Korean War rearmament. As well as these major fluctuations in activity there were marked pauses in expansions—substantial declines in the rate of growth—in 1951–52, 1962–63 and 1967. The fluctuations in the rate of growth of U.S. industrial output are shown in Fig. 1.1 which also indicates the conventional periods of business cycle expansion (from trough to peak in business activity) and contraction or recession (from peak to trough) determined by the National Bureau of Economic Research. These postwar fluctuations differ from those of the interwar period in several ways. As Table 1.1 shows, leaving aside the wartime expansion of 1938–45, postwar expansions have typically lasted longer than those in the interwar period, while postwar contractions have typically been of shorter duration than those earlier. More important, perhaps, is the fact that the extent of contractions, measured by the declines in industrial production, has been much less severe since 1945 than before. After the economy made its rapid conversion from war to peace in 1945, in not one of the four succeeding recessions did industrial production fall more than 15 per cent. In 1920–21,

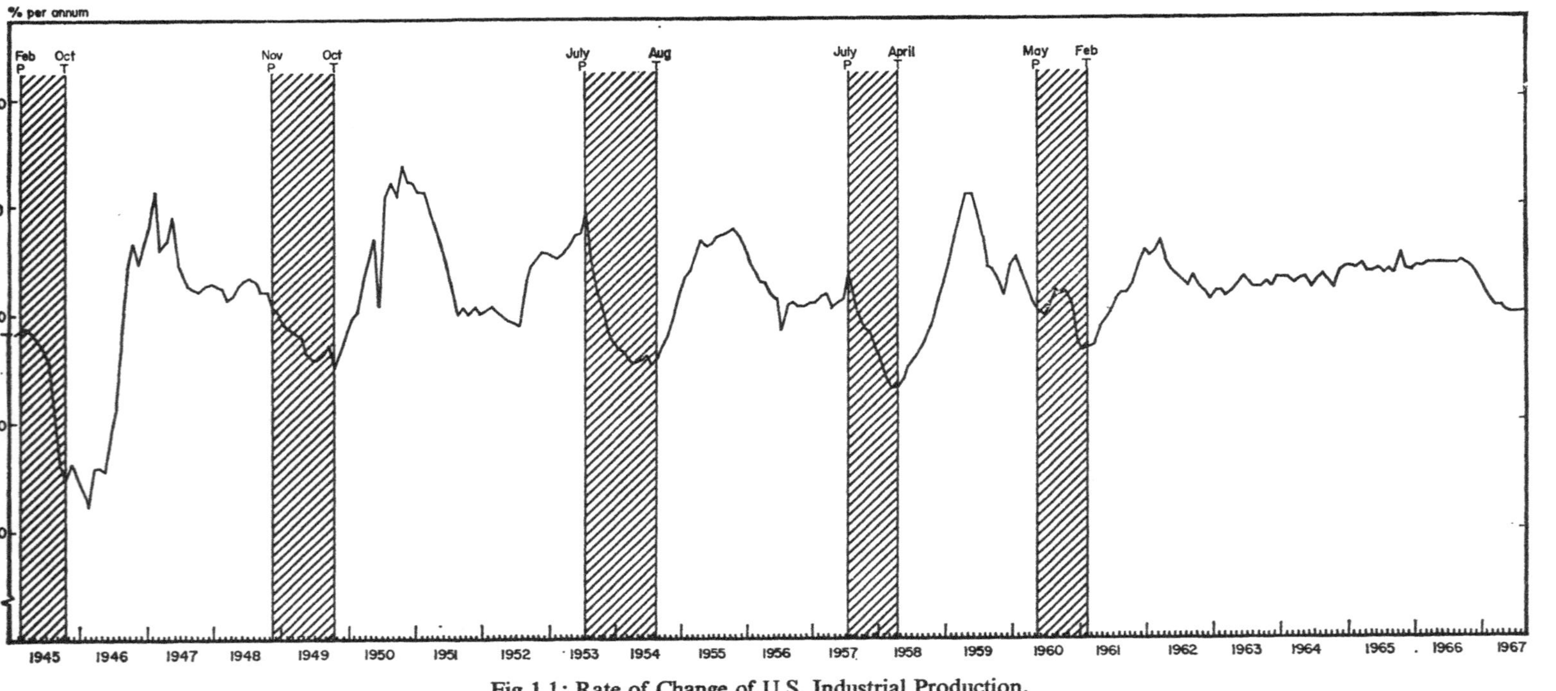

Fig 1.1: Rate of Change of U.S. Industrial Production.

Source: FRB. Shaded areas represent periods of contraction determined by NBER as in Table 1.1.

TABLE I.1: *Chronology and Severity of U.S. Business Cycles 1919 to 1967*

Dates of*		*Duration in months of*		*Percentage Fall in Industrial*
Trough	*Peak*	*Expansion*	*Contraction†*	*Production During Contraction‡*
March 1919	January 1920	10	18	32·4
July 1921	May 1923	22	14	17·9
July 1924	October 1926	27	13	6·1
November 1927	August 1929	21	43	53·4
March 1933	May 1937	50	13	32·4
June 1938	February 1945	80	8	31·4
October 1945	November 1948	37	11	8·3
October 1949	July 1953	45	13	10·0
August 1954	July 1957	35	9	14·3
April 1958	May 1960	25	9	7·5
February 1961		71§		

* As determined by the National Bureau of Economic Research. See G. H. Moore and J. Shiskin, 'Indicators of Business Expansions and Contractions', NBER Occasional Paper 103 (New York: NBER, 1967), Appendix F, p. 113.

† From peak in same line to trough in next line.

‡ Measured from peak to trough in FRB Index of Industrial Production, whose peaks and troughs do not coincide exactly with the NBER business cycle peaks and troughs.

§ Up to December 1967 the expansion since February 1961 had lasted 71 months.

1923–24 and 1937–38 the falls were much greater, while that of 1929–33 was disastrous. Only the 1926–27 fall was lighter than those after 1945. This mildness of postwar recessions is the main explanation of the absence since the end of the war of prolonged bouts of mass unemployment like those in 1921–22 and throughout the decade of the 1930s.

Yet despite the improvement in the performance of the American economy, fluctuations persist and have severe effects on the welfare of both the United States and the world overseas. Between March 1957 and July 1958, unemployment rose from 3·8 per cent to 7·5 per cent of the labour force, and again between May 1960 and May 1961 it jumped from 5·2 per cent to 7·1 per cent which represents an increase of about 1·4 million people. In most recessions the volume of American imports has fallen and prices of internationally traded goods declined, usually creating balance of payments problems and pauses in growth for many developing and developed countries. Fluctuations in American economic activity are still of concern both domestically and internationally.

This chapter provides a survey of postwar fluctuations in activity, together with an outline of a model which provides a useful framework within which the fluctuations can be understood. A brief discussion of the relative importance of regular and irregular influences on household, business and government behaviour concludes the chapter: these influences are explored in greater detail in the subsequent chapters and notes. To allow this chapter to be a short introduction to the subject supporting statistics and authorities are not referred to: it is in effect a preview of things to come, and the student will find references in the subsequent chapters, notes and bibliography.

RECONSTRUCTION CYCLE, 1945–50

The decline in output at the end of the war was due to the rapid ending of defence production and demobilization. After delays due to shortages and strikes civilian production rose in early 1946 to satisfy a high level of demand for all goods and services, partly due to the desire of consumers and businessmen to re-stock, partly to the exceptionally large hoards of savings accumulated during the war, and partly to the strong demand

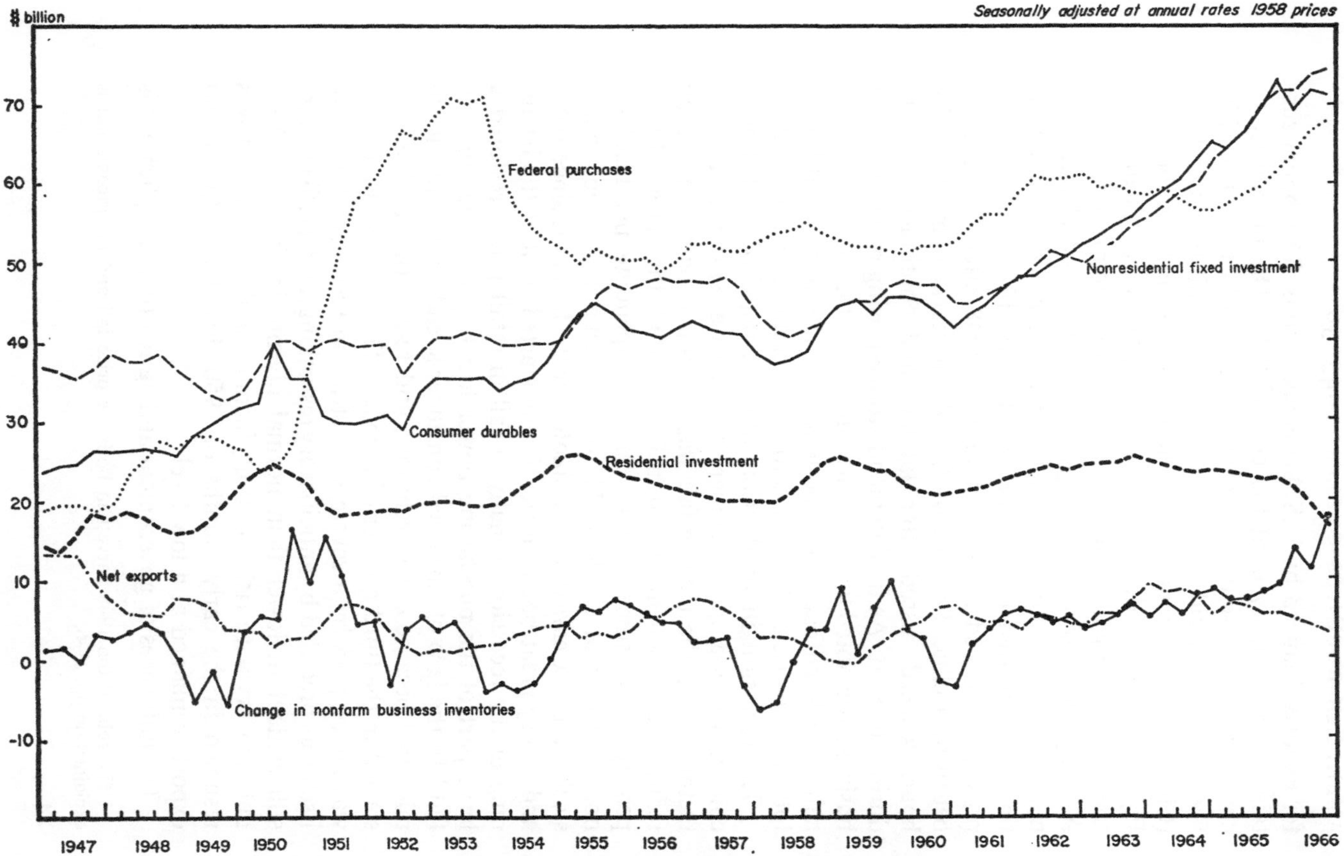

Fig. 1.2: Unstable components of U.S. gross national product.
Source: SCB.

for exports financed by U.S. loans and grants. This boom sustained the economy until the end of 1947. The propensity to consume did not return to normal levels until early 1948 while fixed investment did not start to taper off until the same time. (Changes in components of national expenditure are shown in Fig. 1.2.) Exports declined from mid-1947 as European countries used up their credits or satisfied their immediate needs. Although some serious shortages still persisted—steel and automobiles were the most prominent—excess demand by all indications disappeared during the first half of 1948. The postwar price rise reached its peak in January 1948 after which levels began to decline. Pressure on the labour market—measured by hours worked—eased after January and continued to relax during the year. As final demand stopped rising most sectors of business attempted to reduce inventory investment. In the second half of 1948 cutbacks in production became general, although total inventories did not fall until the second quarter of 1949.

The recession in production was not matched by a fall in consumer spending. Consumer spending was sustained by four factors. First, the income fall was to some extent made up by reduced tax payments and transfers. Second, the marginal propensity to consume rose to maintain spending per head on nondurables and services. Third, the general recession made steel and hence cars freely available (for the first time since 1941) and a very great boom in car buying started right at the beginning of the recession. Finally, a fall in retail prices restored a large part of the purchasing power lost by the money income fall.[1] In the face of sustained consumer spending, inventories in mid-1949 became excessively low, and re-ordering by business started in the third quarter of the year. The process of recovery was interrupted by a severe steel strike in October—the strike itself was preceded by anticipatory restocking, and its effects were still evident in lower than normal inventories in mid-1950—but recovery with rising output, incomes and employment was resumed in the early months of 1950. Fixed investment and exports remained at a low level.

The influences of government and agriculture complicate this

[1] The role of the 1948 harvest in both the price fall and the income fall is explained on pp. 25–6.

story. That of government took several forms. Firstly, in late 1947 rearmament began, and defence expenditures rose until mid-1949. During the final quarter of 1947, when fears of inflation were strong, interest rates were raised and there was a general credit squeeze. The most obvious and important effect was a stifling of the residential mortgage market. Until then the building industry had been booming. After the end of the year new housing starts declined sharply and residential construction fell after mid-1948. The decline was short lived: interest rates started to fall again in early 1949 and with the mortgage market easing again housing starts rose. During the second half of 1949 construction was a powerful force for recovery. Nevertheless in late 1948 the recession in housebuilding both in its direct effect, as well as its influence on inventory accumulation and production of building materials and on purchases of household furnishings and equipment, was a significant factor in the general downturn. Other actions of government were clearly expansionary in late 1948 and early 1949: increased foreign aid, the income tax reductions in the 1948 Revenue Act and the measures to stabilize farm incomes (see below). The overall effect of Federal fiscal actions which had on balance been deflationary in 1947 and early 1948, became clearly expansionary during the course of 1948. This change was reinforced in early 1949 by the operation of the 'automatic' fiscal stabilizers—falls in tax receipts and increases in transfers caused by the decline in business activity.

The second complicating influence is agriculture. After a series of poor harvests and heavy foreign demand for wheat, the U.S. in 1948 experienced an exceptionally large grain harvest. Early prospects of this caused the first break in agricultural prices in January 1948 and after the middle of the year the falling grain prices were causing meat prices to decline also. The resulting large fall in food prices (together with a fall in cotton and hence textile prices) was responsible for the fall in the cost of living in early 1949. The Federal Government responded to the fall in prices in the second half of 1948 and in 1949 with substantial loans and purchases under the agricultural support policies, but despite this farmers' incomes fell by nearly one-third between mid-1948 and mid-1949. The significance of this fall is that after reduction in tax and increases in transfers are allowed for, the fall in total personal disposable income over this twelve month period roughly equals the fall in farm income. This fall was partly compensated by the effect on consumption of the price fall.

The 1948–49 recession was caused by a reduction in growth in aggregate demand which precipitated a fall in inventory investment. The reduced growth of demand reflected primarily the end of the postwar restocking boom in which consumers filled their cupboards and wardrobes (but not their garages), and businessmen restored their inventories and productive capacity; it also resulted from autonomous factors of which the declines in residential building and exports and the fall in farm incomes, were the most important. The fall in inventory investment led to cutbacks in output, employment and incomes, but the declines were of short duration because actual inventory levels quickly fell below desired levels. This was partly due to the short-run stability of consumption of nondurable goods; it was also partly due to a rising Federal deficit and the large rise in automobile purchases due to the increasing availability of steel. By mid-1949 the agricultural changes had ceased to be depressing and were on balance expansionary—farm incomes had stopped falling and declines in retail prices were raising real incomes.

There were at least two inevitable features of the recession. First, after the end of the war business had increased fixed investment to carry out replacements of assets deferred during the war, and to raise civilian production capacity to the expected postwar levels. These levels on the whole were correctly anticipated, and once the capacity was installed excess demand was removed from both directions: supplies became more freely available and demand for capital goods declined. Second, exports had to decline from their abnormally high 1946 and 1947 levels. By contrast one feature was definitely not inevitable: the decline in residential construction; and there was one which probably could not be foreseen: the good harvest of 1948. The marginal propensity to consume was an uncertain factor: it had to decline from its abnormally high 1947 level, but in 1948 the timing of the decline and the effect on it of developments in the car market were unpredictable.

KOREAN CYCLE, 1950–54

In June 1950 the U.S. economy was again operating at a high level of activity. Residential construction was expanding rapidly, inventory investment was rising and the car market was for the first time since 1941 approaching an equilibrium. Industrial employment and hours worked were high (although the unemployment rate was relatively high largely due to the decline in farm employment). For the first time since the late 1920s the U.S. economy was booming without the special stimulus of war or postwar recovery. How long this boom would have lasted, uninterrupted by other events, cannot be measured. With industrial fixed investment starting to pick up again at mid-year, it would almost certainly have continued well into 1951. But the outbreak of the Korean War at the end of June altered every plan.

On the economy the Korean War had two main effects. It caused first a great burst of household buying and inventory accumulation which pulled the output of consumer goods—both durables and nondurables—to high levels. The consumer buying came in two bursts: in the months immediately following the U.S. involvement in the war, and again in the two or three months after the Chinese intervention at the end of November. Part of the increases was due to rising incomes; but a distinct part was for hoarding semi-durables like processed foods and textiles which it was feared would become scarce and for buying durables like cars the production of which might cease as happened during World War II. The second wave of buying subsided in the second quarter of 1951, mainly of its own accord: consumers had in a short period of time bought the durable goods which normally they would have bought over a much longer period: this bunching of purchases was inevitably followed by a fall in demand. Government controls may have had some effect on speculative behaviour: controls on consumer credit were imposed as early as September 1950, and on residential credit in October. Price and wage ceilings set at the end of January 1951 removed the incentive to anticipate price increases. Faced with a tightening mortgage market at the end of July 1950 (the result of official action) housing starts fell after August.

Inventories of consumer goods rose in the final quarter of 1950—the lull between the two bursts of consumer demand—and in the second quarter of 1951 when consumer demand had started to decline. After the first quarter of 1951 retailers found their inventories too high and their attempts to reduce their inventories together with falling sales led to a general fall in the production of consumer goods in the second and third quarters of 1951. This output—especially of durable goods—stayed at a low level until the second half of 1952.

The second main effect of the war was to launch a large rearmament programme. The initial plans laid in 1950 envisaged a gradual rise in the size of the armed forces and in defence production until the mid-1950s when the maximum threat from Russia and her allies was expected. The Chinese intervention caused the date of the maximum threat and the peak defence build-up to be brought forward to 1952–53. The armed forces expanded from just over 1½ millions in early 1950 to about 3½ millions in early 1952. Defence production rose rapidly from August 1950 to the second quarter of 1951, after which it continued to rise for the next two years but at a slower rate. In the early stages, parallel with the placing of military orders, a rapid rise occurred in the inventories of durable goods manufacturers.

From mid-1951 to mid-1952 the level of aggregate activity was remarkably steady. Rising defence production took up the slack left by falling inventory investment and reduced production of consumer goods. The percentage of unemployed in the civilian labour force which had been 5·4 per cent in June 1950, fell to 3·3 per cent a year later and was 3·1 per cent in June 1952. Disposable personal incomes were steady and so were consumer expenditures. Fixed investment—both business and residential—remained unchanged. The unstable factor was traders' inventory investment. As was pointed out above, this was cut back in the second quarter of 1951 when consumer demand receded to normal levels. As production fell inventories actually declined throughout the second half of 1951 and first half of 1952. Partly the decline was due to shortages—especially of durable goods and automobiles. Partly it was due to excessive production cutbacks. By early 1952 it was obvious that consumer demand was not falling, and that inventories were unduly low. At the same time many materials, until then rationed for defence production, became more freely available, while at the end of June controls over consumer credit expired.

There followed around June 1952—and interrupted by the simultaneous steel strike—a strong restocking boom, undoubtedly fed by the feeling that the Korean War was probably over: output of consumer goods—especially household equipment and furnishings—rose strongly in the third quarter of the year. Automobile production, delayed by the strike, followed in the final quarter. Considerable pressure was placed on the labour force: manufacturing employment rose, bringing the unemployment rate down below 3 per cent, while hours worked increased. Personal income rose, and expenditures on nondurables and services increased steadily. There was a sharp rise in expenditures on durables of all types. Traders' inventory investment rose until the end of 1952, after which it slackened off as consumer demand stopped rising.

This small consumer goods boom occurred while major shifts of direction were taking place in rearmament policy. The defence budgets adopted in 1950 and 1951 foresaw defence expenditures rising in the fiscal years 1952, 1953 and 1954. The budget for fiscal 1953, adopted in 1952, had as a background the onset of stalemate in Korea, and the impending presidential and congressional elections. The defence spending authority was cut, with the likely result that new military orders would decline in fiscal 1953 and spending would reach a peak and decline in fiscal 1954. This in fact is what happened. Defence production continued to rise throughout 1952 and early 1953, reached a peak in July–August of that year, and fell by nearly 15 per cent in the next nine months. Defence expenditures reached a peak in the second quarter of 1953 and fell by nearly 20 per cent in the next twelve months. With the fall-off in defence production there was a fall in defence manufacturers' inventories of work in process and materials which accounts for all of the fall in manufacturing inventory investment which took place from mid-1953 to mid-1954. The decline in defence orders stopped at the end of 1953 and during 1954 these orders rose again leading to a small revival of defence goods production in early 1955.

The cuts in defence output began to affect household incomes in August when both hours worked and employment in manufacturing declined. Between July 1953 and July 1954 wages and salaries paid in manufacturing industry fell by over 8 per cent. However, the effect of this and other falls in personal incomes were offset by increased transfers (unemployment and veterans benefits) and reduced taxes. Real personal disposable income fell by no more than half a per cent between the second quarters of 1953 and 1954. Total consumer expenditures remained unchanged, although there was a significant change in composition no doubt reflecting the changed income distribution during the recession: purchases of clothing declined in the second half of 1953, and sales of automobiles fell in the last quarter of 1953 and the first of 1954. The consequence was that output of consumer goods declined between July and December 1953 and there was a fall in retailers' inventory investment during this period. By the second quarter of 1954, however, when it was clear that consumer spending in general was not declining, inventories and output of consumer goods were rising again.

The 1953–54 recession was caused by the fall in defence production, although the effects of this fall were aggravated by the dear money policy of the spring of 1953 and its effect on house building (see below). Most of the fall in inventory investment in the fifteen months after mid-1953 was the direct consequence of falling defence output—reduction in work in process and of stocks of materials in firms making armaments. The initial reduction in defence output and employment stopped personal income from rising, checked the growth of consumer expenditure and caused some reduction in traders' inventories. This secondary effect of the defence output fall was shortlived: personal income was maintained by increased Federal transfers and falls in tax payments. Aggregate consumer spending was maintained during a period when the unemployment rate rose from 2·6 per cent (in July 1953) to 6·2 per cent (in September 1954) and when hours worked fell correspondingly.

The main expansionary force during the recession was residential construction. After its decline at the end of 1950 and in early 1951 housebuilding had remained at a steady level until the end of 1952 when it experienced a small rise following the easing of credit controls and rising personal incomes (the boom in household furnishings and equipment was undoubtedly related to this small rise). The rise was nipped in the bud, however, by the tightening of money markets and general rise in interest rates which followed the raising of the Federal Reserve Banks' discount rate in January 1953. The authorities were concerned about the possibility of inflation, especially with the removal of wage and price controls at that time, and adopted a policy of restraint. It is likely they went too far. In the words of the President's Economic Report of 1954:

'The restrictive monetary and debt management policies pursued in the early months of the year had . . . a more potent effect than was generally expected. . . . The demand for credit that developed in May and June was not, therefore confined to the funds needed for current operations . . . some lenders became reluctant to commit funds for future use. . . . The Federal Reserve authorities responded to the incipient, and possibly dangerous, scramble for liquidity with a degree of promptness and vigor for which there is no close parallel in our central bank history.' (p. 50)

Despite the promptness of the reversal, mortgage yields rose from 4·5 per cent to over 5 per cent in mid-1953 and new housing starts fell by 12 per cent between March and August.

However, with the adoption of an easy credit policy in the second half of 1953 and the beginning of a fall in interest rates after the middle of the year—a fall which continued throughout 1954—the stage was set for a substantial rise in housebuilding. New starts picked up in the last quarter of 1953 and rose throughout 1954. The volume of residential construction rose by 24 per cent between the final quarters of 1953 and 1954 (and continued to rise during the first half of 1955 although the peak in new starts had been passed in December 1954). With this construction went a substantial increase of consumer expenditure on home furnishings and equipment.

The other factors which had expansionary effects at different times in 1953 and 1954 were Federal expenditures to support agriculture which offset to some extent the fall in farm incomes during 1953; the rise in state and local government expenditures, some of which was normal expansion, some attributable to the recession; a slow but persistent rise in exports throughout 1953 and 1954; and the increase in defence orders in 1954.

By the third quarter of 1954 the combined effect of these expansionary forces was offsetting the decline in defence output and disposable personal income was starting to rise. In the last quarter of the year personal consumption was responding and rising strongly, consumer goods output was rising faster and the inventory decline was tapering off.

The significant features of the 1953–54 recession are first, the role of falling defence output; second the use of Federal fiscal policy in sustaining personal income; third, the changes in monetary policy and the cyclical behaviour of residential construction; and finally the unimportance of inventory investment in any role as primary cause either of the recession or of the revival.

PEACEFUL CYCLE 1955–58

At the end of 1954 the economy was recovering rapidly. One of the main forces, residential building, continued to rise until mid-1955 after which rising mortgage rates caused a slow decline until the end of 1957. The recovery in 1955 was maintained by a large rise in fixed investment required to replace old plant and enlarge capacity as industrial production in early 1955 rose above previous peak levels of output. Fixed investment rose to a high level in mid-1956, and maintained this level for another year. Under the stimulus of this and other demands for durable goods, inventory investment by durable goods manufacturers rose to a very high level in the first half of 1956. Real personal disposable incomes increased by over 7 per cent between the end of 1954 and the end of 1955 and consumer demand responded. There ensued a tremendous increase in automobile purchases—they rose by over one-third between the end of 1954 and mid-1955. From the peak in the third quarter of 1955 they declined during the next twelve months back to 1954 levels, but total consumption did not decline. During 1956 both real disposable incomes and consumption expenditures rose at an annual rate of about 2½ per cent.

The end of the boom in 1957 and the recession in 1958 were

brought on by two major influences. First, and most important, was the natural ending of the fixed investment boom. By the second half of 1956 planned capacity equalled desired capacity, although with the lengthy lags in the fixed investment process it was nearly two years before the extra capacity was installed. New orders placed with equipment manufacturers declined from the end of 1956. Production of equipment started to decline in the second quarter of 1956; shipments fell in the final quarter.

The second influence was a fall in defence production. Since 1953 the ordering and output of defence goods had fluctuated. After the big fall in defence orders in 1953 and the consequent decline in defence production there were two successive periods of rising orders, each followed by a rise in defence output. In the first, orders rose in 1954 and fell during the first half of 1955. Output consequently rose during 1955 to a peak in the third quarter, declining by about 10 per cent during the next three quarters. This decline was offset by rising demand for other types of durable goods. In the second period orders rose after the middle of 1955 to reach a high level in mid-1956, after which they fell. Output of defence products consequently, after rising again in the second half of 1956, fell in the second quarter of 1957. Between April 1957 and February 1958 production of defence equipment dropped by 16 per cent. Not only was this fall much greater than that in early 1956, but it occurred when output of other types of durable goods was also falling.

With the fall in equipment orders—both civilian and military—there was an immediate decline in inventory accumulation by durable goods manufacturers: up to the first quarter of 1956 their inventory investment had been rising; thereafter it began to fall and in the final quarter of 1957 and first half of 1958 inventories were substantially reduced.

Other depressing influences were relatively unimportant. Two which played small parts were the fall in exports in 1957 in British, Canadian and Japanese markets (in early 1957 U.S. exports had been swollen by oil exports due to the stopping of supplies from the Middle East); and the dear money policy adopted by the Federal Reserve from August to October 1957, the main effect of which was probably to delay the revival of housing starts. Housing starts, which had fallen throughout

1955 and 1956, showed slight signs of revival in early 1957 when mortgage yields declined. However, a large rise in yields in the second half of the year caused starts to fall again.

In 1957 and 1958 the economy responded to the depressing influences in normal ways. Although the unemployment rate rose from 3·8 per cent in March 1957 to 7·5 per cent in July 1958, and average hours worked per week fell from 40·6 in December 1956 to 38·6 in February 1958, real disposable personal income barely fell in the first half of 1958. The familiar fiscal effects and, on this occasion, a rise in farm income[1] offset the fall in wages. Personal consumption of nondurables fell slightly in the first half of 1958, while car sales slumped. As on earlier occasions the fall in durable goods production led to a fall in output of nondurable goods as manufacturers and traders trimmed their inventories in the face of expected falls in sales. When—again, as on earlier occasions—the inventory trimming went too far in the face of fairly steady sales, traders and nondurable goods manufacturers restocked in the second half of 1958. Output of consumer goods, which had fallen from October 1957 to March 1958, rose strongly in the second and subsequent quarters.

The other expansionary factor was—once again—residential construction. Housing starts reached a very low level during the first three months of 1958. Mortgage yields started to fall at the end of 1957 and by the second quarter of 1958 starts were rising rapidly. Residential construction started to rise strongly in the second half of the year and continued until mid-1959.

DISAPPOINTING CYCLE, 1959–61

In the expansion of 1959–60 the U.S. experienced two phenomena which it had hitherto escaped. In the first place the unemployment rate at no stage fell below 4·9 per cent (compared with, say, 3·8 per cent in March 1957 and 2·6 per cent in July 1953). Industrial capacity was by most measures also correspondingly under-utilized. Secondly, the U.S. started to lose gold reserves on a very large scale. After accumulating gold

[1] Due to a rise in livestock prices following bad seasons with reduced livestock numbers and meat production.

just after the Second World War, the U.S. had on balance lost gold from 1950 to 1957. But the loss after that time was on a much greater scale. The immediate cause of the loss in 1958–59 was a large deficit on current account: a rapid rise in imports as industrial production expanded (this was a normal experience) together with a decline in exports as Western European countries experienced a brief recession.

The situation became worse in 1960. Higher interest rates abroad in the middle of the year caused an outflow of short term funds, and this outflow increased with a loss of confidence in the dollar and rise in the price of gold in London late in the year. The problem was aggravated by the unwillingness of the monetary authorities to raise interest rates because of the signs that the economy was moving into recession.[1] At the end of the year confidence was restored by a Presidential declaration and a number of administrative measures to economize in the use of foreign exchange. However, the basic balance of payments problem persisted in the years ahead.

In early 1959 the economy was expanding rapidly in all sectors—rising consumption, purchases of automobiles, housebuilding, business fixed investment and inventory accumulation were all stimulating the economy. Even exports were rising. This strong boom—GNP rose by 9·2 per cent between the second quarters of 1958 and 1959—was, however, very short lived. The basic causes of its premature decease were three—although there is some interaction between them all.

The first factor was the steel strike of 1959. This began on July 15th, lasted 116 days and did not end until a Federal injunction forced the strikers back on November 9th. The strike had two effects. In the first place it was anticipated several months before it happened, and business in the second quarter proceeded to pile up inventories of steel and metal products to such an extent that manufacturers forced activity up to exceptionally high levels. These high levels of activity were one of the influences which created the inflationary pressures and fears at

[1] The Federal Reserve reduced its discount rates in the middle of the year and eased the credit situation by open market operations. Either the gold loss, or uncertainty as to whether a recession was beginning or not, may have prevented it from going further in the direction of ease. See the reference to residential construction on p. 37.

the time which led the monetary authorities to raise interest rates and restrict credit. In the second place the strike caused a great shortage of steel and a backlog of industrial orders. As soon as the strike was over output of durable goods again rose to very high levels as inventories were replenished in the final months of 1959 and first quarter of 1960. Output of all durable goods, not only iron and steel, was at an all-time high level in January 1960. Fed by a temporary restocking boom, this rate of output had to decline, and after January activity receded from its peak levels—manufacturing employment, hours worked and wage and salary bill all declined.

The second cause is the failure of the revival in business investment to develop into a strong boom as in 1955–57. The reason is probably that the boom of 1955–57 *was* a strong boom and when it tapered off it reflected a state of business opinion which foresaw no large backlog of investment projects. By early 1959 some backlog had again emerged, but it was not large and the additional capacity it represented would not raise the rate of investment to the 1955–57 levels. New orders for equipment which reached a trough at the end of 1957 rose steadily until the first quarter of 1959. Thereafter they tended to decline although not at such a rapid rate as in 1957. Production of equipment stopped rising in mid-1959, although it did not actually fall until the end of 1960. The consequence was that business fixed investment, which had risen quite rapidly until the third quarter of 1959, increased thereafter only slowly to a peak in the second quarter of 1960 (not as high as the 1956–57 level) and declined slowly thereafter.

The third factor inducing recession was Federal monetary and fiscal policy. It was suggested above that the high level of activity generated by the expected steel strike helped to form the climate for anti-inflationary policy in 1959. The balance of payments situation was an influence also. Federal Reserve discount rates were raised in March, and again in May and September. Bond yields rose sharply in the second and third quarters of the year with the usual effect on housebuilding: new starts declined rapidly during this six month period. On the fiscal front the Federal deficit (national income basis) which had been running at an annual rate of about $10 billion throughout

1958, was halved in the first quarter of 1959, and was virtually zero for the rest of the year. During the first half of 1960 the Federal surplus was over $5 billion (annual rate). This substantial swing to surplus of course reinforced strongly the tight monetary policy. In its effect on expenditure it reflected two things. One was that the 'automatic' fiscal stabilizers which worked so well in recession could be equally efficient in expansion. The other was that Federal expenditure did not rise—in fact, fell slightly—in 1959. Defence spending had been planned in 1958 and 1959 to decline, and defence expenditures in fact fell from early 1959 until mid-1960.[1] The only other important category of expenditure to fall was payments to support farm prices. This deflationary influence of Federal policy was not, of course, peculiar to 1959. Federal policy in 1955 had been virtually identical. What made monetary and fiscal policy so dangerous in 1959 and early 1960 was the weaknesses in other parts of the economy: the inventory hump caused by the strike, and the lack of strength in business fixed investment.

The great burst of durable goods inventory accumulation was over by the second quarter of 1960, and with final demand very steady in the middle of the year inventory investment began to decline in other sectors. Between January 1960 and January 1961 production of durable goods of all types fell by about 15 per cent. By May 1961 the unemployment rate was 7·1 per cent. Inventories of consumer goods fell in the last quarter of the year and the first of 1961 as output was reduced slightly. As in other recessions the increase in Federal transfer payments maintained disposable personal incomes. Beginning as early as February consumer goods production was rising again and inventory policy was being reversed. In the second quarter this revival in industrial activity was pushing up wages and salaries and causing a rise in consumer spending. Residential construction had declined until the end of 1960. The lower rates of interest in the second half of the year caused a rise in starts at the end of the year which allowed a small slow rise in construction throughout 1961. Apart from personal consumption expenditures and inventory investment, the main expansionary

[1] This fall resulted from a slow decline in defence orders throughout 1958 and 1959 which did not lead to any significant fall in output of defence equipment.

force in 1961 and early 1962 was defence expenditures arising from increased orders placed in 1960.

THE EXPANSION SINCE 1961

The expansion since the 1960–61 recession—lasting 71 months from the NBER trough in February 1961 to the end of 1967—is the second longest expansion recorded since the 1850s, exceeded only by the expansion of 1938–45 which was dominated of course by the Second World War. The other lengthy expansions were also associated with wars: 1861–65, 1914–18 and 1949–53— except for the recovery during 1933–37 from the Great Depression. The most recent expansion can be divided into several distinct episodes: the rapid recovery of 1961–62 and subsequent slowdown in 1962–63; renewed expansion in 1964 accelerated by the onset of the war in Vietnam in 1965; with inflation and monetary restraints in 1966 leading to reductions in civilian purchases in late 1966 and early 1967.

In the first year of recovery from the 1960–61 recession between the first quarters of 1961 and 1962, GNP grew by 7·6 per cent, with all sectors of the economy except exports expanding. In the following year growth dropped to 4·2 per cent, and the unemployment rate, 7·1 per cent in May 1961 and down to 5·5 per cent a year later, was 5·9 per cent in May 1963. The strong recovery had been followed by a disappointing slowdown—a pause in expansion most clearly reflected in employment and output of durable goods manufacturers. The check came from the decline in defence orders at the end of 1961 which led to large falls in inventory investment and materials output of durable goods manufacturers in early 1962 and the end of the rise in defence production later that year. Defence expenditures fell in the second half of the year. This defence slowdown had little effect on the rest of the economy because of the high levels of other government expenditures, of exports, and of household spending on durable goods and housing. However the fall in the aggregate rate of growth in 1962 resulted in a slight fall in business fixed investment in early 1963. Thus during 1963, although incomes and employment continued to rise, with no strong growth points in the economy the unemployment rate remained high and industrial capacity was under-utilized. At this time there was renewed concern about the failure of the economy to reach its potential levels of output, and pressure on the Administration to use fiscal measures to stimulate faster growth. In 1962 business benefited from changed depreciation rules for tax purposes and from an investment tax credit, and the revival of fixed investment in the second half of 1963 was probably assisted by these measures. A major programme of tax reform proposed by President Kennedy in 1963 was eventually passed by Congress early in 1964. This provided large individual and corporate income tax reductions spread over the next two years.

The pace of expansion started to quicken in the second half of 1963 as fixed investment and exports both rose at a time when consumer spending on durable goods was increasing rapidly. In the second and third quarters of 1964 consumer spending increased sharply following the fiscal reform which had included a reduction in the rate of withholding tax for the purpose of achieving an immediate effect on disposable income. During 1964 the rise in business fixed investment was strongly sustained, although the growth in exports slackened and residential construction stopped rising (see p. 40). Towards the end of 1964 orders for defence equipment started to rise. There was a consequential increase in inventory investment by manufacturers while defence production started to rise at the beginning of 1965.

Until the middle of 1965 the influence of government on the expansion since early 1963 had been exerted through the tax reductions which had resulted in a Federal budget deficit in 1964. The volume of Federal, state and local government purchases of goods and services had not risen, small declines in defence expenditures being offset by small rises in civilian expenditures. With the growth of the American military effort in Vietnam, foreshadowed by President Johnson's request to Congress on July 28, 1965, for increased military resources, the impact of the government on expansion became more pronounced. (Following this request there were widespread expectations of a repetition of the Korean boom, but in the event the boom was orderly because markets were in a more settled state—most commodities were in plentiful supply, retail shops were well stocked, and consumers did not expect shortages.) Government purchases between the first quarters of 1965 and 1967 rose by nearly 25 per cent. The rate of growth of output remained virtually unchanged, about one-third being due to the rise in government purchases and one-half to the rise in consumer expenditure.

With this sustained and relatively high rate of growth, inflationary pressures appeared, and during 1965 official concern changed from fiscal pump priming to fiscal and monetary restraints. The labour market gradually tightened and the unemployment rate which was 5 per cent in December 1964 fell to 4·1 per cent a year later. During 1966 it averaged 3·8 per cent. The peak pressure on the labour market, measured by hours worked in manufacturing, appears to have been from February to May 1966. Prices, at both retail and wholesale levels, rose rapidly during the first half of 1966. Interest rates in money markets and bond yields had risen very strongly during the first three quarters of 1965. In the fourth quarter, however, the rising demand for credit was reflected in a large increase in rates and yields. The official policy of restraint was marked by the raising of Federal Reserve discount rates in December, and during the first three quarters of 1966 all interest rates rose rapidly. Fiscal policy also exerted some restraint, and tax increases became effective in early 1966.

The restraints had an immediate impact on housebuilding, and a delayed effect on business investment. Housing starts had risen since the 1961 recovery until the middle of 1963, after which they had fluctuated slightly about a high level as mortgage rates remained low. With tightening credit at the end of 1965, mortgage rates started to rise in November and followed the steep rise in interest rate levels during 1966. Despite government aid there was a big drop in residential mortgage lending, and between December 1965 and October 1966 housing starts were halved. The volume of residential construction fell severely in the twelve months after the middle of 1966. This particular decline stopped the hitherto rapid growth of consumer purchases of furniture and household equipment. On business investment the impact of fiscal and monetary restraints was slow to take effect. Business fixed investment expanded until the end of 1966, and it was not until the first half of 1967 that expenditure fell. This fall was accompanied by a very large fall in inventory investment and a small decline in industrial production, concentrated mainly in durable goods manufacturers of both consumer and business equipment.

By September 1966 some of the pressures in money markets subsided and interest rates tended to fall. Credit once again flowed into residential mortgages and, assisted by government measures to make housing finance easier to obtain, housing starts rose after October from their very low levels. Towards the end of the year Federal Reserve policy became slightly less restrictive and during the first half of 1967 monetary policy was reversed in the direction of making credit more readily available. By mid-1967 expenditures on consumer durables were rising again and manufacturers had ceased to cut back inventories. In the third quarter output of household durables was increasing and activity in the durable goods manufacturing industries was approaching the peak 1966 levels. Severe strikes in the automobile industry in September and October reduced output but expansion was continuing at a rapid rate in most sectors of the economy at the end of the year.

THE THEORY OF U.S. FLUCTUATIONS

The explanation or model of U.S. fluctuations in the post-1945 period which is outlined here is intended as a flexible framework, designed to be applied to each of the major episodes in activity as set out above, capable of interpreting the effects of the special circumstances which prevailed from time to time. The model derives features from Samuelson's multiplier-accelerator mechanism, Metzler's inventory analysis and Hick's general cyclical theory.[1]

Purchases of GNP are divided into two categories.[2] In the

[1] See P. A. Samuelson, 'Interactions between the multiplier analysis and the principle of acceleration', *R. Econ. Statist.*, *21*, May 1939, pp. 75–78; L. A. Metzler, 'The Nature and stability of inventory cycles', *R. Econ. Statist.*, *23*, August 1941, pp. 113–29; and J. R. Hicks, *A Contribution to the Theory of the Trade Cycle*, Clarendon Press, Oxford, 1950.

[2] In what follows the exposition is simplified by neglecting imports of goods and services. Imports depend on GNP and represent a reduction of income available for domestic spending. Their effect on the model would simply be to reduce the value of the multiplier.

first are exports, fixed investment, residential construction and government purchases. It is assumed that none of these expenditures are affected by short period changes in aggregate income and output, and in this sense they are autonomous expenditures. In the second category of purchases are consumer expenditures and inventory accumulation. Consumer expenditures depend on income and can be approximated by some simple function of GNP (a consumption function). Inventory accumulation depends on the change in aggregate sales of goods and can be

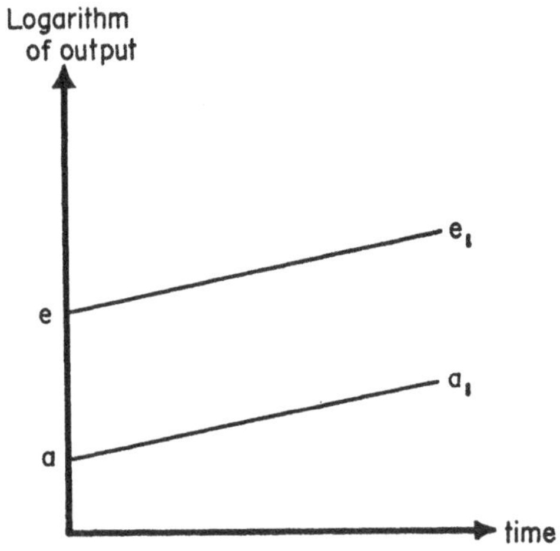

Fig. 1.3: Equilibrium output model: steady growth.

represented by another simple function of change in GNP (an inventory accelerator, or induced investment function). Given the level of autonomous expenditures, the definitions of the consumption and inventory accelerator functions determine a level of output where desired saving and investment, and actual saving and investment, are all equal. This we call equilibrium output. The case of constant rates of growth of autonomous expenditures is shown in Fig. 1.3. aa_1 is the growth path of autonomous expenditures; ee_1 is equilibrium output, derived from aa_1 by the multiplication of autonomous expenditures by a given parameter (the Hicksian super-multiplier).

The effect of a change in the rate of growth of autonomous

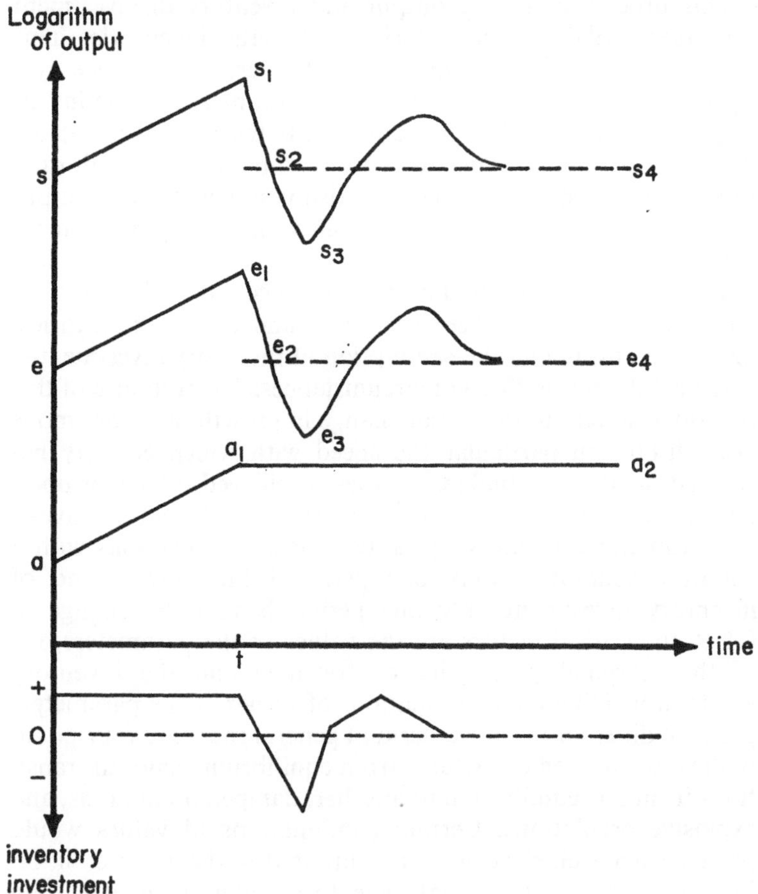

Fig. 1.4: Equilibrium output model: absorption of shock.

expenditures is illustrated in Fig. 1.4. Suppose autonomous expenditures, hitherto growing at 5 per cent per annum, cease to grow at time t. Desired inventories had been growing along the path ss_1 and at t cease to grow. Inventory investment is cut to zero, and equilibrium output falls from e_1 to e_2. Consequently desired inventories fall from s_1 to s_2, inventory disinvestment begins and output declines along the path e_1e_3.

This process of falling output and inventory disinvestment continues until desired inventories equal actual inventories. This is shown on the diagram by the point where the distance s_3e_3 equals *se* (this distance, being a logarithm, measures the inventory-output ratio and *se* by definition is the desired ratio). At this point of equality inventory disinvestment is at a high rate. In such circumstances, inventory disinvestment ceases, output rises and desired inventory rises also. Inventory investment commences.

The particular pattern of events described—the fall in output, the closing of the gap between actual and desired inventories, the rise in output and the resumption of inventory investment—may be different in different circumstances. The response of this economic system to the initial change in growth of autonomous expenditure—in particular the speed with which equality between desired and actual inventories is achieved—depends upon the particular forms of the consumption and inventory investment functions. In the simplest case of linear functions with a lag of consumption only one period behind GNP, and of inventory investment only one period behind the change in GNP, the critical factors are the values of the parameters, i.e. of the marginal propensity to consume and the inventory accelerator. Different combinations of values of the parameters produce different responses, and in general there are four possibilities: unchecked departures from equilibrium, smooth transitions from one equilibrium to another, damped oscillations, and explosive oscillations. Certain combinations of values would produce unchecked declines in output (for there is no 'floor' in our model) with actual inventories always greater than desired inventories. In the case of *increases* in the growth of autonomous expenditures such combinations of values would be explosive upwards. In contrast, other combinations of values would result in a smooth change from one equilibrium position to another. Yet other combinations of values would produce persistent oscillations—output always overshooting the equilibrium level e_2e_4 and inventories fluctuating about the equilibrium desired level s_2s_4. For instance, after the rise in output from the trough level e_3 desired inventories would lag behind actual inventories and inventory investment would rise to a high rate before the gap was closed. Then the process would swing into reverse again: inventory investment ceases, output falls, desired inventories decline, and so on. These oscillations can in general be damped or undamped depending on the values of the parameters. Persistent oscillations of this sort, whether damped or not, are what are normally thought to be involved in an 'inventory cycle'. Sequences of changes in the rate of growth of autonomous expenditures would keep a damped cycle oscillating as well as making the cycle quite complex.[1]

It does not appear that the cycle in U.S. activity and inventories is of the persistent oscillating type. Such a cycle would imply a state of semi-permanent inventory disequilibrium which is not apparent in the evidence. Instead, U.S. recessions and recoveries appear to be associated with distinct declines and increases in the rate of growth of autonomous expenditures, and the corresponding falls and rises in inventory investment are short-lived responses to the changes in equilibrium output and equilibrium inventory following the changes in autonomous expenditure. Inventory investment is predominantly intended investment, and not the unintended result of the overshooting of equilibrium levels. When the level of equilibrium inventory declines the transition from one level to another (or from one growth rate to another) will be relatively smooth. Just as there may be some delay in reducing inventory investment, with consequently some unintended investment, there may be some overshooting of the new lower level of desired inventories, but this unintended disinvestment will not be large enough to cause a reaction strong enough to bring about a general recovery—

[1] As Hicks shows when the consumption and inventory accelerator functions are linear and with or without lags, the equilibrium level of output is a simple function of autonomous expenditures only in special cases, e.g. the stationary state and the regularly progressive economy. If autonomous investment fluctuates, quite different fluctuations may be produced in equilibrium output (see Hicks [1950] Appendices 17, 18 and 29, pp. 182–84, 197–99). In the case of the regularly progressive economy, equilibrium output will grow at the same constant rate as autonomous expenditures. For the general solution to Hicks' second order difference equation, with an autonomous expenditure function of any given shape, see R. Frisch and A. K. Parikh, 'Parametric solution and programming of the Hicksian model', in *Essays on Econometrics and Planning*, ed. C. R. Rao, Pergamon Press, Oxford, 1965.

even temporary—from the recession.[1] The recovery can come only from a rise in autonomous expenditures (or an increase in their growth rate) which reverses the previous change in equilibrium output and equilibrium inventory. In the absence of this, inventories would quickly settle down to their recession equilibrium. In other words, the response of the economic system to a change in equilibrium is either a smooth movement, or a heavily damped oscillating movement, to the new equilibrium. In a recession, the typical changes in inventory investment, following the fall in autonomous expenditure, are a rapid fall to a high level of disinvestment, succeeded by a recovery to zero investment. In the post-1945 recessions any subsequent development of this partial but clearly damped cycle has been swamped by the external shock of recovery. In the recovery, the typical inventory investment changes have been a rapid rise, succeeded by a decline to a lower—but not zero—level about which investment has fluctuated slightly until the end of the general economic expansion: the overall pattern is one of a very heavily damped oscillating rise to the new equilibrium level of investment. Any damped oscillation produced in this way is a unique and transient phenomenon and cannot be regarded as something which dominates economic change, creating a regular short business cycle possibly sustained by outside disturbances. In the economic system envisaged here, the shocks—changes in autonomous expenditures—cause recessions and expansions. Induced inventory investment amplifies the response to the shock but does not itself lead to important fluctuations in business activity independent of the shocks.

This conclusion about the so-called inventory cycle is based partly on the evidence studied in this book of the fluctuations in output, inventory investment and autonomous expenditures, and partly on the likely properties of the formal model just described. It must be agreed that our knowledge of the actual values of important parameters in the model—like the marginal

[1] In the brief recessions since 1945, the reaction to excessive inventory disinvestment in some nondurable goods manufacturing and trading industries (especially textiles) has contributed through restocking booms to the early stages of recovery in those industries. But this has not been general (it is not apparent in the durable goods industries) and in the absence of general recovery the booms must have died down.

propensity to consume and the inventory accelerator—is tentative and not firmly based, and that the extent to which the formal model is a working representation of reality is a matter on which opinions vary. Granted this basic uncertainty, however, currently available econometric evidence suggests that the parameter values lie in certain ranges and that the functions have certain shapes. By inserting plausible numerical values into the equations describing plausible, if simplified, models, the likely stability properties of the model can be examined and the likely nature of the response mechanism studied.

The most probable values of the long run marginal propensity to consume out of GNP, and the marginal ratio of inventory to quarterly GNP are 0·64 and 1·00 respectively.[1] In the simple linear model described above, and which underlies Figs. 1.3 and 1.4, where consumption is a fixed proportion of output lagged one period, and inventory investment is a fixed proportion of change in output, also lagged one period, the response of the model to a displacement from equilibrium is just inside the oscillatory side of the line between a non-oscillating return to equilibrium and a damped oscillation. The short run marginal propensity to consume is probably lower than 0·64 because of the short run stability of consumption suggested by empirical studies. This stability can be represented by a linear consumption function in which consumption in a period depends not only on output a period later but on output two periods later (and possibly even further back in time). The affect of this modification on the model is to stabilize the response mechanism more strongly, increasing the dampening factor and making non-oscillatory returns to equilibrium more likely. Investigations of the more general cases of distributed lags in both consumption and inventory investment suggest that while the possible cyclical behaviour becomes richer in variety, the general pattern of stability properties is unaltered. Thus the introduction of more complicated or more realistic lags into the simple linear model is unlikely to alter the general conclusions we have reached, viz. that the response of the economic system to a disturbance from equilibrium is likely to be either a relatively

[1] These are discussed below in this chapter and in Notes B, C and M.

smooth transition to a new equilibrium or a damped oscillation which rapidly approaches the new equilibrium.[1]

REGULAR AND IRREGULAR FACTORS IN PRIVATE SPENDING

We now briefly review present knowledge about the consumption, inventory investment and other expenditure functions.

The consumption function

In the years immediately before the Second World War and in the years since 1950, the ratio of personal consumption expenditures to disposable personal income has been about 0·91. This ratio has altered only slightly as income has tended to rise over the period, and consequently it appears that both the long run average and long run marginal propensities to consume are about 0·91. During the war years 1941–45 the ratio of consumption to income was considerably lower because of shortages and high voluntary saving. Between 1946 and 1950 the propensity rose to abnormally high levels: the need to restock

[1] Let c_t, i_t and y_t be respectively consumption, inventory investment and output at t all measured as deviations from equilibrium values. Let a and b be respectively the marginal propensity to consume and the marginal inventory accelerator coefficient.

Assume $$y_t = c_t + i_t \tag{1}$$

$$c_t = ay_{t-1} \tag{2}$$

and $$i_t = b(y_{t-1} - y_{t-2}) \tag{3}$$

Then $$y_t = (a + b)y_{t-1} - by_{t-2} \tag{4}$$

This is the second order linear difference equation analysed in the text above. It has a single Robertson lag in the receipt of income and its expenditure, no Lundberg lag between sales and output (and hence no unintended change in inventories) and a zero Metzler coefficient of expectations.

Suppose consumption has a distributed lag, e.g.

$$c_t = a_1y_{t-1} + a_2y_{t-2} \tag{2.a}$$

where $$a = a_1 + a_2$$

so that $$y_t = (a_1 + b)y_{t-1} - (b - a_2)y_{t-2} \tag{4.a}$$

The effect of a_2 is to reduce the coefficient of y_{t-2} and increase the stability of the system. For a general solution of the second order equation see R. G. D. Allen, *Mathematical Economics*, 2nd ed., Macmillan, London, 1959, Chapter 7. The introduction of a Lundberg lag with unintended inventory change and a positive coefficient of expectations increases the restrictiveness of the stability conditions, i.e. reduces the values of a and b below which initial displacements return rapidly to equilibrium (see Metzler [1941], especially Table 5, p. 123, and Chart 9, p. 128).

The more general case of distributed lags is considered by both Allen, loc. cit., and Hicks [1950] appendices 19–26, pp. 184–93.

wardrobes, houses and garages, the desire to spend freely after years of war and shortages, and the high level of accumulated savings, pushed the ratio up to 0·95 in the peak period of abnormal expenditure in 1947. In 1948 the ratio was starting to fall, but it rose again in 1949 when Americans indulged in the final stage of their postwar spending spree, this time on automobiles. By 1950 the spree was ending and with the finish of the great car boom the propensity was declining permanently.

The propensity to consume shows also a high degree of short-term variation, arising first from the slowness of consumption levels to change when income changes. This effect is perhaps more pronounced when income falls: consumption of services and nondurable goods tends to be maintained and savings decline. Sudden increases in income are normally saved for a period; steady rises usually result in a corresponding steady rise in consumption.

The other source of short period variation arises from the special influences—over and above income—upon purchases of durable goods. Part of purchases of furnishings and household equipment is associated with new family formation and the rate of house buying. The most sensitive factor appears to be short run changes in new housebuilding which depends on the cost and availability of credit. Automobile purchases are still difficult to explain. Credit terms are important, and short run increases in income are clearly responsible at times for increased purchases. However, when allowance is made for all measurable factors there is still a significant part of automobile purchases which is random from the point of view of short period fluctuations.

We have, then, a consumption function with a stable long run propensity to consume of about 0·91, and a systematic tendency to rise when income declines and to fall back when income increases. To these regular features are added erratic influences affecting purchases of consumer durables which while certainly not destroying the regularity at times reduce it.

The inventory accelerator function

A flexible version of the accelerator appears to operate as a determinant of business investment in inventories. The relation is strongest and most pervasive amongst manufacturers of durable goods. Fluctuations in the inventory investment of these manufacturers have tended to dominate changes in inventory investment since 1945, and a substantial part of their inventories is work in progress reflecting lengthy periods of fabrication. Because there is a large amount of production to order by these manufacturers they have unfilled orders which bear a direct relationship to work in progress.

The basic hypothesis of the flexible accelerator theory is that demand for inventory depends on the need to have goods in the production and distribution pipeline because of normal delays in ordering, fabrication and delivery. For firms producing or ordering for stock the level of inventory—finished goods, work in progress and materials—will depend on expected sales. For firms producing or delivering to order (mainly durable goods manufacturers) the level of inventory—predominantly work in progress and materials—will depend on the stock of unfilled orders.[1] Where these dependencies are expressed as simple proportions the factors of proportionality are the constant marginal ratios of inventory to sales and unfilled orders, or accelerator coefficients. The evidence for making a judgement of the size of the aggregate marginal inventory-GNP ratio is by no means clear,[2] but the provisional estimate—a working hypothesis—used here is that the ratio lies between 0·5 and 1·3, and is most likely in the region of unity.[3]

This value of the marginal inventory-GNP ratio and that of the marginal propensity to consume (the propensity to consume out of GNP is in the region of 0·64) place the response-cycle of our model in the class of damped oscillations. While the quantitative evidence is by no means clear-cut, it is at least plausible and consistent with the more general considerations set out earlier. The case for a heavily damped cycle, with no persisting

[1] This is the simplest statement of the hypothesis. Other factors may modify the relationships in certain circumstances, e.g. the length of the delivery period for materials.

[2] It is reviewed in Note L below.

[3] The time unit in the model outlined above on pp. 41–8 is one quarter. The accelerator coefficients are consequently the ratio of inventory to quarterly sales, or (in the marginal sense used here and in the model) the ratio of quarterly inventory investment to change in sales during the quarter.

inventory fluctuations, has most of the evidence pointing in its favour.

Housing investment function

Residential construction in the formal model above is treated as autonomous. This is only a first approximation. At any point in time homeowners and owners of rental units wish to hold a stock of housing units which depends on the demographic structure, on expected real income and on the expected user costs of home ownership. This desired stock will be a relatively stable quantity unless expected income changes substantially or the demographic structure alters considerably due to, say, the end of a war. The potential demand for new units is the difference between actual and desired stock, and this is of course a less stable variable than the desired stock.

What part of the potential demand results in new starts at any point in time depends on the conditions of supply of housing credit (residential mortgages), of which the two most important aspects are the yield on mortgages and the proportion of the value of the work done required as a cash payment. The yield and the proportion can vary in the short run and have a rapid effect on the level of housing starts.

The conditions of supply of housing credit can be directly influenced by the Federal government and its agencies. Public housing has been a very small part of total housebuilding since 1945, but over one quarter of housing units started since 1945 have had mortgages guaranteed or insured by Federal agencies. In some years the proportion has been nearly one-half. By varying the conditions of mortgage guarantee and insurance—in particular varying the maximum allowable yield and minimum down payment—the housing authorities have been able to influence housebuilding.

More important than this, however, has been the regulation of the flow of mortgage funds into housing by changes in interest rates. When the yields on government securities rise and a gap is created between bond yields and mortgage yields the flow of money into mortgages normally dries up. Mortgages become difficult to get; mortgage yields themselves rise. When the gap closes, or when other yields fall, money again flows into mortgages. The typical pattern has been for rising interest rates and credit shortages to appear—usually with official approval if not encouragement—as a boom nears full employment (or its peak). Mortgage yields rise and housing starts fall. The onset of recession—which as we have seen may not immediately follow a decline in residential construction (e.g. 1956–57)—will induce lower interest rates and easier credit, normally with official assistance—and a rise in starts.

Residential construction is not an endogenous variable like inventory investment or personal expenditure on nondurables; nor is it exogenous in the sense that exports are. Although the housing start 'tap' is not entirely automatic (the level of interest rates and the ease of obtaining credit are endogenous factors), it depends very much on official monetary and housing policies, and there has been an 'administrative cycle' in monetary management which through changes in monetary policy has curbed housing in the boom and stimulated it in recession. This cycle is not stabilizing in any simple sense: the fall in house-building has been a factor in the onset of most recessions, although all revivals have been stimulated by increases in housing starts.

The fixed investment function

Fixed investment does not show very much short run variability. Its behaviour is, however, affected by the cumulation of short run influences. The simplest working hypothesis to explain capital accumulation starts with a desired stock of capital. The difference between desired and actual stock of capital is the demand for capital and this with various lags due to planning, ordering and construction will over time be translated into new investment. The lags and the delays are important. Given an initial change in the demand for capital, the rate of investment will, after delays associated with planning the new investment, and placing contracts and orders, rise to a peak and subsequently fall off as the project is completed. The average lag from beginning planning to completion of construction has been estimated to range from seven quarters in the case of durable manufacturing to two and a half years in the case of nondurables.

The desired stock of capital is a forward-looking concept. It is the productive capacity which business wants to have available in the near future (say, two or three years ahead) and reflects the expectations of business about that future, particularly with respect to sales, prices and costs (including long term interest rates and tax rates). These expectations will be based on current and past experience, and in particular on the current rate of growth of sales.

This hypothesis leads to an accelerator relationship, although unlike the inventory accelerator, the fixed investment accelerator has very long lags and hence slow responses to changes in sales and other factors. If current sales are rising and are expected to continue to rise, the desired stock will rise and the rate of fixed investment will be maintained. If sales cease rising and are not expected to renew their growth, the desired stock will not rise and the rate of fixed investment will fall. If at the beginning or end of a war there is a large gap between desired and actual stock of capital, investment will rise to close the gap. Unless expectations alter so as to cause the desired stock to grow, investment must fall after a while.

A fall in fixed investment is thus likely to be the result of decisions taken more than two years previously. In the case of the two major falls since 1945, that of 1948–49 was the result of the end of the postwar expansion of capacity: business in 1945–46 forecasted levels of sales in 1947–48 and when capacity appropriate to these levels of sales had been installed the rate of investment declined. In the case of the fall in 1957–58, business in 1955 and 1956 did not expect sales to rise above their prevailing levels and consequently decided not to increase desired capacity further. In neither case did business find it necessary to revise its expectations or forecasts.

The model outlined above could incorporate a fixed investment accelerator. The possibility of persisting oscillations, probably with quite long periods, would arise. However, separate treatment of fixed investment has the advantage of flexibility which is important both when the model is used as a tool of historical analysis and also in view of the fact that in the post-1945 period there have been only three strong investment booms (1964–66 being the third).

Imports and exports

Changes in imports of goods and services are closely dependent upon changes in domestic activity. Part of imports of finished goods and services can in fact be included in the consumption function and depend on disposable personal income. Imports of raw materials and semi-manufactures depend on manufacturing production and inventory investment. Both finished imports and the others are sensitive to changes in foreign prices relative to U.S. prices. The quantitative evidence can be summarized as follows. The long run marginal propensity to import all goods and services (with respect to GNP) is about 0·05, the effect of any change in GNP being spread over several quarters. Estimates of the effect of price changes are not very reliable, but suggest that the aggregate long run elasticity (with respect to relative prices) is between one-half and unity.

Such supposed long run regularities are considerably distorted by month to month erratic changes in imports, and from other short run factors such as dock strikes. In 1949 government stock piling of strategic materials prevented imports from falling more than they would otherwise. In 1957–58 American import demand was swollen by the successful competition of European car manufacturers with their small 'compact' types. In 1946–47 and in 1951, although industrial activity was high and rising, high prices caused some imports to fall severely probably for speculative reasons.

U.S. exports have clearly been influenced in the first instance by level of demand in foreign markets, and the rises in activity in Europe in 1951, 1955–56, 1959–60 and 1963–64, and the falls in 1949, 1952, 1957 and 1962, have caused corresponding rises and falls in U.S. exports of both goods and services. As well as this, exports were sustained by aid policies in the postwar years up to and including the Korean war. The fall-off in aid between the early postwar programmes and the Marshall Plan was a factor in the decline in exports in 1947–48.

GOVERNMENT EXPENDITURES AND FISCAL AND MONETARY POLICY

Fluctuations in government purchases have been dominated by changes in the rate of defence expenditures. In early 1948, in 1956–57, in 1959–60, in 1962–63 and in 1965–66, but particularly in 1950–51 and 1953–54 changes in defence expenditures have had important effects on aggregate demand and on the capital goods industries in particular. Change in defence expenditure has usually had effects well in advance of actual work done or payments made. An impact is evident as soon as military orders or contracts are placed: manufacturers respond rapidly by purchasing materials for inventory and recruiting labour. In some cases the rumour of new orders or announcement of a new defence policy encourages stockpiling. Correspondingly, a fall-off in orders results in a decline in work in progress and a fall in inventories of materials. Inventory investment is very sensitive to rearmament policy.

Defence policy has been the major government influence on short term fluctuations, although other government policies and actions have had an effect. The effect of housing and monetary policies upon housebuilding has been mentioned above. In its stabilizing or destabilizing effects, defence expenditure has been remarkably similar to housebuilding. Declines in each have tended to be factors causing or contributing to recessions. Increases in each have been forces assisting recovery from recession, and these increases on different occasions have been encouraged through the speeding up of defence ordering and through cheap money policy as deliberate anti-recessionary measures.

An important role has been played by the automatic fiscal stabilizers. In all recessions except 1948–49, personal disposable income was sustained by automatic falls in tax payments and increases in unemployment payments. (In the model the effect of a reduction in tax payments or an increase in transfers can be shown as an increase in output equal to the product of that part of the increase in personal disposable income spent and the supermultiplier. Thus in Fig. 1.4 between e_1 and e_3 output is raised by varying amounts depending on the changes in tax and unemployment payments.) The most important automatic stabilizer has been the change in corporate tax liabilities: in recessions when profits have fallen, after-tax profits have fallen considerably less. In the upswings the stabilizers of course work in reverse, slowing the rises in disposable personal income and in after-tax profits.

Other government policies have been partly accidental, partly discretionary. For instance, in late 1947 when a tighter monetary policy was enforced, the Federal budget surplus which until that time had been offset by large purchases of securities from the public by the authorities, became particularly deflationary. This undoubtedly was a factor in the change in business opinion in early 1948 which led to the fall in commodity prices. In 1948–49 loans and purchases under Federal farm price support schemes equalled some 16 per cent of farmers' incomes. In 1959, as has been described, fear of inflation led to severely deflationary fiscal and monetary policies which cut residential construction and weakened further an already weakening boom. In most recessions some government expenditures were speeded up as part of deliberate expansionary policy. In all recessions state and local governments have hastened expenditure on public works and other construction schemes. In 1954 the Federal government speeded up some defence expenditures and public works schemes and stockpiled some materials. In 1958–59 funds for highway construction were released, public works were speeded up and unemployment compensation was temporarily extended. In 1961–62 there were similar actions, and as well a special veterans insurance bonus was paid, defence ordering speeded up and farm prices supported. Except in 1961–62 these actions were on a relatively small scale, and in all cases were effective after revival had commenced—although the official announcements of the impending policies may have encouraged business confidence.

The conclusion to be drawn from this summary review of government policy is that the single most important influence (measured by frequency and size) upon changes in U.S. activity since 1945 has been changes in the defence effort. The automatic fiscal tools have had a clearly stabilizing influence. Discretionary fiscal actions have assisted revival but only when it has been under way. The enforcement of dear money in boom periods has at all times had a clearly deflationary result, via housebuilding.

The emphasis above on the destabilizing effects of government policy should not hide the fact that the U.S. economy since 1941 has avoided a major slump, and that this is in no small part due to the large and pervasive role of government, and in particular the large volume of government expenditure. If instability arising from fluctuations in this large volume of expenditures and from changes in government policy is the price that has to be paid for the avoidance of major slumps, it is a small price to pay. Nevertheless one may hope that the instability can be reduced further.

Whether the American business cycle can be expected to be a regularly recurring phenomenon depends on whether one expects certain structural features and behaviour patterns of American economic life to persist. Some regularities will not cause a persisting business cycle: I have argued that the forms of the consumption function and the inventory accelerator will not lead of their own accord to a continuous inventory cycle. Only a sequence of disturbances from changes in defence expenditures, housing starts or business fixed investment could cause a sequence of expansions and recessions.

Although changes in defence expenditures can be, and have been, used to counter recessionary tendencies, these expenditures and the decisions on which they depend must be treated as exogenous factors—as random shocks imposed on the economic system from outside. Business fixed investment, while exogenous in the short run, is clearly endogenous in the long run. However, on the evidence of the last twenty years it cannot be said that a fixed investment accelerator will generate a sequence of cycles: the lags are too great and the structural properties of the rest of the system lead to such a degree of stability of output and income that a persisting sequence of short or medium term cycles is most unlikely. We are left with changes in residential construction as our best candidate for the cause of a persisting oscillation. There is no doubt that housebuilding has been an unstable influence; but whether the instability has a regularity depends on whether the alternation of dear and cheap money is a basic regularity of the economic system. It seems there are elements of regularity offset to some degree by random influences. The regularities spring from the combination of dear money arising in periods of boom and the authorities' habit of 'leaning against the wind'—attempting to avoid inflation by making money dear. In recession the opposite combination occurs. But it is obvious that while both the natural dear money and the policy of the authorities (and the opposites in recession) are induced by the change in business activity, there is nothing necessarily automatic in this 'monetary accelerator', nor is there any reason why the alternation of cheap and dear money should persist with any degree of regularity.

I conclude this review of postwar U.S. business fluctuations by referring again to the analogy between business fluctuations and the motion of a rocking chair. Both the shocks the economy experiences, and the type of response of the economy to the shocks, determine the nature of the fluctuations. The relative importance of shock and type of response can vary, and in general a wide variety of explanations of business fluctuations is possible depending upon this relative importance. For the postwar decades the variety can be narrowed down to two main types. One is that inventory investment is so unstable that small changes elsewhere in the economy start or reinforce a largely self-perpetuating fluctuation in investment in stocks. I find no evidence for this whatsoever. The part played by inventory investment in the fluctuations has been to aggravate rises and falls in the growth of demand, not to generate an inventory cycle. The other type of explanation emphasises the shocks, and in particular the changes in defence expenditures and in monetary policy, with strikes and changes in car sales and exports being at times important. If these were regular changes they would probably generate a regular cycle in business activity. If the response of the economy were very sensitive to shocks, even irregular changes might have generated a regular cycle. Neither of these possibilities appears important since 1945. Instead, the shocks have been irregular and the response of the economy has been relatively insensitive. Each contraction, expansion and pause has been a unique historical episode associated with a unique combination of shocks, and the characteristics of each episode have been determined by the strength and timing of the shocks of which the most prominent and frequent have been changes in defence expenditures and monetary policy. Whatever may have been the cause of the American business cycle in the distant past, during the last two decades the influence of the Federal government in the economy has been so great that, despite its record of maintaining high degrees of employment and activity, it must bear the main share of responsibility for causing economic fluctuations.

CHAPTER 2

Legacies of Depression and War

THE DEPRESSION OF THE 1930S

The Great Depression of the early 1930s reached its trough in 1933 when about one-quarter of the civilian labour force was unemployed. Thereafter there was a slow recovery with rising output and incomes, and falling unemployment, interrupted in the second half of 1937 by a severe decline in activity. This lasted until mid-1938 when the revival from deep depression was resumed. Average unemployment in 1937 was 14·3 per cent, and GNP just equalled the 1929 level. In 1939 and again in 1940 GNP rose by 8½ per cent over the previous year, pushed up at first by rising government expenditures and housebuilding, and later by the revival of business fixed investment. Inventory investment rose during the recovery but rearmament played only a small role. In 1940 GNP per head and PCE per head surpassed the 1929 levels for the first time. America had at last struggled out of her decade of misery.

By 1941 the upswing was receiving the stimulus of large military orders and purchases as rearmament got under way, together with a high level of investment. There was a very strong inventory boom and consumers also were buying goods in anticipation of shortages as war threatened. The average rate of unemployment which had been 9·9 per cent in 1940 fell to 4·7 per cent in 1941. Thus when war did descend in December 1941 the economy was once again operating with nearly fully utilized resources and expanding rapidly. Furthermore, it is unlikely that at the end of 1941 there were any major physical deficiencies or shortages arising from the low output and incomes of the depression. There is no evidence to suggest that stocks of houses, automobiles or industrial plant and equipment in 1940 and 1941 were significantly different from long term desired levels.

Rather than any physical deficiencies, the economic legacies of the depression were the twin beliefs that a slump must naturally follow inflation or a period of boom, and that public policy must be directed towards managing the economy to avoid slumps like that of the 1930s. The latter belief lay behind the passing of the Employment Act of 1946 which, primarily a declaration of intent, said it was the responsibility of the Federal government 'to promote maximum employment, production and purchasing power'.[1] The former belief was founded not only on the experience of the 1930s, but also on the memory of the severe slump of 1920–21 following the postwar boom. As Friedman and Schwartz put it in referring to expectations in the years 1946 to 1948:

'The major source of concern about inflation at that time was not the evils of inflation *per se*—though no doubt these played a role—but the widespread belief that what goes up must come down. . . . Those expectations were partly a product of the severe 1929–33 contraction, which fostered a belief that severe contractions were the peacetime danger if not indeed the norm; and partly a product of the 1920–21 price collapse, which fostered a belief that major wars were followed by deflation and depression'.[2]

This fear of inflation and expectation of impending doom did influence the behaviour of government, business and households in the early postwar years.

WAR

For three and a half years, 1942 to mid-1945, the U.S. economy was operated at full capacity to produce large quantities of

[1] Government responsibility in creating postwar full employment was stated as early as January 1942 by the National Resources Planning Board. The Act was the outcome of a lengthy congressional debate during 1945 and 1946.

[2] M. Friedman and A. J. Schwartz, *A Monetary History of the United States 1867–1960*, NBER Studies in Business Cycles No. 12, Princeton University Press, 1963, pp. 584–85.

goods and services for war while still maintaining high standards of civilian consumption. Taxation and patriotic saving reduced private spending, supplemented by a wide range of direct controls over production, purchases, wages and prices. Unemployment in 1944 declined to 1·2 per cent of the civilian labour force, while 11·4 million out of a 66·0 million labour force were in the armed forces. Residential construction and production of consumer durables virtually ceased. Business investment was channelled into increasing the capacity of essential munition plants. Wide ranges of ordinary consumer goods became unobtainable. The gap between consumer aspiration and fulfilment grew as household purchasing power rose.

THE END OF THE WAR

Some time in the first half of 1945—probably in the second quarter—total output of goods and services reached its wartime peak.[1] During the second half of 1945 output declined by $57 billion or about one-sixth. Thereafter, for about a year and a half, output stayed at a virtually unchanged level. The graphs in Fig. 2.1 show a continued small fall until 1946 I, and a small rise in the next six months, but such small changes in the estimates during this period are unreliable and should be disregarded. Reduced production for military purposes, together with demobilization, was the dominating cause of the 1945 fall in output. As Table 2.1 shows, government military expenditures fell by $75 billion or 46 per cent in the second half of the year, and together with a fall in other government expenditures more than offset the small rises in private expenditure. During the following fifteen months military expenditures continued to fall, but were now offset by rising other government and private

[1] GNP, seasonally adjusted at annual rates, and at 1958 prices, is estimated to have been $356·6 billion in 1945 I and $361·7 billion the following quarter. The 1945 and 1946 estimates at 1958 prices are unofficial, rough estimates described in Note A. Due to the problems of deflation it is impossible to say in which quarter from 1944 III to 1945 II government purchases at constant prices reached a wartime peak, but it was probably during the half year 1944 IV to 1945 I. The problems of measuring personal consumption during the period when prices were controlled and during the period of decontrol are referred to on pp. 79–82 below.

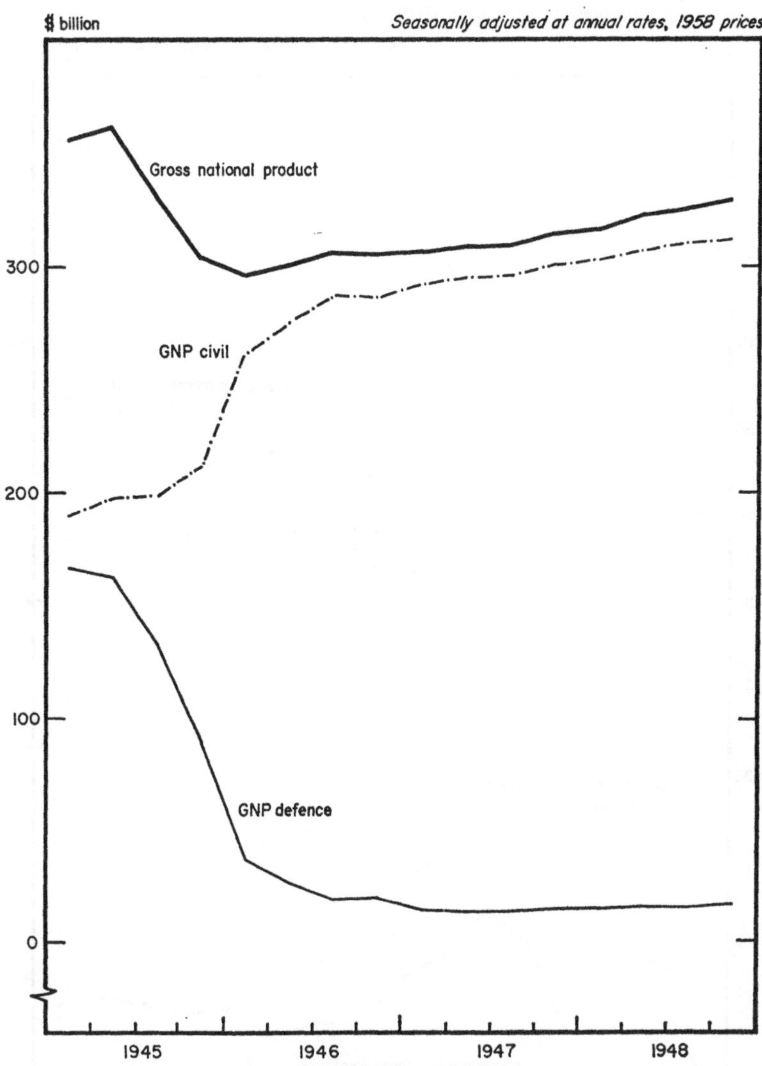

Fig. 2.1: Gross national product.

Source: 1945–46: Table A.1 with GNP and PCE (B).
1947–48: SCB. GNP defence is Federal National defence purchases deflated with Federal purchases price index.
GNP civil is total GNP less GNP defence.

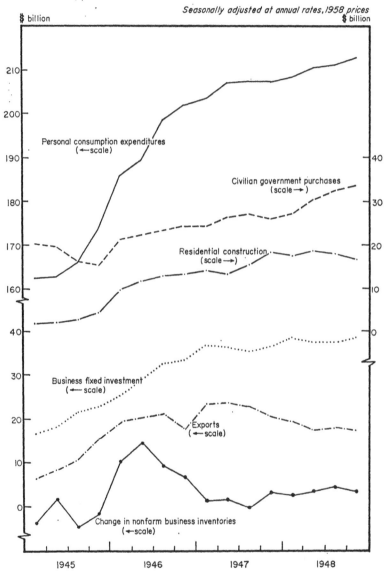

b. Components of civilian GNP
Seasonally adjusted at annual rates, 1958 prices
$ billion
$ billion
Personal consumption expenditures (←scale)
Civilian government purchases (scale→)
Residential construction (scale→)
Business fixed investment (←scale)
Exports (←scale)
Change in nonfarm business inventories (←scale)
210
200
190
180
170
160
40
30
20
10
0
40
30
20
10
0
1945
1946
1947
1948

TABLE 2.1: *Changes in GNP 1945 to 1947*

(based on seasonally adjusted data at annual rates, 1958 prices)

	$ billion	
	1945 II to IV	*1945 IV to 1947 I*
Government purchases		
National defence	−75·1	−74·5
Other*	−4·3	8·6
Private expenditures		
Personal consumption	11·1	29·4
Investment†	11·0	38·5
Gross National Product	−57·3	2·0

* Other Federal, state and local.

† Gross private fixed investment, change in business inventories and net exports.

Source: 1945–46 Table A.1 with GNP and PCE [B].
1947 SCB, with Federal defence purchases deflated with implicit Federal purchases price index.

expenditures. Until the middle of 1946 the fall in military expenditures and the rise in other expenditures was rapid. After mid-1946 both changes slowed down. Mid-1946 marks the return to a predominantly civilian economy.

The impact of the decline in military expenditures on employment and industrial production was swift. Industrial production had reached its peak wartime level in the last quarter of 1943 and, although it subsequently receded slightly from that level, output remained at a high and steady rate during 1944 and the first quarter of 1945. Production of durables began to fall in April (before the German surrender in May) but the big drop was during August and September after the end of the war with Japan. The main part of the production of the durable goods industries was munitions (aircraft, guns, ships, land vehicles, etc.) which reached their peak levels in 1944. Munition production had been declining at the end of 1944 and early 1945, but rose again during March to May in response to increased military orders following the German offensive in the Ardennes in late 1944. These orders however rose only temporarily and declined—as originally planned—in early 1945. Munition production accordingly started to fall substantially in June and July, although the big falls occurred in August and

September.[1] Output of nondurables also fell in the third quarter, and by October total industrial production was only 69 per cent of what it had been in March (see Fig. 2.2).

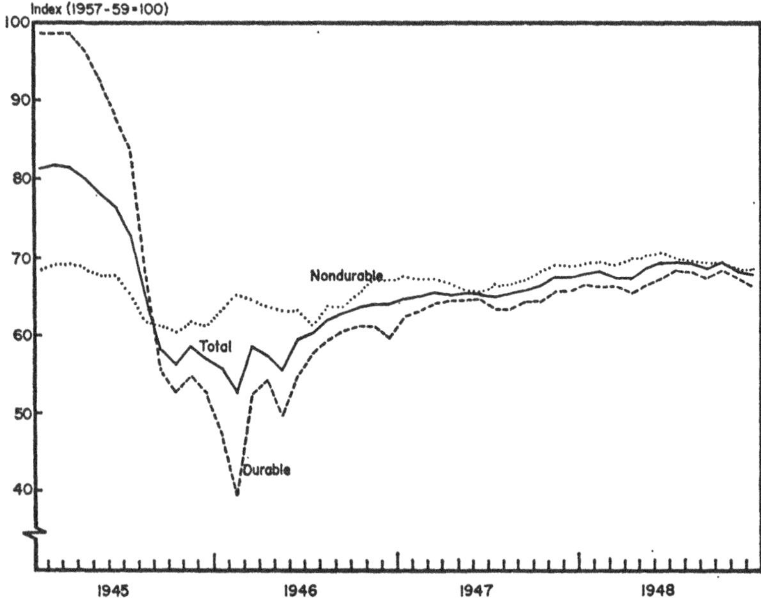

Fig. 2.2: Indexes of industrial production, 1945–48.
Source: FRB.

In May 1945 out of a total labour force of 66·5 millions, 12·1 millions were in the armed forces and only just over half a million of the rest (1·03 per cent of the civilian labour force) were unemployed.[2] The demobilization of the wartime labour force was accomplished very rapidly after May; the first main reduction taking place on the civilian side (see Table 2.2).

[1] Index of Munitions Production, 1943 = 100, 1944 = 110:

1944	N	109	1945	M	109	1945	J	84
	D	107		A	105		A	56
				M	104		S	26
1945	J	106		J	95			
	F	102						

Source: SCB, January and February 1946.

[2] The unemployment rates quoted in this paragraph are from G. H. Moore (ed.), *Business Cycle Indicators*, NBER Studies in Business Cycles No. 10 (Princeton N.J.: Princeton University Press), Vol. 2, Series 14.0, p. 1122. These differ slightly from those derived from seasonally adjusted data in Table 2.2 below.

TABLE 2.2: *Changes in Labour Force, 1945–46 (million)*

	Total	*Armed Forces*	*Civilian Labour Force*	*Employed*	*Un-employed*
May 1945	66·509	12·130	54·379	53·818	0·561
Change May–Sept. 1945	−2·266	−0·410	−1·856	−3·071	1·215
Change Sept.–Dec. 1945	−2·869	−3·930	1·061	0·740	0·321
Change Dec. 1945–March 1946	−0·689	−3·320	2·631	2·384	0·247
Change March–June 1946	−0·212	−1·400	1·188	1·227	−0·039
Change June–Dec. 1946	0·358	−1·180	1·538	1·494	0·044
December 1946	60·831	1·890	58·941	56·592	2·349

Source: SCB 1949 Statistical Supplement, p. 53. Seasonally adjusted with factors for 1948–49.

Between May and September civilian employment declined by over three million people while at the same time the armed forces released 400,000. More than two-thirds of this reduction —about 2·3 million—left the labour force. The remainder raised the unemployment rate to 3·73 per cent. In the last quarter of the year was felt the main impact of military demobilization: the armed forces declined by nearly four millions, while civilian employment rose by about three-quarters of a million. Almost three million people left the labour force with the result that the rise in unemployment was very small, the unemployment rate rising only to 4·07 per cent.[1] Demobilization continued in the first quarter of 1946 when the armed forces declined by another 3·3 million. Civilian employment was now increasing swiftly, rising by 2·4 million this quarter, but with only 700,000 leaving the labour force another quarter of a million unemployed raised the unemployment rate to 4·32 per cent. The main impact of demobilization was nearly over. 1·4 million people left the armed forces in the second quarter of 1946, and

[1] These changes in the labour force in 1945 IV hide a movement of civilian workers out of the labour force (women leaving employment and men retiring) and a corresponding movement of demobilized veterans into civilian employment.

after 200,000 had left the labour force the balance were all absorbed in employment. During the last six months of 1946 a further 1·2 million left the armed forces, and although the total labour force at last stopped falling and started to increase, employment increased by 1½ millions. From May 1945 to December 1946 the armed forces had fallen from 12·1 to 1·9 millions, the labour force from 66·5 to 60·8 millions, and civilian employment had risen from 53·8 to 56·6 million. The unemployment rate had risen from 1·03 per cent to 3·97 per cent. During the intervening twenty months the economy partly by retirements from the labour force and partly by expansion of civilian employment had absorbed this enormous demobilization with the rate of unemployment never once rising above levels which are not high for the American economy.

THE SOURCES OF HOUSEHOLD DEMAND

From 1941 to the second quarter of 1945 disposable personal income had risen by 64·2 per cent. Under the influence of wartime shortages, lack of choice and opportunity to purchase, and voluntary restraints, the proportion of income spent fell sharply as the following table shows:

TABLE 2.3: *Ratio of PCE to DPI*

1939	0·950
1940	0·936
1941	0·869
1942	0·757
1943	0·744
1944	0·740
1945 I and II	0·776

Source: SCB.

Expenditures on consumer durables fell absolutely. The relation between these expenditures and income shows little stability even on an annual basis, but in the light of pre- and postwar average relationships, expenditures on durables from 1942 to 1945, fluctuating at about $10 billion each year, were below what would have been expected from prevailing levels of income by an amount which rose from $10 billion in 1942 to $15 billion in 1945.[1] About half of this reduced consumption was at the expense of furniture and equipment, actual expenditures on which in 1944 were about half of what would have been normal for prevailing levels of income. The other half of the reduced consumption fell on automobiles and parts, expenditures on which almost ceased. (The situation of car stocks at the end of the war is considered in more detail below, p. 70.

Expenditures on nondurables and services did not fall during the war years, but the gap between actual expenditures and what might have been expected in the light of pre- and postwar consumption-income relationships was large. On nondurables, the expenditure gap was approximately $10 billions in each of the years 1942–44. On services the gap was about the same, and continued in 1945. Expenditures on clothing and shoes were only slightly below normal; expenditures on food were below normal by approximately one-tenth in 1942–44, while service expenditures as a whole were below normal by about one-sixth. Expenditures on some goods, such as gasoline, showed dramatic falls.

The effect of these reduced and retarded purchases was that during the four years 1942–45 personal consumption was below normal by amounts which totalled about $95 billion at the end of 1945 (at 1945 prices). This estimate is based on pre- and postwar relationships between income and consumption for the three groups durables, nondurables and services, and is a measure of the abnormal personal savings of the war years which caused households to accumulate exceptionally large holdings of financial assets such as currency, bank deposits, savings bonds, and other securities by the end of the war. The estimate is higher than that suggested by some alternative methods of estimating normal consumption (for details see Note C) but is supported by estimates of excess household holdings of financial assets derived from postwar relationships between income and assets. At the end of 1945 the value of financial assets as defined in the FRB held by households was about $110 billion greater than that suggested by the 1948–58

[1] The sources of these estimates and those in the following paragraphs are explained in Note C. The underlying theories of consumer behaviour are outlined below on pp. 85–6 and in Note B.

relationship between income and assets, while a similar relationship based on Goldsmith's estimates of intangible assets (financial assets plus equity in business) gives excess holdings in the region of $70 billion. The picture that emerges from a study of the entire household balance sheet is one with total equity or net worth in 1945 not excessively high, but a large surplus holding of intangibles offset by a large shortage of consumer durables and houses. Thus all the evidence points to an abnormally large holding at the end of 1945 of financial assets due to abnormally high wartime savings, with the excess holding being in the region of $80 to £100 billions—between one-half and two-thirds of DPI in 1945.

Thus if incomes were maintained after the end of the war, consumers were in a position not only to raise their expenditures on services, food, and other nondurables, but also to replenish stocks of durables which had been run down during the war. The situation of consumer durables was paralleled by housing, and a more detailed look at the automobile and housing markets will emphasize the enormous backlog of household demand that was available to be met when hostilities ended.

Automobiles

Production of cars ceased in early 1942, and manufacturers', dealers' and distributors' stocks which were estimated to be about 538,000 on January 1, 1942, were taken over by the government to be released for essential purposes only. Whereas registrations of new passenger cars had totalled 3·731 millions in 1941, in 1942 they fell to 305 thousand, in 1943 206 thousand, in 1944 66 thousand, and from January to September 1945 about 13 thousand. The stock of cars—measured by Chow as new car units per 100 people—was 9·178 at the end of 1941. As Table 2·4 shows, with virtually no new purchases depreciation eroded the stock steadily away until by the end of 1945 it was as low as 3·513 units per 100 people. At the automobile prices which had prevailed in 1941, and with allowance for the rise in disposable personal incomes, the demand relationships existing in both the pre-1942 and post-1946 periods suggest that the desired stock of cars would have been at the end of 1945 10·307 units—nearly three times as great as the actual stock. At the price levels which

TABLE 2.4: *Automobile Stock, Annual Purchases and Price, 1939 to 1954*

Year	*Automobile stock per 100 persons New car units*	*New purchases per 100 persons*	*Relative price of automobiles 1937 = 100*
1939	7·719	2·079	104·9
1940	8·221	2·622	97·1
1941	9·178	2·797	120·1
1942	7·420	—	119·0
1943	5·790	—	204·7
1944	4·457	—	356·3
1945	3·513	—	449·3
1946	4·057	—	338·6
1947	5·291	2·198	263·4
1948	6·101	2·381	236·2
1949	8·076	3·234	159·7
1950	10·256	4·170	161·8
1951	11·463	3·278	161·2
1952	11·194	2·648	169·6
1953	12·057	3·594	152·4
1954	12·052	3·408	141·3

Source: G. C. Chow, 'Statistical demand functions for automobiles and their use for forecasting', in *Demand for Durable Goods*, ed. A. C. Harberger, University of Chicago Press, 1960, Tables 1 and 2, pp. 157, 164.

were eventually established in 1949–51, the desired stock would have been more than twice as large: 8·355 new car units.[1]

To equate supply and demand the level of average automobile (second hand) prices had risen 4·78-fold between 1941 and 1945, and had risen in relation to the average level of prices 3·74-fold. At the end of 1945, to get automobile prices back to the prewar relationship with the general price level would have required about 9·5 million new cars—almost three times the annual production of 1940–41. There was thus a potential demand for about three years production, plus the effect of any rise in incomes after 1945, plus the replacement demand (about one-quarter of the stock in a prewar year), less the effect of a higher relative price of cars should automobile manufacturing costs after the war be higher relative to prices in general than before the war. (In the light of the relative prices of 1949–51,

[1] For the basis of these calculations see Note D.

this last offsetting effect was equivalent to nearly one prewar year's new car purchases.)

Housing

After low rates of residential building during the early 1930s, construction—measured by new non-farm dwelling units started—rose from 93,000 in 1933 to 620,000 in 1941, the figure of the latter year approaching those of the mid-1920s. It is unlikely that the housing market was very greatly out of long run equilibrium in the years 1940–41. With war and the imposition of controls over building and materials, starts declined to 301,000 in 1942, 184,000 in 1943 and to the trough of 130,000 in 1944. These low rates were continued in the first quarter of 1945, but some expansion took place after the first quarter, particularly during the last three months of the year. For the whole year starts were only 208,000.[1]

By the end of the war, however, houses built during the war had not kept up with the growth in population and depreciation on existing stock. At the end of 1945 the stock of accommodation per head was of the order of 15 per cent below the 1941 level.[2] At the same time the growth in real incomes, after allowing for increased cost of construction and low interest rates, is estimated to have raised the demand for accommodation per head by some 10 per cent over the 1941 level. Allowing for population growth during wartime, this suggests that the aggregate demand for housing at the beginning of 1946 was between one-quarter and one-third greater than was available at that date. At the 1941 rate of residential construction the lower limit of this range was between five and six years work; at the rates achieved in the early 1950s it was about three years work.[3]

[1] Figures from L. Grebler *et al.*, *Capital Formation in Residential Real Estate: Trends and Prospects*, NBER Studies in capital formation and financing No. 1, Princeton University Press, 1956.

[2] The estimates in this paragraph are explained in Note D.

[3] For figures on which these comparisons are based see L. Grebler *et al.* [1956] Tables B7 and D1. Note that while Grebler's housing stock estimates appear to be close to other benchmark estimates prewar, the former estimates may underestimate the postwar stock (op. cit., pp. 368–76). If this is so, the estimate of the housing shortage above in the text may be too great if the wartime reduction in the stock has been overestimated. Additionally and alternatively, if the postwar rate of construction has been underestimated by Grebler *et al.*, the burden on the construction industry of the shortage is correspondingly less.

THE SOURCES OF BUSINESS DEMAND

Fixed investment

Business fixed investment in plant and equipment had fallen to low levels during the early 1930s and by 1941 the stock of capital was less than it had been in 1929. Although GNP was nearly one-third greater than it had been in 1929, if we allow for technical progress during the 1930s which may have reduced the optimum ratio of capital to output, and for the building boom of the 1920s, it seems unlikely that the age of both structures and equipment in 1941 was abnormally high.[1] In 1940 and 1941 as business activity rose so did fixed investment, but after the onset of war investment declined sharply. In manufacturing, for example, during the years 1942–44 gross investment in structures did not cover depreciation, while investment in equipment allowed no more than a 10 per cent increase in the real value of the stock. By the end of the war the average age of capital in the economy had almost certainly increased since 1941, although the deficiencies in the capital stock were more obvious in structures than in equipment, and the capital stocks of some industries such as aircraft production were virtually wartime creations. If output was to be maintained at the higher, wartime levels the need to re-equip industry was likely to be a major element in postwar demand.

Estimates of desired and actual capital stocks at the end of the

[1] Stocks of fixed assets as measured by the Office of Business Economics (*SCB*, December 1966 and February 1967) declined after 1929 for: manufacturing structures until 1941, manufacturing equipment until 1936, non-farm, non-manufacturing structures until 1947, non-farm non-manufacturing equipment until 1936, farm structures until 1946, and farm equipment until 1935. The ratio of net stocks at 1958 prices to GNP was

	Structures	*Equipment*
1929	0·746	0·257
1941	0·467	0·196
1965	0·342	0·184

The fall in the capital-output ratio in the 1930s was much more pronounced in structures than in equipment. Some part of this fall must be due to changes in technology; some part probably reflects the youthfulness of structures arising from the building boom of the late 1920s (in other words 1929 is not a good year for purposes of comparison). The equipment ratio over a forty-year period exhibits a fairly constant value and that for 1941 does not appear unduly low.

war are shown in Table 2.5. The detailed derivation of the estimates is explained in Note E.

TABLE 2.5: *Stock of business plant and equipment*

$ billion, 1954 prices

	*All industries**		*Manufacturing*	
	Desired Capital	Actual Capital	Desired Capital	Actual Capital
1945	—	234·8	—	51·9
1946	305·1	249·0	67·3	59·4
1947	309·1	265·4	70·3	65·9
1948	319·7	279·5	76·0	71·2
1949	321·4	287·9	75·9	73·1

* All industries are those included in the GNP definition of the business sector (including farming and government enterprises) with the exception of mining—but not petroleum extraction—and real estate.

Source: Desired capital (average over year): see Note E. Actual capital (at year end): B. G. Hickman, *Investment Demand and U.S. Economic Growth*, Brookings, Washington, D.C., 1965, Table B-4, p. 228.

Desired capital is the stock planned for long term equilibrium, given the expected levels of output, prices and costs, and is estimated from a relationship between capital stock and output (with allowance for a declining trend in the desired capital-output ratio) based on 1949–60 data. Only a fraction (about one-quarter) of any capital deficiency, i.e. the difference between desired and actual stocks, is made good during one year—the response to the deficiency is a lagged response. The figures in Table 2.5 show that in all industries the stock of capital at the end of 1945 was only three-quarters of what was desired in 1946.[1] The deficiency was $47 billions in 1946 prices, and in normal conditions (i.e. conditions of the 1950s) about one-quarter of this amount would be made good during 1946. In other words, planned net private business investment could be expected to be in the region of $12 billion in 1946. To this could be added some $9 billion to cover depreciation giving planned private business expenditures during 1946 on gross

[1] In 1946 desired stock depends on output in 1946 alone, while in later years it depends on a weighted average of current output and output lagged one year. See Note E.

fixed investment of about $21 billion which would be 50 per cent above 1941 levels (allowing for price differences).[1] As Table 2.5 shows the proportionate difference between desired and actual stock in manufacturing industry—13 per cent—was almost as large as it was in other industries, despite the wartime investment which had been concentrated in expanding plant for munition production.

Business was in a favourable situation to finance the fixed investment expected in the early postwar years. With rising output after 1940 corporate profits as well as the income of unincorporated business rose rapidly, although increases in taxation after 1941 prevented profits after tax from rising very much from 1942 on. Dividends after rises in 1940 and 1941, which did not bring the total up to the 1937 level, remained roughly steady for the remainder of the war. Hence undistributed profits, after their initial large rises in 1940 and 1941, rose only slowly during 1942 and 1943 and in 1944 actually fell. However, during the war as has been mentioned above (p. 73) business fixed investment declined, and the consequence was the accumulation of financial assets and growing liquidity of business. The situation is reflected in corporate balance sheets at the end of the war.

At the end of 1945 the relationship of equity to the income of non-financial corporations was about the same as prevailed during the period 1947–58, on the basis of Goldsmith's data.[2] Tangible assets, according to this evidence, were no more than about $10 billion below the level to be expected from 1945 corporate income. However intangible assets, in the light of the asset-income relationship for 1947–58 were almost $40 billion above normal. This is likely to be too high an estimate of 'excess' assets as the relationship appears to have altered during the late 1950s. Using 1947–54 data, the excess would be nearer $20 billion. The liquid asset (currency, demand deposits and short term government securities) relationship is not very clearly defined in the data, but from the relationship prevailing in the early 1950s it appears that excess holdings of liquid assets were

[1] Estimate of depreciation from Hickman [1965], Table B-2, p. 226, changed from 1954 prices to 1946 prices.

[2] For the source of data and description of the relationships see Note E.

of the order of $10 billion. Business was clearly in a position to finance internally from liquid reserves a large part of its anticipated postwar investment.

By the end of the war the level of business inventories in relation to sales was substantially below the levels of 1939–41. For example, at the end of 1945, if the average 1941 inventory-sales ratio had applied, total manufacturing and trade inventories would have had to have been about $6 billion or one-sixth greater than they actually were.[1] This deficiency in stocks was spread throughout the business sector. Only in durable goods manufacturing was the 1945 ratio higher than in 1944 (due to the decline in munitions production) and this ratio was still less than one-half of the prewar ratio. The purchased materials ratio in nondurable goods manufacturing and the goods in process ratios in both durable and nondurable goods manufacturing had not fallen during the war, but in both branches of manufacturing inventories of finished goods in relation to sales had fallen dramatically as production to military order replaced production for stock, and as shortages caused stocks to be run down. The value of durable manufacturers' stocks of finished goods was about 10 per cent lower at the end of 1945 than it had been at the end of 1941, and the special shortage of durable goods was reflected in the low levels of retailers' stocks of these goods which were at the end of 1945 about one-quarter below the levels at the end of 1941.

In view of the likely rise in household spending and production for civilian purposes after the end of the war, businessmen could be expected to attempt to raise their inventories by large amounts. While the output necessary to raise inventories to optimum levels would not equal that needed to raise business plant and equipment or housing to desired levels, the inventory restocking boom could be expected to have its impact in the early months of peace.

The foreign demand for U.S. goods and services

As output and incomes rose in most countries in the second half of the 1930s the demand for U.S. exports increased, and from

[1] The average 1941 ratio, 1·58, was only slightly above the average ratio of 1951 to 1958. The inventory situation described in this paragraph is based on figures from *SCB*, Business Statistics 1963 edition.

1933 to 1941 the volume of exports of goods and services rose by nearly 60 per cent, although the level in 1941 was not quite the 1929 level. After 1941 war and war production caused exports to decline and in 1943 they were only 61 per cent in volume of the 1941 levels. They rose only slightly in 1944 and early 1945.

A return to prewar levels was not likely to be the major source of increased demand for U.S. exports in 1945. The major factors were the destruction of means of production in Europe and Eastern Asia, the shortages of food, clothing and shelter and—in the countries like the United Kingdom whose output and income had risen rapidly during the war—a greatly expanded effective demand for consumer and producer goods of all kinds. The war had left the world with a great demand for all goods and services to satisfy both the immediate postwar needs of relief and reconstruction, and the increased real incomes of the fortunate countries; the United States was the only large country with the immediate capacity to meet the demand.

UNRRA was established in 1943 in anticipation of the needs of countries occupied by the Allies. The original U.S. contribution was $1·25 billion. At the end of the war in Europe, to meet immediate needs, Congress agreed to double the original UNRRA contribution, and to continue shipments of civilian supplies on lend-lease terms until mid-1946. At the same time the Export-Import Bank (set up in 1934 to finance U.S. exports) had its total lending authority raised to $3·5 billion.

CHAPTER 3

Reconstruction, 1945 to 1947

INFLATION

As Table 2.1 and Fig. 2.1 show, half of the postwar fall in war expenditures took place in the second half of 1945, and more than offset rises in private expenditure, the fall in Federal defence expenditures being $75 billion compared with a decline in total GNP of $57 billion. In the fifteen months after 1945 IV defence expenditures fell another $75 billion but were completely offset by rising private and other government expenditure. As far as the balance between military and civilian output is concerned, the postwar reconversion may be said to have been completed by mid-1946, although as was seen in the previous chapter demobilization was not completed until the end of the year. But before the changes in the main categories of expenditure can be discussed it is necessary to review the effects of the suppressed wartime and postwar inflation.

Inflation is a sustained rise in prices; deflation is a sustained fall in prices; suppressed inflation can be covered by these definitions if a distinction is made between nominal and actual prices. The basic model used in this book to explain inflation and deflation is the Keynesian theory of excess demand. If, in a market, demand exceeds supply at given prices, prices will rise. The price rise will depend upon the workings of the particular institutions for price fixing (such as wage negotiations), and price changes in one market, e.g. for goods, will lead to changes in other markets, e.g. for factors of production. In this theory, monetary factors such as the ease and cost of obtaining credit, and the degree of liquidity, influence the willingness of business and households to spend and pay higher prices. While this model may not be appropriate in periods when business and households have become accustomed to substantial and sustained rises in prices, it provides the most useful explanation of the price changes of the early postwar years.[1]

Wartime price controls were continued with some alterations until the second half of 1946 when they were removed in two main stages in July and in early November.[2] Between June 1945 and June 1946 the Consumer Price Index of the Department of Labour records a 3·3 per cent rise; between June and December 1946 the index rose by 15 per cent. With excess demand for goods and services during and just after the end of the war price controls had created a condition of suppressed inflation. As Lerner, writing in 1948 in a *Review of Economics and Statistics* Symposium on the inflation, said

[1] For a review of modern inflation theory see H. G. Johnson, *Essays in Monetary Economics*, Allen and Unwin Ltd., London, 1967, Chapter III, 'A survey of theories of inflation'. Johnson comments (p. 126) 'for the mild type of inflation typical of the United States and other advanced countries in recent years, however, the [quantity theory] approach has not proved nearly so useful . . . Neither the Keynesian nor the quantity theory approach to inflation, of course, is very well adapted to dealing with the problems of suppressed inflation.'

[2] The Emergency Price Control Act, and the Stabilization Act, both of 1942 and due to expire on June 30, 1945, were extended with some amendments by Congress in June 1945 until June 30, 1946. Wage controls were relaxed substantially in August 1945 when employers were permitted to make wage increases without official approval on the condition that such increases would not be used as the basis of claims for increases in price ceilings. In his budget message of January 21, 1946, President Truman said that 'today inflation is our greatest immediate domestic problem', and he asked Congress to extend the price controls immediately for one year. After extensive investigation and debate Congress passed a Bill which extended controls for a year but removed much of the ability to stabilize prices by linking ceilings to industry-wide cost increases. The President vetoed the Bill on June 29th on the grounds that it was inflationary.

All price controls ended on June 30th, and during July Congress prepared a new Bill extending controls until June 30, 1947, modifying the cost increase provisions of the vetoed Bill and decontrolling major farm products including livestock, milk, grain and tobacco. A Price Control Board was to consider whether price ceilings should be reimposed on some of these commodities. The President signed the Bill with obvious reluctance on July 25th. The use of subsidies to control prices was part of the price control controversy, and the bill which the President signed reduced the limit on subsidies and the terminal date to April 1, 1947.

For brief periods until November price controls were reimposed on some commodities: livestock prices were controlled again, for example, from September 11th to October 16th. On November 9th after the elections in which the Republicans gained control of Congress, President Truman announced the removal on November 12th of all remaining price and wage controls except for ceilings on rents, sugar and rice.

'Rising prices are a symptom of too much spending. Prices in general can rise only if the amount of money spent increases in relation to the amount of goods sold, and if the amount of money does increase in relation to the amount of goods sold, prices have to rise. If prices are not permitted to rise openly and on a free market, they will rise secretly and in a black market.'[1]

Other economists regard the black market as only one of several ways in which supply and demand were equated in suppressed inflation.[2] Goods were withheld from the market, customers were forced to accept goods of unsuitable specification (such as unnecessarily high quality at a high price, or poor quality at the controlled price[3]), delays in delivery and other services were frequent, while black markets flourished. The implication is that actual or effective prices rose to equate supply and demand. Actual prices rose more rapidly than nominal controlled prices and hence the use of the latter overstates the rise in real private consumption during the war. When price controls were removed in 1946, nominal prices rose to the level of actual prices. Thereafter inflation was no longer suppressed.

This analysis of suppressed inflation is of importance not only in underestimating the price changes and the effect of the removal of controls, but also in interpreting the changes in personal consumption in the second half of 1946. Table 3.1 shows the official index of consumer prices and the estimates of the volume of PCE that result from deflating money expenditures by the price index. These are called the [A] estimates, and reveal a 5 per cent fall in consumption in the second half of 1946. In Note A below I review the statistical evidence from the side of production and retailers' inventories and conclude that there is no statistical support for the view that consumption fell.

[1] A. P. Lerner, 'Rising prices', *R. Econ. Statist.*, *30*, February 1948, p. 24. See also Lerner's contribution to a later symposium on the same subject. 'The inflationary process: some theoretical aspects', *R. Econ. Statist.*, *31*, August 1949, pp. 193–200.

[2] See for instance Friedman and Schwartz [1963], pp. 557–58.

[3] 'The effort to associate price with quality standards was a disastrous abortion. . . .' J. K. Galbraith, 'The disequilibrium system', *Amer. econ. R.*, *38*, June 1947, p. 298. After the war textile raw materials were processed into uncontrolled luxury lines at the expense of controlled cheap lines. See the 6th Report of the Director of War Mobilization and Reconstruction, April 1, 1946, *passim.*

TABLE 3.1: *Personal Consumption, 1946–47*

	[A] estimates		[B] estimates		[C] estimates		
	PCE at 1958 prices $ *billion*	*Implicit price index* 1958=100	*PCE at 1958 prices* $ *billion*	*Implicit price index* 1958=100	*PCE at 1958 prices* $ *billion*	*Implicit price index* 1958=100	*PCE at current prices* $ *billion*
1946 II	208·4	66·8	189·5	73·5	203·4	68·5	139·3
III	203·0	72·8	196·9	75·1	203·4	72·7	147·9
IV	198·3	76·7	198·3	76·7	203·4	74·8	152·1
1947 I	203·4	76·2	203·4	76·2	203·4	76·2	155·0

Source: [A] Table A.1 and Note A.
[B] and [C] explained in text.
PCE at current prices: *SCB.*

On the statistical evidence alone the safest conclusion is probably that consumption remained unchanged: this assumption leads to the [C] estimates of Table 3.1. The [C] price index shown is that implied by the official estimate of PCE at current prices and the assumed unchanged volume of consumption. It can be regarded as an index of actual prices, in contrast to the [A] index which is of nominal prices. The [C] estimates are unsatisfactory on two grounds. The first is that the [C] price index in 1946 II is only 2½ per cent above the [A] index, implying that at that time actual prices were only 2½ per cent above nominal, controlled prices. In view of the large rise in prices after decontrol, this does not accord with the suppressed inflation hypothesis. The second ground for objection is that while food production did not change very much from quarter to quarter during 1946, demobilization was still taking place during the second half of 1946, and the number of civilian mouths to be fed rose by 2 per cent between June and December. Some continued rise in civilian consumption from demobilization alone could be expected.

I have accordingly constructed yet another set of estimates [B]. Nominal prices rose by 15 per cent between 1946 II and 1946 IV. Some part of this rise must be ascribed to open inflation, and some to profiteering in the wake of decontrol. As a result I have put the excess of actual over nominal prices in 1946 II at the round figure of 10 per cent. Actual prices rose at a steady rate until 1946 IV when actual and nominal coincide.[1] The [B] consumption series results from deflating the current price expenditures by the [B] price index, and shows a 4 per cent rise in consumption in 1946 III and smaller rises thereafter. While 4 per cent was a large rise to have occurred in one quarter, it is not excessively large when compared with the 16 per cent rise (which we do not question, see Note A) between 1945 II and 1946 II. Furthermore, business inventory investment declined in 1946 III, and during August when the largest increase in nondurable retail sales (at current prices) occurred, the book value of retailers' inventories actually fell. Retailers probably stockpiled in anticipation of the removal of controls, and other suppliers (e.g. farmers) brought to market increased supplies once controls were discarded. The rise in consumption in the second half of 1946 is thus not implausible.

Which estimate [A], [B] or [C], should we adopt? None is better than the assumptions and arguments behind it: each simply quantifies an economic analysis. [A] must be discarded: it flies in the face of all the other evidence. [C] is a safe assumption, but unrealistically minimizes the degree of suppressed inflation in early 1946. [B] is in some respects the most hair-raising estimate, but it explains more facts than either of the others. I accept it, with its overall hypothesis of suppressed inflation and its implications.[2]

PERSONAL INCOME AND CONSUMER EXPENDITURES

As Fig. 3.1 shows, DPI actually fell during the second half of 1945 as government wage and salary payments dropped and manufacturers reduced their labour force. The $12 billion fall in incomes from these sources was offset to some extent by a $5 billion increase in government transfer payments: mainly

[1] The rapid ending of suppressed inflation and the 4 per cent rise in actual prices during the last half of 1946 make it possible to ascribe the price stability of 1947 I to a temporary disappearance of excess demand. No special significance need be attached to the small (0·65 per cent) fall in the official [A] implicit price index between 1946 IV and 1947 I. The CPI rose until December 1946, remained unchanged for the next two months, and rose again in March. The main unstable factor was the movement of food prices, which reached a peak in November and fell during the next three months. In March they rose again.

[2] The [B] estimates are incorporated in the output and expenditure series used here. See Table A.1. The [B] price series is used in the analysis behind Fig. 3.1.

Fig. 3.1: Composition of changes in PCE and DPI, 1945–50.

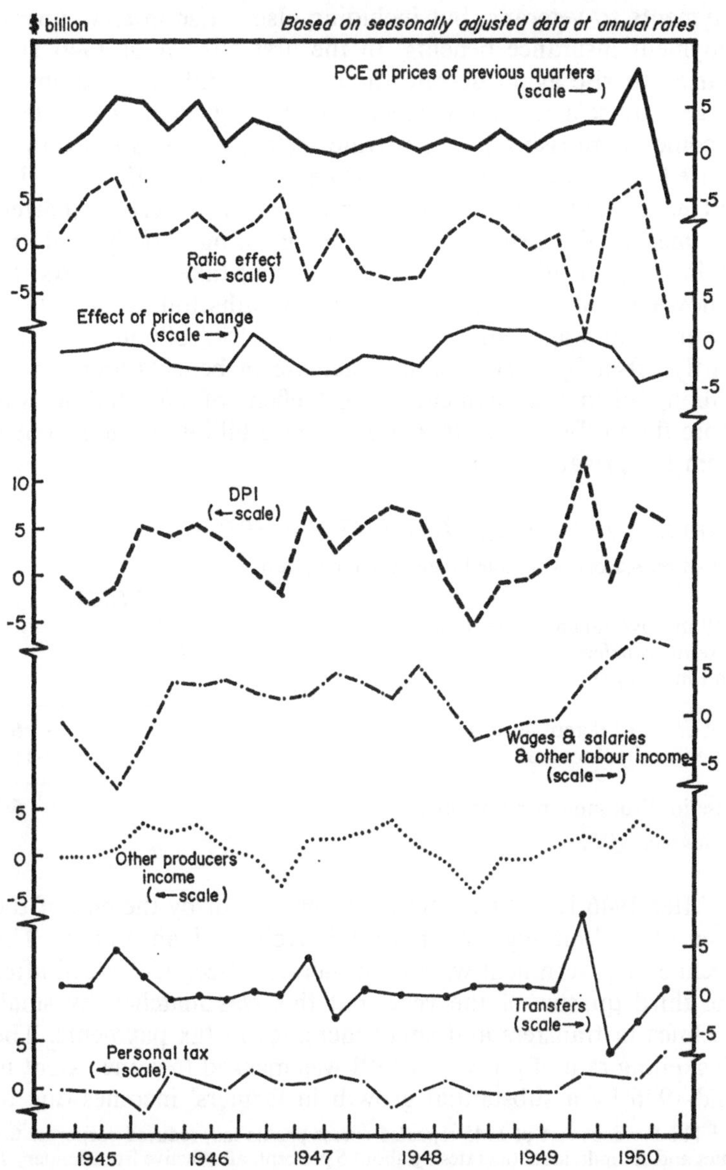

Source: SCB. *PCE:* change in volume of PCE between $t-1$ and t valued at prices of $t-1$. *Effect of price change:* change in prices between $t-1$ and t multiplied by volume of PCE at t. *Ratio effect:* Change in PCE between $t-1$ and t, *minus* PCE at $t-1$ multiplied by the proportionate change in DPI between $t-1$ and t (this is the difference between the actual change in PCE and the change if the ratio of PCE to DPI had been unaltered). For price index in 1945 the CPI is linked to the implicit PCE price index. The price index 1946 II to 1947 I is [B] series Table 3.1.

payments to veterans, but including also a rise in state unemployment insurance benefits. In the first quarter of 1946 DPI started to rise again despite the continued fall in government wages and salaries and a slackening in the growth of transfers. Incomes were rising in the private sectors as industrial output started to expand, while the Revenue Act of 1945 allowed a fall in personal taxes of nearly $3 billion.[1] By the second quarter, incomes in the private sector were growing rapidly and the main postwar adjustment in incomes had taken place. As the following table shows, in the twelve months following 1945 II government wages and salaries fell by $15·7 billion and were partly offset by a $6·7 billion increase in benefits and a $2·7 billion fall in tax payments. The 'deficit' of $6·3 billion was more than offset by an increase of $11·5 billion in the incomes from the private sector.

TABLE 3.2: *Change in DPI 1945 II to 1946 II*

(based on seasonally adjusted data at annual rates)

		$ billion
Fall in government wages and salaries	−15·7	
Rise in transfers	+ 6·7	
Fall in income tax	+ 2·7	
Net effect of demobilization		− 6·3
Rise in other incomes		+11·5
Rise in disposable personal income		5·2

Source: SCB.

After 1946 II, DPI continued to grow, but by the end of the year at a declining rate both relatively and absolutely. The decline in government wages and salaries effectively ended after the third quarter of the year, but this was matched by small declines in transfers and small increases in tax payments. The slackening rate of growth of DPI was masked to some extent in mid-1946 by a substantial growth in farmers' incomes due to

[1] The Revenue Act of 1945 repealed excess profits tax, reduced corporate tax rates and cut individual tax rates by about 5 per cent, all effective from January 1, 1946. A scheduled rise in social security tax was postponed. The estimated revenue loss was $5·9 billion, of which over $2 billion was due to the reduction in tax on personal incomes.

the great rise in the prices of farm products as price controls broke down or were discarded.[1] With farm incomes ceasing to rise in 1947 I and falling sharply in the second quarter, and in the absence of strong income growth in other parts of the economy, the rise in DPI stopped.[2] Apart from farming, the pause in growth of DPI in the middle of 1947 was marked particularly in manufacturing wages and salaries, and to a lesser extent in the service industries and in noncorporate business. In all these sectors growth had been resumed by the last quarter of the year, assisted by an exceptional payment of veterans benefits of about $4 billion in the third quarter.[3]

The model used to explain consumer spending behaviour in the years dealt with in this book is based on modern versions of the Keynesian consumption function.[4] The model embraces three relationships between consumption (PCE) and real income (DPI). The first is the normal, long-term relationship between PCE and DPI: consumption is a fixed proportion of income (the marginal propensity to spend equals the average propensity). For the postwar period we assume this fixed proportion to be 0·91.[5] This normal, long run relationship depends on the expected long run growth in real income, the expected long run rate of interest, attitudes about inheritance of wealth and the prevailing set of social habits and conventions. In the short run, the level of consumption will not be greatly influenced by changes in income. Thus the second, or short-period, relation-

[1] The average index of prices received by farmers during 1946 III was 15 per cent above the previous quarter and 21 per cent above 1945 III. The index in 1946 IV was 9 per cent again above the third quarter. For the removal of price controls see pp. 79–80.

[2] The volume of farm production was in 1947 nearly 3 per cent below that in 1946. The fall in income in the middle of 1947 was due primarily to the fall in output, and to a lesser extent to a price squeeze when farm product prices temporarily stopped rising in the second quarter of the year. (Farm sales and cash receipts, however, remained high due to a large reduction in farm inventories concentrated mainly in the second and third quarters of the year.)

[3] Terminal Leave Bonds were cashed. Originally these bonds were irredeemable for five years, but Congress in 1947 made them redeemable as from September 1st.

[4] A review of the theories and the econometric evidence is contained in Note B.

[5] This is based on the relationship between DPI and PCE 1939–64 excluding the war and early postwar years. See Note C.

ship between PCE and DPI, expresses the stability of levels of consumption, and the slowness of expenditures to alter in response to changes of income. In particular, changes in income judged to be of a temporary nature will not influence the level of PCE, while when changes do influence spending the effects are considerably delayed. There is one important exception to the short run relationship as described: purchases of new cars may depend to a large extent on changes in income from their long period expected level.[1]

The third relationship in the model is the temporary, abnormal expenditure caused by the wartime underspending and the high level of liquid assets held by households at the end of the war. The abnormal expenditure was incurred both to 'restock' houses and garages with durable equipment, automobiles and clothing, and to indulge in a short spending 'spree' after the wartime years of deprivation. This expenditure was spread from the end of the war to 1950, fluctuated over the period depending on the availability of goods, and in its peak periods rose to 4 per cent of DPI, i.e., it temporarily raised the long term propensity to spend out of income up to the high level of about 0·95.

Up to the middle of 1947, the quarter to quarter changes in PCE are dominated by the rise in the propensity to consume from its abnormally low wartime level, and the postwar restocking and spending spree. Price changes, and their effect on real income or purchasing power, were also important in the early postwar years. Consequently, in analysing the changes in PCE in these years I have divided the change in real PCE into three parts depending on change in current DPI, change in prices and change in the ratio of current PCE to current DPI. The breakdown is shown in Fig. 3.1. The ratio is the short run average propensity to spend, and for convenience is called here

[1] Another way of expressing the relationship between expenditures on durables such as cars and income is to say that changes in income of a temporary nature affect consumption—defined to include the services of durables instead of expenditures on them—only through the increase in wealth. Since expenditure on durables is a form of investment, temporary income receipts may increase spending on durables. The logical extension of modern consumption theories to durable goods is a portfolio theory of investment but no suitable quantitative theory is at present available for our purposes.

the consumption ratio. The rise in this ratio back to its long term, normal value—and beyond—is shown in Fig. 3.2.

During the second half of 1945, when DPI fell, the rapid rise in the consumption ratio from 0·781 to 0·869 much more than offset the fall in DPI or the small depressing effect of price increases and allowed substantial increases in real expenditures as Fig. 3.1 shows. The situation in the various consumer markets differed as can be seen in Fig. 3.2. For nondurable goods as a

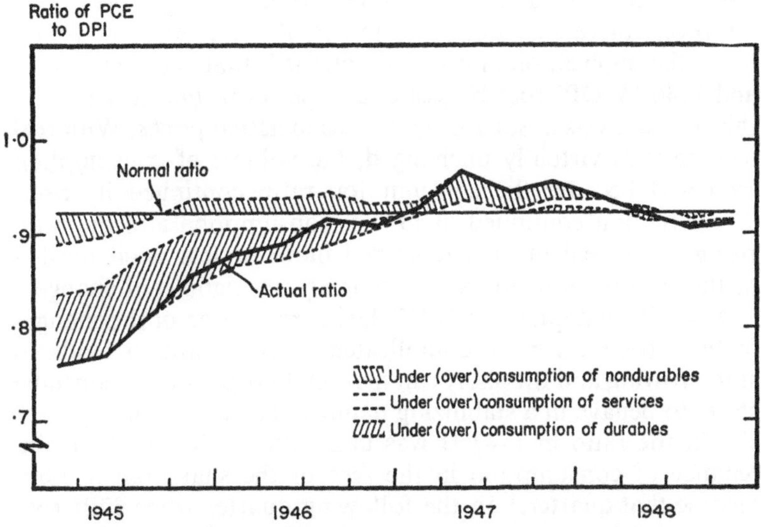

Fig. 3.2.: The consumption ratio, 1945–48.

Source: SCB. *Normal ratio:* based on equation $C_t = 2{\cdot}9 + 0{\cdot}909\,Y_t$ (see Note C, p. 230). *Under (over) consumption of durables, services and nondurables:* based on difference between actual expenditures and those calculated from Equations 1, 2 and 3, Note C, p. 230.

whole, expenditures were back to normal by 1945 III, and were substantially above normal in the fourth quarter. Under-consumption of services had declined a little by the end of the year, but expenditures on durable goods were still well below normal.

The roles of income and ratio change were reversed during the first half of 1946. The ratio rose only from 0·869 to 0·885 between

1945 IV and 1946 II. Instead DPI increased and offset the effect of price increases (important in 1946 II), with the result that real PCE continued to rise. Nondurable expenditures remained abnormally high (mainly on foodstuffs and clothing), while expenditures on services (especially on housing) and on durable goods remained low.

As price controls were removed during the second half of 1946, prices rose, and I have already (pp. 80–2) given reasons for believing that the main part of the rise was the increase in nominal, controlled prices to the level of actual, effective prices. However, there was some rise in actual prices also. In round terms the implication of my assumptions is that between 1946 II and 1946 IV DPI rose by just over 5 per cent, but nearly all of this increase was absorbed by the rise in actual prices. With real income thus virtually unchanged, the volume of consumption increased because the consumption ratio continued its rise.[1] This situation continued in 1947 I, consumption and the ratio rising while real income remained more or less unchanged—neither income nor prices experiencing any significant change.

After the first quarter of 1947 the interpretation of the changes in PCE becomes more complicated as consumption tends to stop growing and the short run marginal propensity to consume starts to behave in a stabilizing manner. The exceptionally large rise in the ratio in 1947 II was undoubtedly due to the maintenance of consumption in the face of the sharp fall in farm income that quarter.[2] In the following quarter when DPI rose because of the temporary increase in veterans benefits the ratio declined, rising again in the final quarter of the year. These short run fluctuations appear to be superimposed on a historically high ratio which was reached in 1947 II and continued at a steady level until the end of the year. During this time consumption of nondurables and services was very steady, although at an abnormally high level in relation to income. Expenditures

[1] In Fig. 3.1 the allocation of these changes is made between the IIIrd and IVth quarters, but the allocation is essentially arbitrary. In view of the fact that the rise in the consumption ratio was part of a rise begun at the end of the war and continued into 1947 it is not necessary to stress the increased supply of goods, greater variety and better quality, following the ending of controls, as factors in causing the rise, although these factors may well have played some part.

[2] See p. 85.

on durables were at normal levels in relation to income, although were still restrained by shortages, especially of cars.[1]

Why was there no postwar slump in consumption? The end of the war found consumers with reduced stocks of durable goods, high levels of liquid assets and a disposition to spend freely after years of war and shortages. If it had been possible to increase the supply of civilian goods and services quickly at the end of the war, consumers would presumably have quickly raised their consumption ratio above the normal long term propensity and equally quickly have brought it back to normal. The supply of goods and services could not of course be increased speedily. Reconversion took time, particularly in the durable goods industries, and textiles were in short supply throughout 1946. Automobiles did not become available in sufficiently large numbers until 1949. Demobilization in the armed forces, while swift, was not finally completed until the end of 1946 and early 1947. In actual fact, therefore, the growth of consumption was slowed down by shortages and the normal delays of demobilization. A consumption boom which in theory might have been over within a year of the end of the war was still in progress at the end of 1947. Instead of a rise and fall in PCE, there was growth until mid-1947. The significance of this delaying and smoothing of the boom was not only that there was no sharp fall in household spending during the reconversion period, but that when expenditures on nondurable goods and services reached limits in the second half of 1947 set by the eventual return of liquid assets to levels which were normal in relation to income, and by the subsidence of the desire to spend freely, incomes had risen to the point where that level of PCE could be sustained. In other words, by the beginning of 1948 consumption was at a level determined by the long run normal consumption function. This explains the stability in the level

[1] M. Sapir wrote 'It is the phenomenal and quite unexpected rise in nondurable expenditures since the war that has been most striking. ... It appears that consumer income, which could not find customary outlets in durable goods during the first postwar year, has 'spilled over' into the nondurable goods areas, in which supplies have been more abundant, prices possibly relatively favourable, etc.' [See 'Review of economic forecasts for the transition period', *Studies in Income and Wealth*, XI, New York, NBER, 1949, pp. 308–9.] The fact that during 1947 the actual aggregate consumption ratio was higher than the normal ratio would appear to cast doubt on the spillover hypothesis.

of consumption during that year. (Shortages of automobiles remained, however, and as is explained in the following chapter, changes in the car market during the next two years made the early 1948 return to normality only temporary.)

INVESTMENT

Housing

The tremendous shortage of houses at the end of the war has been described above (p. 72). While incomes and population had increased since 1941, housebuilding had been controlled and kept at very low levels. On top of the basic shortage, there was a boom in family formation as veterans married and set up house. Despite the rapid expansion of the construction industry after the end of the war (employment rose by about 60 per cent in the twelve months after May 1945) shortages of materials limited the amount of work done by the industry until early 1947. As part of the immediate postwar bonfire of controls, the War Production Board in October 1945 abolished all restrictions on building except limitations on the use of materials in short supply. The rate of private housing starts immediately rose very quickly and by March 1946 was about six times what it had been a year previously. This great rush to build created such shortages that not only were controls over materials strengthened, but the rate of starts declined by 20 per cent for six months after March 1946 due to the difficulties in obtaining materials.[1]

These bottlenecks, and the decline in starts, stopped in the final quarter of 1946 the postwar growth in the volume of building. By the third quarter of 1946 the volume of residential

[1] In December 1945 a Housing Expediter was appointed with broad powers over housing priorities and material allocation (government policy was particularly concerned with providing housing for veterans) and during 1946 not only were attempts made to rigidly control the use of steel and lumber, but low cost housing received special encouragement. In December 1946 the allocation system was replaced by a permit system. This expired on June 30, 1947, after which there were no remaining controls on new construction. For details of postwar housing policy see reports of Federal Housing Administration and the Director of War Mobilization and Reconversion, the *Monthly Labour Review* and the *New York Times*. The explanation of the drop in starts in 1946 is suggested by L. Grebler, *Housing Issues in Economic Stabilisation Policy*, Occasional Paper No. 72, NBER, New York, 1960, note b to Table 22, p. 107.

building had risen to over $15 billion, compared with just under $10 billion in 1941 and just over $10 billion in 1929, and was five times the 1945 III level. Private housing starts rose again at the end of 1946 as controls were removed. Shortages of materials, however, still remained, and with lengthy delays in construction the renewed boom in starts was not translated into a rising volume of building until the second half of 1947.

Business investment

As in the case of housing, there was a great backlog of investment to be undertaken by business after the war. The deficiencies were particularly evident in the case of industrial buildings and other structures which had not been replaced or repaired during the war. The backlog, and the favourable financial position of business has been described above (pp. 73–6). After the ending of fighting and the beginning of demobilization, the general background favourable to a rising rate of investment was reinforced by the expansion of private demand. Although government purchases fell, private purchases of goods and services rose by nearly 40 per cent in the twelve months following 1945 II.

After the fall in profits immediately at the end of the war, internal sources of finance for corporations tended to rise—despite short period fluctuations—from early 1946 to mid-1948.[1] Internal sources declined during the second half of 1945 as war production was halted and before peacetime output was resumed. Corporate profits fell sharply, and undistributed profits declined from about $7 billion in the first quarter of the year to about $3 billion in 1945 IV. At the beginning of 1946, however, internal sources rose rapidly: corporate tax liabilities were reduced by some $2 billion when the Revenue Act of 1945 took effect in 1946 I.[2] In the second half of the year profits rose about $10 billions, the main part being due to inventory profits as prices rose swiftly. With taxes and dividends absorbing some

[1] Internal sources are defined as cash flow, net of dividends (i.e. capital consumption allowances plus undistributed profits), less inventory profits (inventory valuation adjustment).

[2] This Act repealed excess profits tax and reduced corporate profits tax, both with effect from January 1, 1946. For the alterations in individual tax rates, see above (p. 84).

$4 billions of the rise, internal sources did not rise at all. Thus the net effect of the late 1946 inflation on internal sources of funds for corporations was zero: the inventory profits (which are not a source of funds) generated a tax liability which absorbed the increase in undistributed profits from other sources. In early 1947 the reverse movement started. Inventory profits were cut as prices stopped rising, and taxes fell by about $1 billion between 1946 IV and 1947 III. Internal sources rose rapidly throughout 1947, more than doubling between 1947 I and 1948 I. There is no evidence in 1946 or 1947 that businesses curtailed investment because of shortage of finance, although the excess liquidity built up during the war had been used up by the end of 1946.

At the end of the war in 1945 II business investment was running at about $20 billion, double the low levels of 1943, and nearly as great as the 1941 rate. Reconversion and expansion had been planned in many industries with government assistance since 1944, and in some cases retooling for civilian production was under way early in 1945. Industrial building and construction, rising throughout the early months of 1945, expanded rapidly after 1945 III to reach a high level of activity in the first half of 1946 (greater than any year since 1929). This level remained steady throughout the remainder of 1946 and during 1947. Investment in equipment—which had not been cut to the same extent as construction during the war, and which was at relatively high levels in the first half of 1945—rose less rapidly. Its growth was probably restrained by shortages of materials and difficulties in expanding output in the durable goods industries in early 1946, because when output in those industries expanded in the second half of the year, expenditures on equipment rose rapidly, and by 1947 I were at the very high level which continued throughout 1947.

Inventory investment

The ending of the war and the decline in munitions production resulted during the second half of 1945 in a large fall in the goods in process and stocks of materials of durable goods manufacturers. During these months most other inventories changed very little from their low wartime levels, except for the stocks held by retailers of nondurable goods which declined in the last quarter of the year as sales rose rapidly.

By January 1946 restocking had commenced and was taking place in all sectors of the economy—manufacturing, wholesaling and retailing—and was nearly as large in nondurable goods as in durables.[1] In the manufacture of durable goods, the ending of reconversion and the resumption of civilian production during the first half of 1946 generated exceptionally large rises in inventories of goods in process and in stocks of materials. As Fig. 3.3 shows, by the middle of 1946, amongst most durable and nondurable goods manufacturers, with the important exception of durable finished goods, the volume of inventories in relation to sales—measured by the inventory-sales ratios—had reached a normal level which was to be maintained during the following years. Stocks of durable finished goods of both manufacturers and traders were still below optimum levels at the end of 1946. Despite rapid restocking and rises in the inventory-sales ratios during the year, retailers' and wholesalers' ratios were still below normal at the end of it, while as has been pointed out above there were still many shortages of goods such as steel, building materials and automobiles.[2]

In contrast to the situation in durable goods, at the end of 1946 and early in 1947 inventories of nondurable goods traders were nearly restored to normal levels. Retailers, in particular, despite the heavy household demand, had quickly replenished their depleted stocks. Fig. 3.3 shows that from November 1946 to April 1947 the nondurable goods retailers' monthly inventory sales ratio, averaging about 1·20, was not very far below the level of about 1·23 which was typical of the period from early

[1] For rough estimates of investment divided between durable and nondurable goods industries see Note F.

[2] The extent of the unsatisfied inventory demand was probably not very large in relation to output as a whole. Leaving aside the special cases of automobiles and steel, durable goods retailers' inventory-sales ratio in 1946 IV was 0·65, about 20 per cent below the level of 0·80 which was reached in early 1948 and subsequently tended to be maintained (Fig. 3.3 shows the monthly ratio; the quarterly ratio is shown in Fig. 6.4, p. 173). This unsatisfied inventory demand—say, one quarter of the end-1946 inventory—would have been about 6 per cent of durable goods output or 20 per cent of output of consumer durables excluding automobiles in 1947 I.

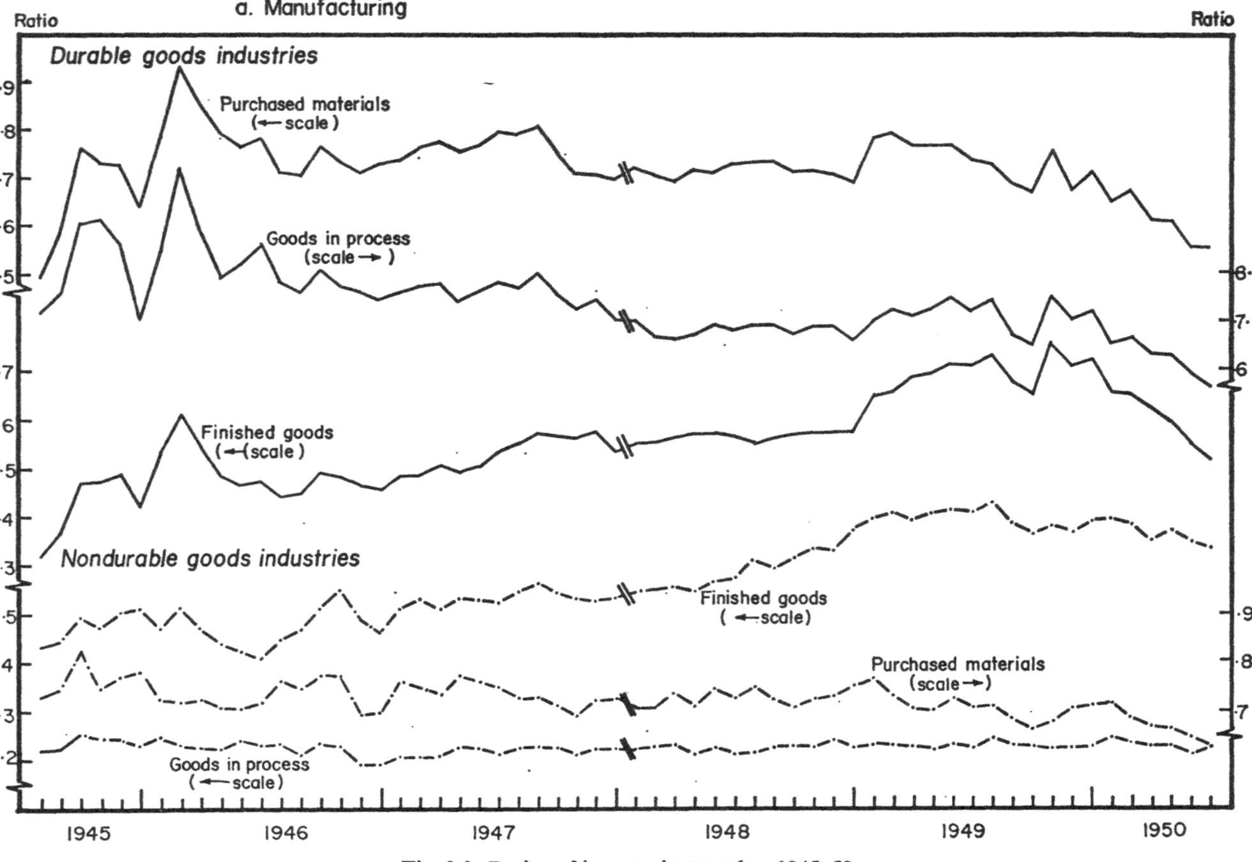

Fig. 3.3: Ratios of inventories to sales, 1945–50.

b. Retail stores and merchant wholesalers

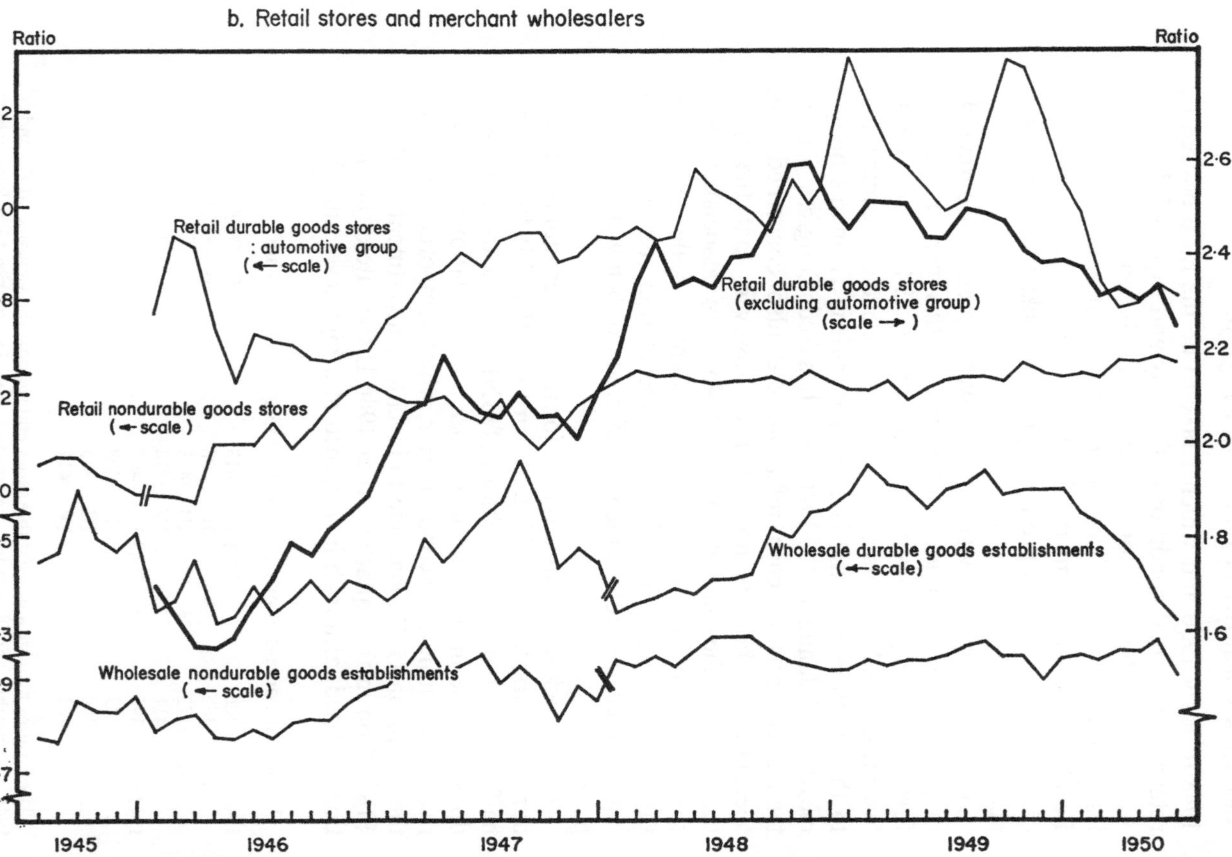

Source: Office of Business Economics. Broken lines indicate links of series with different benchmarks. Inventories are undeflated, end of month, book values; sales are monthly current values. Both series seasonally adjusted.

1948 to early 1950 and which I take to be the ratio desired by retailers in normal conditions of supply and expected demand. Accordingly the inventory deficiency at the end of 1946 was less than 2½ per cent of desired inventories although as Rendigs Fels has suggested to me it is likely that because of the difficulty of getting orders filled promptly greater stocks than usual were needed.[1]

The fear of inventory speculation was expressed prominently in government economic statements in this period, e.g. the President's budget message of January 9, 1945, warned that 'we must avoid speculation in inventories such as contributed to the inflation after the last war'. President Truman's budget message of January 21, 1946, which asked Congress for extended controls to curb inflation, was also concerned with speculation. There is no evidence, however, that the price increases in the second half of 1946 were associated with speculation in inventories on any extensive scale, except for the special case of farmers' speculation on the ending of price controls which is referred to below (footnote[2], p. 98).

The restocking boom was a major factor in economic activity during the first half of 1946. Between 1945 IV and 1946 II, nearly half the rise in private purchases of GNP was due to the tremendous increase in the rate of inventory accumulation: the sharp rise in output in the second quarter, which temporarily arrested the decline in GNP, was due to inventory investment of almost $18 billion in that quarter. After 1946 II the rate of accumulation declined, although it remained at a high level until 1947 I.

[1] The ratios of end of quarter inventory to quarterly sales are:

1946	I	·328	1948	I	·413	1950	I	·427
	II	·365		II	·408		II	·429
	III	·372		III	·413			
	IV	·411		IV	·414			
1947	I	·396	1949	I	·407			
	II	·383		II	·408			
	III	·366		III	·405			
	IV	·403		IV	·417			

These ratios provide a more stable series and support the view that at the end of 1946 nondurable goods retailers had raised their inventories to a level which was, in the light of subsequent practice, normal in relation to sales.

Foreign trade

Expanding exports had a considerable effect upon GNP immediately after the end of the war.[1] In the three quarters after 1945 II, the rise in exports contributed nearly $13 billion to the growth of civilian output. Over one-half of these rising exports were financed directly or indirectly by the U.S. government through loans or grants, and until the middle of 1946, grants in kind in the form of supplies to UNRRA and civilian supplies distributed by the armed forces, together with loans by the Export-Import Bank, were the main forms of government assistance. In early 1946 (when receipts were swelled by a revival of income from foreign investment) the growth of exports slackened and the level actually fell later in the year. Part of this was due to the difficulties overseas buyers were finding in financing commercial imports. Some of these difficulties were removed when the proceeds of the British loan became available in late 1946 and early 1947, and during the first half of 1947 export expansion was resumed.

Commercial imports did not respond to the decline in late 1945 of industrial production largely because the stability of household incomes maintained the demand for foodstuffs and beverages. As output rose again during 1946 imports grew slowly, restrained by shortages and slow growth in productive capacity in supplying countries. During 1947 the slight recession in the textile industries caused a fall in textile imports, while consumer resistance to high coffee prices led to a decline in coffee imports. By late 1947 industrial expansion was again leading to a growing import demand.

THE RETURN TO EQUILIBRIUM

In most industries the trough in the immediate postwar decline in output was reached in October 1945, and as Fig. 2.2 shows

[1] Since the 1965 National Income revisions, foreign transactions in the national income accounts include government nonmilitary grants in cash and kind (such as exports under UNRRA, Interim Aid and European Recovery Programme schemes) and private remittances. Government purchases and PCE correspondingly exclude these items. Military grants however are recorded as government purchases, not as exports. Similarly U.S. imports financed under reverse lend lease are excluded.

the production of both durable and nondurable goods was rising by November. Between October 1945 and January 1947 nondurable manufacturing production rose by 14 per cent, and all industries with the exception of tobacco products shared the rise. During 1946 growth was steady, with several industries—in particular textiles—operating at capacity and experiencing supply shortages.[1] As we have seen, both household demand and merchants' demand for restocking was strong. The only major industry whose growth was not steady in 1946 was meat packing, whose output in the second quarter of 1946 (after allowance for seasonal factors) was only 70 per cent of that in the first quarter due to a substantial drop in cattle slaughterings.[2] Leather tanning was consequently also seriously affected in the third quarter. Cattle slaughtering did not return to normal until the final quarter of the year, and these changes in the meat packing industry account for the decline of 6 per cent in the index of total nondurable production from February to July 1946, and the rapid rise thereafter.

The high level of nondurable output changed very little from November 1946 to March 1947. Most merchants completed their restocking, and the growth in household demand was slowing down. By the second quarter of 1947 consumption had stopped growing and production in some industries was falling as merchants and manufacturers ceased accumulating inventories. Output of processed fruits and vegetables declined substantially during the first half of the year, and production of apparel fell by 3 per cent in the second quarter. Declining

[1] 'One of the most acute and paradoxical dislocations in the economy today is the shortage of low and moderately priced textile products. Although military procurement was held to a minimum and total textile production increased during the first quarter of 1946, civilian, industrial and agricultural consumers found it was more difficult than at any time during the war to buy the kinds of apparel and fabric they most urgently needed' [6th Report of the Director of War Mobilization and Reconstruction, Washington, April 1, 1946, p. 37].

[2] Activity of meat packers was disturbed by the disruption of the channels of meat distribution caused by price controls. Packers' buying and selling prices were firmly controlled and in the second quarter of 1946 and again when controls were reimposed in September farmers reduced their shipments of cattle to regular markets and hence the packers were unable to buy normal quantities. Farmers were speculating on the end of controls; at the same time it is likely that some cattle shipments were made direct to restaurants, butchers, etc., at black market prices. See the *NYT* throughout June 1946.

export orders contributed to the decline in production. In the aggregate, nondurable goods output fell by 7½ per cent between February and July 1947. Although textile output did not recover until the end of the year, food production started to rise again in July, and total nondurable output resumed its growth during the second half of the year.

The revival of durable goods production after October 1945 was delayed by strikes, particularly those in the steel industry in January and February, in coal in April and May, 1946 (which caused shutdowns in steel) and in the automobile industry which started in November 1945 and did not end until the following March. In February the steel mills were operating at only 20 per cent of capacity and the reduced deliveries of steel affected in varying degrees machinery makers, the motor industry and other manufacturers. Recovery from the strike period did not come until July when output of durables rose above the November 1945 level.

During this period of severe shortages while the pressure of demand for both producer and consumer durables was very great, inventories of durable goods were nevertheless raised substantially, and by third quarter of 1946 when durable goods output was rising rapidly the bulk of manufacturers' restocking was completed. In the fourth quarter production settled to a steady rate of increase which lasted until the middle of 1947.

The slight recession in output in mid-1947 was, like the fall in nondurable output, concentrated in consumer goods—such as appliances and television, which fell slightly in July and August —and was due to falls in consumer expenditure around the middle of the year. The cuts in output were not great enough to prevent inventories of durable goods from rising in 1947 III.

As Fig. 3.4 shows, the rate of growth in civilian production reached its maximum in the first quarter of 1946. Growth in the second and third quarters of the year was still at historically high levels, but by early 1947 the rate had settled down to about 4 per cent per annum which was to become normal in the succeeding years. Most categories of civilian expenditure experienced the initial burst of growth and subsequent slackening in the rate. In the early stages from 1945 III to 1946 II, consumption, inventory accumulation and the balance (fixed investment,

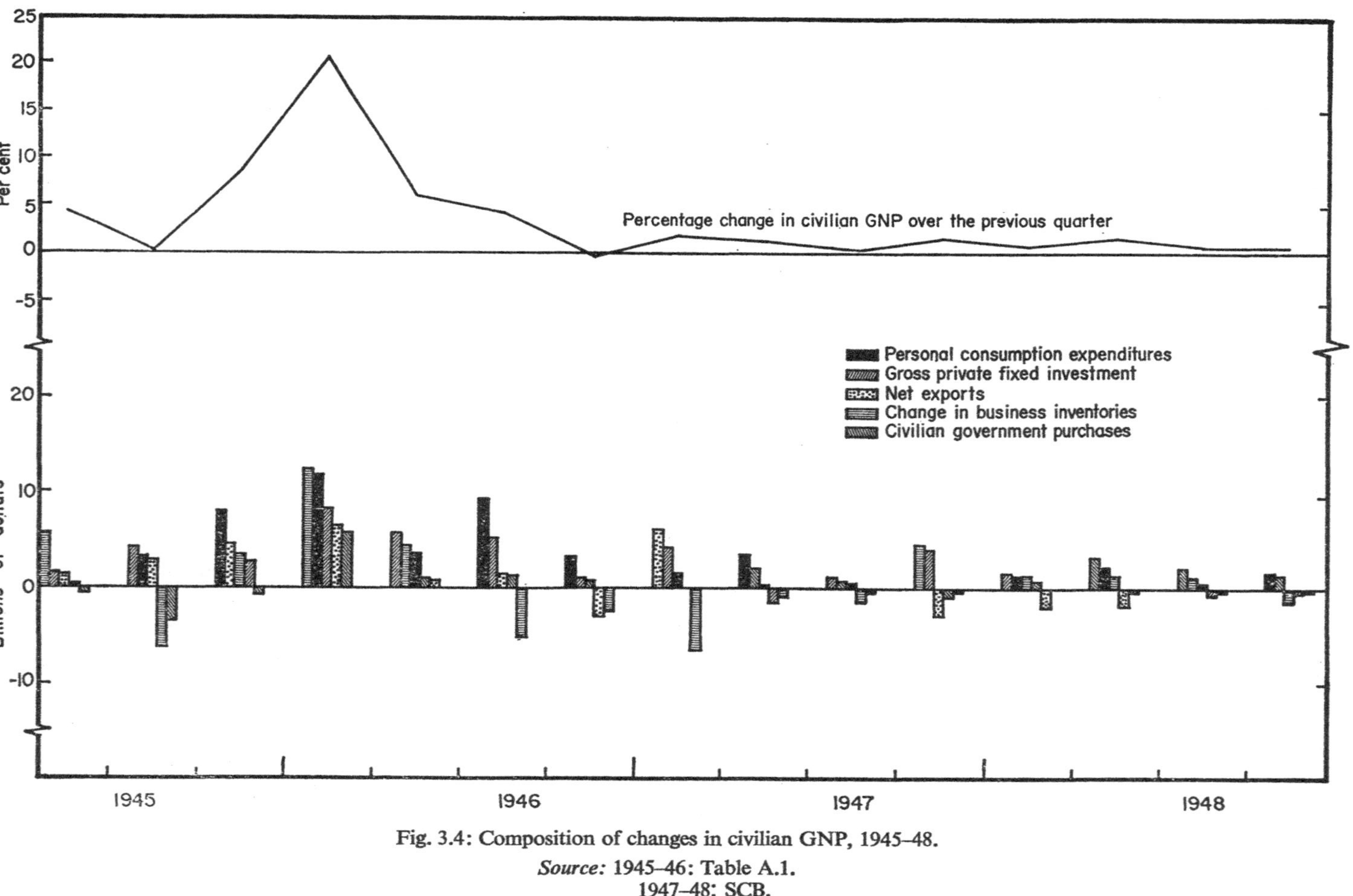

Fig. 3.4: Composition of changes in civilian GNP, 1945–48.

Source: 1945–46: Table A.1.
1947–48: SCB.

net exports, civilian government purchases and changes in farm inventories) contributed roughly equally to the growth. During the following period to 1947 I, when aggregate civilian growth temporarily stopped, consumption growth of $14 billion, and growth in the balance by a similar amount, were partly offset by the reduction in inventory accumulation of $13 billion. Thus the period from the end of the war to early 1947 was characterized by an initial rapid burst of growth of final civilian sales coinciding with a very strong inventory restocking boom, succeeded by a much slower rate of growth of final sales coinciding with the end of the restocking boom. By mid-1947, growth of final sales had almost ceased, and although there were still shortages of durable goods, inventory accumulation on balance was zero.

The ending of the rapid phase of growth of civilian output in mid-1946, and the reduction in inventory investment are two aspects of the same phenomenon: the recovery of production to capacity levels. As we have seen, nondurable goods output had recovered by early 1946, and despite fully occupied capacity there were shortages—in particular of textiles—during the year. Durable goods industries did not recover high rates of output until the middle of the year. Until that time manufacturers were building up their work in progress and stocks of material to normal levels. When normal levels of working were reached the buildup stopped and manufacturers' inventory investment declined. The manufacturers' restocking boom of 1945–46 was thus linked directly to the rise in output.[1] The emergence of capacity working was not a sudden event. Capacity was being expanded in most industries, and bottlenecks developed and were removed at different times in different places. The labour force was still benefiting in the second half of 1946 from the final stages of demobilization. Nevertheless, on the evidence of rates of growth of production and civilian labour force, the middle of 1946 saw the general emergence of fully employed physical capacity and labour force.

The background to the changes just described was inflation. From the end of the war until the end of 1946 there was excess demand for goods and services in general. The price increases

[1] Traders' restocking continued beyond the middle of the year.

which would have occurred were kept in check by the wartime price controls, and the inflation was largely suppressed. I have assumed (see pp. 81–2 above) that by mid-1946 actual prices were some 10 per cent above nominal prices and that there was excess demand at that time. After mid-1946 price controls ended. The immediate reason was a political attack on the system of controls which the Administration was unable to resist, especially after the return of a Republican dominated Congress in the elections of November 1946. The economic forces pressing for removal were also strong: it is likely that the divergence between nominal and actual prices had reached a point where the distribution system was functioning inefficiently and some change was essential.

This divergence between nominal and actual prices may have been widened in mid-1946 by an increase in the degree of excess demand which developed in the second and third quarters of the year. There is of course no direct evidence that such an increase occurred. It is however indirectly supported, and provides a useful hypothesis to relate the main changes of 1946. The argument is as follows. During the second half of 1945 and the early months of 1946 civilian demand for goods and services rose rapidly. Output responded, but not quickly enough to satisfy demand. Inflationary pressures developed, being partly suppressed by controls. As output gradually reached capacity levels, and hence as its rate of growth slowed down in mid-1946, inflationary pressures were strengthened. In other words, effective demand continued to grow at a given rate, but output growth slackened. Consequently not only were the economic pressures to remove controls strengthened, but the inflation caused a large increase in actual prices (on p. 88 above I assumed it was 5 per cent in six months).

By the end of the year excess demand had disappeared. Several months of price stability followed with adjustments both up and down as new relationships emerged after the years of control. But price rises do not cure inflation: their function is to equate supply with demand. Inflation can end only when excess demand ceases to appear; the basic reason for price stability in early 1947 was the end of growth of consumption—the end of the household spending spree—and the consequent decline in the growth of demand to a level similar to that of productive capacity. The above argument is really the extension of the hypothesis about suppressed inflation with which this chapter began. As was remarked there, that hypothesis explains more facts than any other. The reasonableness of the hypothesis is not critically dependent upon the inference that excess demand increased in the middle of 1946, but the two assumptions complement each other.

This explanation of the events of 1946 does not attribute any important role to inventory investment in the inflation. Inventory investment is a passive performer. In the absence of a background of excess demand, a productive build up as occurred at the beginning of the Korean War can be expected to lead to a rise and fall in prices. The increase in manufacturing inventories involves an increased demand for materials and labour, the price of which will rise, while when the build up is completed and inventory investment declines some fall in material prices will result. Thus in our period with a background of excess demand, the growing inflationary pressures would have been somewhat offset by the related inventory cycle. But the excess demand was so strong that the effect of the inventory cycle was insignificant in the overall picture. Of course in early 1947 price stability depended upon stable demand, and the low level of investment at that time was a factor in the stability.

Some writers have emphasized the role of expectations in early 1947. B. G. Hickman, for instance, suggests that the decline in inventory investment may have been due to anticipations of deflation, and cites the President's Economic Report which referred to fears of a drop of general consumer demand.[1] R. Fels has drawn my attention to confident statements by economists and journalists in the second quarter of 1947 that the postwar recession had at last arrived. It is possible that mistaken forecasts of the business situation led to some inventory disinvestment. However a more comprehensive explanation is provided by the argument above: the decline in excess demand and ending of inflation, which depended to some extent on the decline in inventory investment, allowed the underlying

[1] B. G. Hickman, *Growth and Stability of the Postwar Economy*, Brookings, Washington, D.C., 1960, p. 61, and *Economic Report of January 1947*, p. 16.

fears of postwar deflation to become prominent. Some inventory disinvestment may have been consequently induced. But the high level of final sales was not affected by the false warnings and businessmen did not allow themselves to be talked into a slump.

The pause in growth in mid-1947 represents the achievement of a position where the forces of growth and recession, inflation and deflation, were temporarily in balance. The emphasis must be on both the balance and its temporary nature. On the one hand, two years after the end of the war, inflation had ceased and the economy was enjoying high levels of output and employment. On the other hand, there were still shortages of steel and of cars, exports were falling, output growth was not sufficient to encourage businessmen to extend their existing plans to increase capacity, and some deflationary fiscal and monetary pressures were building up. To these we turn in the next chapter.

CHAPTER 4

Sources of Growth and Change, 1947 to 1950

HOUSEHOLD SPENDING

PCE remained unchanged during the second half of 1947 over its second quarter level, and while consumption per head was at the highest level ever reached in the U.S. economy such stability lasting for nine months was unusual. Furthermore, although this period undoubtedly marked the return to more normal economic and commercial conditions with the ending of most shortages of goods and the restocking of household inventories, the stability did not result from stability in the underlying determinants of consumer behaviour. The main trends in the volume of consumption until the middle of 1950 are shown in Fig. 4.1. Expenditures of food, clothing, other nondurables and services declined in 1947 IV and although they rose rapidly during the first half of 1948 the mid-1947 levels were not reached again until mid-1948. The early 1948 rise stopped during 1948 III, but was resumed in the last quarter of the year, continuing at a declining rate throughout 1949 until the first half of 1950 when a rapid growth occurred. Purchases of automobiles which had been declining slightly in mid-1947 increased in the final quarter of the year to a level which stayed roughly unchanged throughout 1948 (except for a drop in the second quarter). In 1949 I there began a large rise which continued throughout 1949 and 1950. Household expenditures on equipment, furnishings and other durable goods tended over these years to fluctuate slightly around a constant level. After a rise in 1948 II they showed a slight tendency to decline in the second half of the year—a tendency which became a pronounced fall

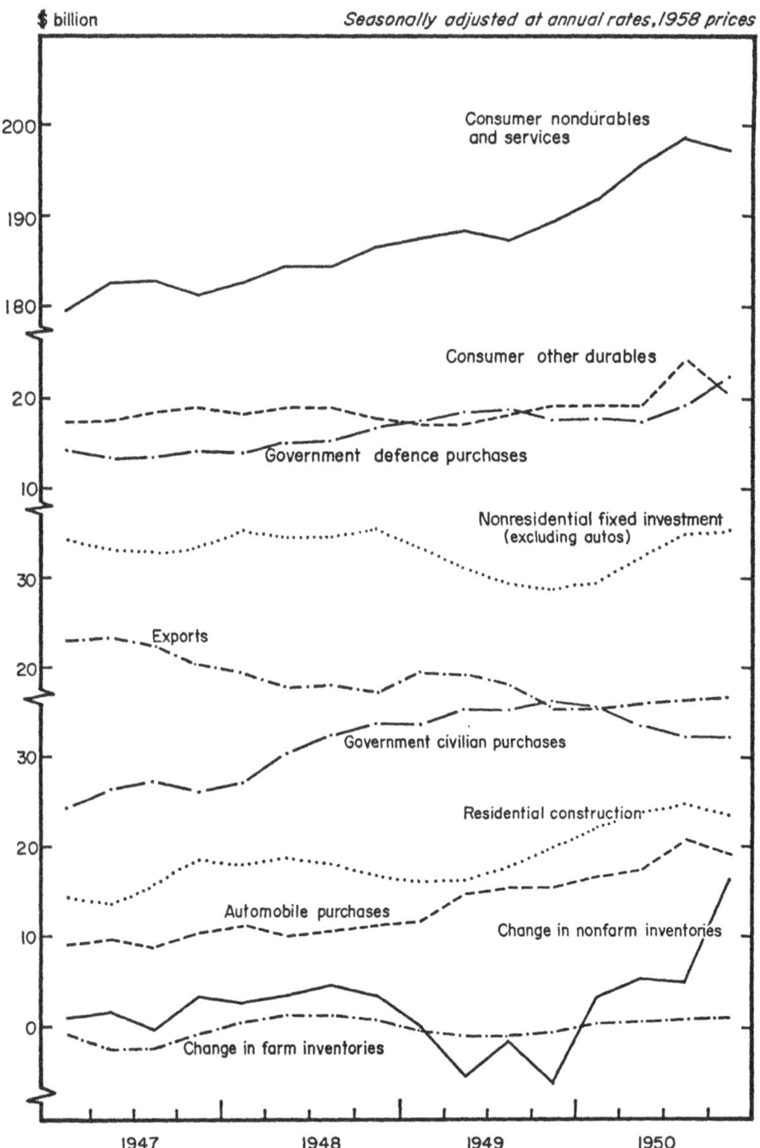

Fig. 4.1: Components of gross national product, 1947–50.
Source: Tables 6.1 and 6.2.

in the first half of 1949. These expenditures rose again in the second half of the year and were back at their early 1948 level during early 1950. In what follows I consider the movements of the main influences upon PCE—income, prices and the consumption ratio.

After its recession in the second quarter of 1947, DPI grew rapidly from the third quarter of that year until 1948 II, after which the rate of growth slackened, DPI actually falling by $5 billion in 1949 I. Disposable income remained virtually unchanged for the next six months, but in the final quarter of the year began a steady rise which was interrupted in 1950 I by an exceptional increase of $13 billion.

The sequence of surge and recession in incomes was experienced in most parts of the economy. Wage and salaries rose strongly in 1947 IV and 1948 I and again in 1948 III.[1] In 1947 III farm incomes started to rise from their low levels of the middle of the year, and by the second quarter of 1948 had reached an all-time peak from which they began to decline in the second half of the year as farm prices fell. Transfer payments from government showed no change from 1947 IV until 1949 I when unemployment benefits and assistance to farmers rose slightly (under $1 billion). It was on tax payments, however, that government action was effective in 1948. On April 2nd, over President Truman's veto, Congress passed the Revenue Act of 1948 which reduced individual tax rates, increased personal exemptions and permitted income splitting by married couples. The act was retroactive, liabilities for the calendar year 1948 being reduced by the full amount. Reduced withholding rates became effective on May 1st. The Treasury estimated that the reduction in income tax in a full year, based on total personal income of $200 billion, would be $4·7 billion (together with another $250 million from reduced estate and

[1] These rises were partly due to labour force increases, partly to higher rates of remuneration. For example, in manufacturing industries between September 1947 and March 1948 employment rose 0·8 per cent, hours remained unaltered and hourly wages rose 3·2 per cent. Between June and September 1948 while employment increased 2·8 per cent, hours fell by 1·0 per cent and hourly wages rose 3·5 per cent. These third quarter wage increases reflect the substantial wage increases negotiated during the summer by the unions particularly in the durable goods industries. See below, pp. 162–3.

gift tax). Total personal income in 1948 turned out to be $210 billion and the cost of the income tax reduction was about $5·0 billion.[1]

Personal taxes fell in the second quarter of 1948 by $2·1 billion (seasonally adjusted at an annual rate), and by another $0·8 billion in 1948 III. A delayed effect of the tax rate changes came in the first quarter of 1949 when refunds rose by some $0·6 billion at an annual rate, roughly seasonally adjusted.[2] Consequently, the tax reductions were important in swelling DPI in 1948, although of the $14·1 billion increase in DPI between 1948 I and 1948 III, one-half was due to increased wage and salary bills and another $2·8 billion to increased farm incomes. In 1949 I the increased refunds of $0·6 billion account for the entire fall in net personal tax compared with 1948 IV. In the second quarter refunds remained high but net personal taxes fell further because of the fall in income.[3]

The recession in incomes began with the small dip in farm incomes in 1948 III, followed by the larger drops in 1948 IV and during the first half of 1949.[4] The rise in wages and salaries and noncorporate business income tapered off in 1948 IV and these incomes declined at a decreasing rate during the following three quarters. From 1948 IV to 1949 IV the drop was $6·6 billions.[5] The declines were offset over the same period by a fall in personal taxes of $2·6 billion and a rise in government transfers of $2·1 billion, of which $1·4 billion was due to un-

[1] For the details of the Act and its expected effects see A. E. Holmans, *United States Fiscal Policy 1945–1959*, Oxford University Press, 1961, pp. 97–100, and W. Lewis Jr., *Federal Fiscal Policy in the Postwar Recessions*, Brookings, Washington, D.C., 1962, pp. 92–96.

[2] Basic data from Lewis, op. cit., Table B-1, p. 282.

[3] The importance of the tax reductions of 1948 is compared in Chapter 5 with that of other policy changes.

[4] Farm prices had reached a peak in January 1948, and fell substantially in February. Subsequently they recovered (especially meat prices) and by July were on average only slightly below the January level. In August a decline commenced and between July and December the average level of prices for farm products fell by 11 per cent. June was the month farm income reached its peak, and between July and December income fell by 17 per cent. For the farm situation see below pp. 127–32.

[5] Wage and salary payments reached a peak in November 1948 and a trough the following September, falling during the period by 4·5 per cent. The most important immediate cause of the decline was a fall in average hours worked. Over the period, employment in all industries fell by only 1·4 per cent.

employment benefits and $0·8 billion to aid for farmers. Consequently after 1949 I DPI fell only slightly. The changes between the peak and trough quarters and also between 1948 IV and 1949 III are summarized in Table 4.1.

TABLE 4.1: *Components of Change in DPI*
(based on seasonally adjusted data at annual rates, not deflated)

	$ *billion*	
	1948 III to 1949 III	*1948 IV to 1949 III*
Wage and salaries*	−3·9	−5·2
Farm income	−6·4	−5·0
Other non-labour income	0·4	−0·1
Transfers	1·6	1·9
Personal Taxes† (decline)	1·9	2·2
Disposable personal income	−6·5	−6·3

* Including other labour income.
† Including personal contributions for social insurance.
Source: SCB.

Non-labour income was the first to recover with dividends, rental and interest income rising by $0·6 billion in the final quarter of 1949 and farm and business proprietors' income increasing slightly. These incomes increased more rapidly in the first half of 1950. With the factory work week rising again after May 1949, and manufacturing employment after July, wages and salaries started to increase again in September despite the continued downward drift in average hourly earnings (which lasted until the beginning of 1950). The wage and salary recovery was interrupted by the strikes of October and November, however, and steady growth was not resumed again until December and January. During the first half of 1950 wages and salaries rose rapidly as employment, the average work week and average earnings all increased.

The effects of tax and unemployment benefit changes on the recovery of DPI were partly offsetting. With no changes in tax rates, personal tax payments reached a trough in 1949 IV and in the next two quarters rose by $1·7 billion. Unemployment benefits reached a peak in 1949 IV and fell by $0·8 billion during the first half of 1950. The major effect, however, was from the payment in the first half of 1950 of National Service Life Insurance dividends.[1] These increased personal incomes in 1950 I by \$8·4 billion (4 per cent) at annual rates, and by \$2 billion in 1950 II. The combined effect of these changes between 1949 III and 1950 II was as follows:

TABLE 4.2: *Components of Change in DPI 1949 III to 1950 II*
(based on seasonally adjusted data, at annual rates, not deflated)

	\$ billion
Wage and salaries	9·3
Farm income	0·6
Other non-labour income	3·4
Transfers	2·1
Personal taxes (rise)	−1·8
Disposable personal income	13·6

Source: SCB.

The increase in DPI in the fifteen months after mid-1947 was largely offset by a decline in the consumption ratio and by rising prices (see Fig. 3.1, p. 83). During the first six months of 1947 the rise in consumer prices had slackened considerably, there being virtually no change in price levels from March to June.

[1] National Service Life Insurance was a low cost government insurance introduced in 1940 and which until 1951 any serviceman could buy and continue after discharge. After the end of World War II, because mortality experience was better than had been originally expected, the Veteran's Administration (VA) was in a position to pay bonuses or dividends. On March 4, 1949, the VA announced that dividends would be paid by mid-1950 while on June 20th the payment of a special dividend of \$2·8 billion was authorized and the conditions of payment were published. Applications were to be made in August and the first payments would be made in January 1950.

At the time of the announcements it was agreed by economists that the payment would stimulate consumer spending, and although there is no direct evidence it seems obvious that the Administration decided to make the payment when it did because of the decline in business activity and the difficulty of knowing in early 1949 how far the decline would go. As it happened, the administrative problems in making the payment were so great that the actual payments did not begin until nearly a year after the first announcements and the Administration was accused of trying to influence the November 1950 elections (*NYT*, July 4, 1949).

On January 16, 1950, the first payments were made and by the end of February 43 per cent of the refunds were completed. By May 30th the payment was ending. Altogether \$2·6 billion were distributed to 16 million veterans. See *NYT* March 4, June 9, June 20, July 4, July 24, November 19, December 31, 1949, and *SCB* March 1950, 2–3, and August 1950, 7.

In the second half of the year however the rise was resumed, and between June and December the level rose by 6·3 per cent. The fall in food prices during the first quarter of 1948 slowed down the average rise, but other prices continued to increase, and from March to September 1948 prices rose another 4·6 per cent. After September the consumer price level receded slightly. The effect of these price rises was thus particularly marked during the second half of 1947 when more than two-thirds of the rise in DPI was offset by rises. Most of the remainder was offset by the effect of the fall in the consumption ratio.

During the first nine months of 1948, when incomes reached their postwar peak, one-half of the rise in DPI was offset by the continued fall in the consumption ratio, and one-third by the price rises. The result was the slow resumption of growth of household expenditures mainly during the first half of the year.

The decline in DPI after 1948 III was more than offset by a rise in the consumption ratio and the price declines. In 1948 IV when DPI stopped rising, the rise in the ratio and the fall in prices allowed PCE to grow by nearly 1 per cent. In 1949 I when DPI fell by 2·7 per cent, the rise in the ratio and the fall in prices exactly offset the income decline. During the next six months when DPI was virtually unchanged, the ratio continued to rise and prices continued to fall so that PCE rose even faster. Thus during the year 1948 IV to 1949 III when DPI stopped rising or fell, the total fall in DPI was exactly offset by the rise in the consumption ratio, while two-thirds of the fall was offset by the fall in consumer prices.

The maintained growth of consumption during the year 1948 IV–1949 III can be explained as follows:

TABLE 4.3: *PCE Changes 1948 III to 1949 III*

	%
Population	1·7
Disposable Personal Income	−3·3
Nondurable PCE at current prices	1·6
Nondurable PCE prices	−5·0
Services PCE at current prices	1·6
Services PCE prices	2·1
Durable (excl. autos) PCE at current prices	−2·7
Durable PCE prices	−2·5

Source: SCB.

During the period disposable personal income fell by 3·3 per cent. The price of nondurables fell by 5 per cent, and with population growing at 1·7 per cent p.a., real nondurable consumption per head was able to be maintained without any change in the savings ratio. Prices of services, however, continued to rise, and for real consumption of services to be maintained—as it was—the savings ratio had to fall despite a reduction in purchases of household furnishings and equipment. Thus, if we leave purchases of motor cars out of account, it appears that the level of nondurables and service consumption per head was maintained in the face of a 3·3 per cent fall in DPI partly by reduced purchases of household equipment and furnishings, partly by a fall in the proportion of income saved. The main part, however, of the fall in the savings ratio was due to the 40 per cent increase in purchases of new cars over the period.

Purchases of consumer durables were affected to some extent by the changes in instalment credit controls. The expiry of the wartime controls on November 1, 1947, probably played only a small part in the rise in car sales in 1947 IV and 1948 I. On September 20, 1948, under PL80-905 signed by the President on August 16th, the Federal Reserve Board reimposed controls requiring minimum downpayments on autos and appliances, and limiting repayment periods. Sales of appliances must have been affected by this regulation, for sales declined in 1948 IV, before DPI had fallen very much and while prices were declining. On June 30, 1949, the controls lapsed and appliance sales rose sharply in the following quarter. Auto sales do not appear to have been influenced by the September 1948–June 1949 reimposition.

Purchasers of durable goods were exposed to other special influences as well as changes in credit controls. Cars had continued to be in short supply throughout 1948, although output was higher in 1948 IV than in 1948 III. The car market remained unchanged during the first quarter of 1949 but as output of cars started to rise in the second quarter the situation altered. Prices of cars fell and sales of cars rose rapidly.[1] Residential building declined after the middle of 1948 and played some part

[1] For the special circumstances of the car market see Note H.

in the fall in purchases of furniture and household equipment in 1948 IV and the subsequent two quarters. Sales of television sets started to become commercially important during 1947 and rose swiftly throughout 1948. Television growth continued to increase in 1949: between 1948 IV and 1949 I sales increased by about 30 per cent and between 1949 I and 1949 II by 40 per cent.[1] Thus on balance while the total of expenditures on durables was pulled down from mid-1948 to 1949 I by the fall in sales of furniture and household equipment, after 1949 I the consumer durables markets were dominated by the great surge in car sales.

The more rapid rise in consumption after 1949 III was due to the resumption of growth in income. Consumer prices were virtually unchanged in 1949 IV and 1950 I, and rose only slightly in 1950 II. The NSLI dividend of $8·4 billion in 1950 I and $2·0 billion in 1950 II appears to have been all saved, at least in those quarters—the consumption ratio fell in the first quarter and rose again in the second so as to offset all of the dividend.[2]

[1] The television boom was not of course able to offset the decline in sales of furnishings and household equipment. The relative importance of these expenditures was:

	1948	*1949*
	$ billion	
Furniture	2·786	2·702
Kitchen and other household appliances	3·444	3·113
China, glassware, tableware and utensils	1·442	1·391
Other durable house furnishings	2·742	2·679
Radio and television receivers, records and musical instruments	1·450	1·675

Source: SCB.

[2] A substantial literature has arisen on the light that the uses of the NSLI dividend throw on consumer behaviour and, in particular, on Friedman's permanent income hypothesis. The hypothesis (see Note B) suggests that consumption is not correlated with transitory income, although it allows that purchases of consumer durables and net change in assets may be. The dividend is generally regarded as a windfall to the recipients, and hence as transitory as distinct from permanent income. Its disposition can thus be used to test Friedman's theory.

There was in 1950 a BLS consumer survey which provides cross-section data to test the alternative theories. The data refers to the whole year, and thus includes the first six months of the Korean War when consumer expectations undoubtedly changed: this apart from anything else makes interpretation difficult. The main conclusions are *first* that the main part of the dividends was spent during the year (this was the main result of Bodkin and Jones cited below). From our quarterly analysis we know that if this is correct, the dividends were

Between 1949 III and 1950 II DPI (excluding the dividend) rose by $11·6 billion while PCE rose by $9·6 billion. In 1958 prices PCE rose by $10·8 billion or 5·0 per cent. Expenditures on nondurables and services rose by $8·1 billion (4·3 per cent) representing a rise in real consumption per head of over 2 per cent per annum.

A MODEL OF CONSUMPTION EXPENDITURES

The most important facts arising from our survey of household behaviour can now be summarized. From mid-1947 to mid-1949 real consumption per head (including expenditures on automobiles and other durables) remained virtually unchanged, but rose by about 3 per cent in the year before the outbreak of the Korean War. The consumption ratio (ratio of PCE and DPI) reached its postwar peak in 1947 II and continued at a high level until the end of 1947 as Fig. 3.2, p. 87, shows.[1] By 1947 IV on all the major groups of consumer goods and services—durables, nondurables and services—spending was in excess of what would have been expected if the long term, postwar relationship

spent during the second half of the year after the war had broken out. R. Bodkin, 'Windfall income and consumption'. *Amer. econ. R.*, XLIX, September 1959, p. 607, estimated that in his sample $97 out of every $100 was spent on consumption (including durables). The *second* conclusion (based on Reid cited below) is that a large part of the dividends was used to purchase consumer durables—furnishing, equipment and automobiles—and to make down payments on housing. M. G. Reid, 'Consumption, savings and windfall gains: a reply'. *Amer. econ. R.*, LIII, June 1963, p. 444, suggests that out of every $100 dividend $62 went to consumer durables: this implies that the $2·6 billion dividend raised PCE on durables by $1·6 billion in the second half of 1950, or $3·6 billion as an annual rate at 1958 prices. See also R. C. Jones, 'Transitory income and expenditure on consumption categories', *Amer. econ. R.*, L, May 1960, pp. 584–92, M. G. Reid, 'Consumption, savings and windfall gains', *Amer. econ. R.*, LII, September 1962, pp. 728–37, and R. C. Bird, 'Consumption, savings and windfall gains: a comment', *Amer. econ. R.*, LIII, June 1963, pp. 443–44. As well as the Korean War, a further complication in interpretation was the early warning that the dividend would be paid (see footnote[1], p. 110 above). The first statement was in March 1949 and in July it was announced that the first payments would be made the following January. At the end of the year the *NYT*, December 31, 1949, reported that some effect of the dividend had already been felt through credit purchases. If this was so, the Bodkin–Reid evidence suggests it was slight.

[1] As was pointed out above on p. 88 the short period marginal propensity to consume started to offset fluctuations in income at this time, and the high ratio in 1947 II is partly due to the temporary fall in farm incomes that quarter.

of income and expenditure had held.[1] After 1947 IV the ratio and the excess spending declined. By 1948 II the excess had disappeared and during the second half of 1948 the actual ratio was no higher than the long term ratio. By late 1948 consumption per head of most services and nondurables was at its normal level: normal, that is, in relation to current income and current expectations of future income. Expenditures on some durables were probably still high due to the replenishment of stocks, but stock levels themselves were at or approaching a similarly defined normal level. In mid-1948 only cars were still in short supply and constituted an abnormal element in household spending.

The model of postwar household spending is outlined above.[2] It involves three assumptions, summarized again as follows. The first assumption is that there is a long term marginal propensity to spend out of disposable income. This is a propensity which applies to normal times, i.e. not war or postwar recovery, and allows households time to respond to income and other changes in their economic environment. I have estimated it as 0·91 for the period 1939 to 1964 with abnormal periods omitted. The marginal propensity is approximately equal to the average propensity, i.e. PCE is a constant proportion of DPI.[3] The second assumption is that during the years 1946 to 1950 the long term propensity was temporarily increased by the need to restock durable goods and the desire to indulge in a spending spree. In 1947 high levels of expenditure on nondurables and services drove up the consumption ratio to 0·95; in 1948 it fell temporarily to normal—temporarily because cars were still in short supply; in 1949 and 1950 when cars became generally available for the first time since 1941 the ratio rose again.

The third assumption is that expenditures do not respond quickly to changes in income, but that instead they respond, with a delay, to what are judged to be permanent increases in income. Apart from the complication of postwar abnormality, these ideas represent a translation of the set of theories associated with Duesenberry, Modigliani and Friedman, and a

[1] The long term relationship is based on the experience of the years 1939–40, and 1947–64. See Notes B and C.

[2] Pp. 85–6. [3] See Note C.

particular application of a model of Modigliani and Ando.[1] The application is illustrated in Fig. 4.2.[2]

The axes of the figure measure real PCE and DPI per head of population. *oo'* is the long run consumption function, and the slope of *oo'* is the normal marginal propensity to consume. *pp'* and *qq'* are short run expenditure functions, drawn to represent a high degree of short run stability in consumption per head. The arrowed line traces the changes in quarterly consumption and income.

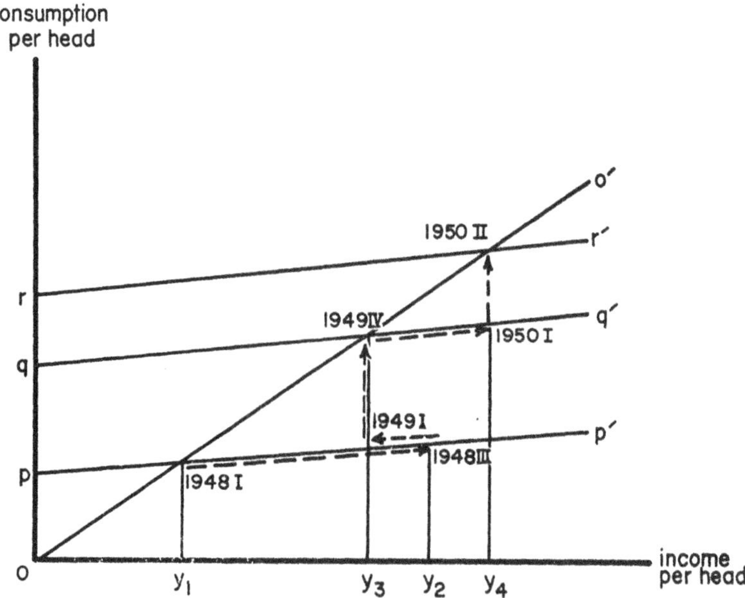

Fig. 4.2: Short run changes in consumption, 1948–50.

The interpretation of the main changes in 1948–50 is as follows. The decline of the consumption ratio from its abnormal 1947 level to the normal, long run level in early 1948 was temporary, depending on the continued shortage of automobiles. In what follows I start by disregarding the abnormal

[1] For the theories see Note B, and for the Modigliani-Ando model see Fig. B.1, p. 222.

[2] For an econometric analysis of the model see Note G.

postwar factor in consumer spending, and conduct the analysis with the normal long run and short run functions. At the end the abnormal factor will be reintroduced.[1] In 1948 I income was oy_1 and consumption was determined by the normal function oo'. Between 1948 I and 1948 III income rose to oy_2. Consumption remained virtually unaltered, moving along the function pp'. This was followed in 1948 IV and 1949 I by a fall in income to oy_3 resulting in consumption moving back along pp'. In fact, the rise and fall in income was completely offset by the fall and rise in the average propensity.

From 1949 I to 1949 IV income per head was virtually constant. The changes from early 1948 until early 1949 had kept consumption unaltered although income was now higher than it had been at that time. Consumption was below the level determined by the normal propensity and consequently after 1949 I consumption started to rise. We know this took the form first of a rise in durable expenditures and later a rise in non-durable and service expenditures. In the figure this consumption growth can be regarded as a rise in the short period expenditure function from pp' to qq'.[2]

For income oy_3, the intersection of qq' and oo' represents an equilibrium level of consumption. In 1950 I however, income was increased considerably to oy_4 by the NSLI dividend. There was a big movement along the short run function qq', and consumption rose by a large amount. After 1950 I the growth of other income made up for the NSLI dividend and income per head remained at the new high level of 1950 I. Consequently in 1950 II consumption increased, the short period function rising from qq' to rr'.

This explanation of the relationships between income and consumption inevitably omits some factors required for a complete explanation of all the changes. Most important were the changes in the car market. Consumer spending in 1948 was lower than it otherwise would have been because of the shortage of cars. By the second quarter of 1949 the material shortages

[1] From the point of view of presentation it is easier to do this than to work with a given abnormal propensity, temporarily depressed in early 1948.

[2] If the intercept op measures net wealth, as it does in the Modigliani-Ando model, the rise in the function is the result of a rise in net wealth due to the temporarily high rate of saving measured by the difference between oo' and pp'.

which had held back output had been overcome and output was rising rapidly. Consumers could at last complete their postwar restocking and finally satisfy their desire to spend lavishly. During the fifteen months before the Korean War expenditures on cars rose to high levels and the propensity to consume rose again to an abnormally high level. In terms of Fig. 4.2 the entire set of long and short run functions temporarily rose. The functions and the propensity would gradually have returned to normal as restocking was completed. With allowance for the temporary setback in automobile production caused by the steel strike in the last quarter of 1949, consumer spending would probably have returned to normal during the second half of 1950, had it not been for the new influences arising from the Korean War.

The car market is the major abnormal factor in 1949. In late 1948 sales of furnishings and household equipment declined as fewer new houses were built and instalment credit controls were imposed; later in 1949 sales rose again as house building revived and the controls were removed. In 1949 the realization that the postwar slump had been experienced with only minor falls in income and no serious deflation—unlike what had been generally expected since the end of the war—probably gave consumers greater confidence in the future. However, despite these complications, the simple framework of the long and short period consumption functions provides an empirically adequate as well as a theoretically satisfactory explanation of the most important aspects of consumer behaviour.

BUSINESS FIXED INVESTMENT

Following the rise in the second half of 1946, business investment stayed at a high level until the end of 1948 after which it declined to a low point in the fourth quarter of 1949. As Fig. 4.3 shows, the stability in 1947 and 1948 hid diverse trends. Investment by the commercial sectors had been falling since the middle of 1947. Plant and equipment expenditures by manufacturers reached a peak in 1948 I and declined thereafter for nearly two years. These two groups of industries accounted for some two-thirds of non-residential fixed investment. The other third, consisting of the investment of the regulated industries

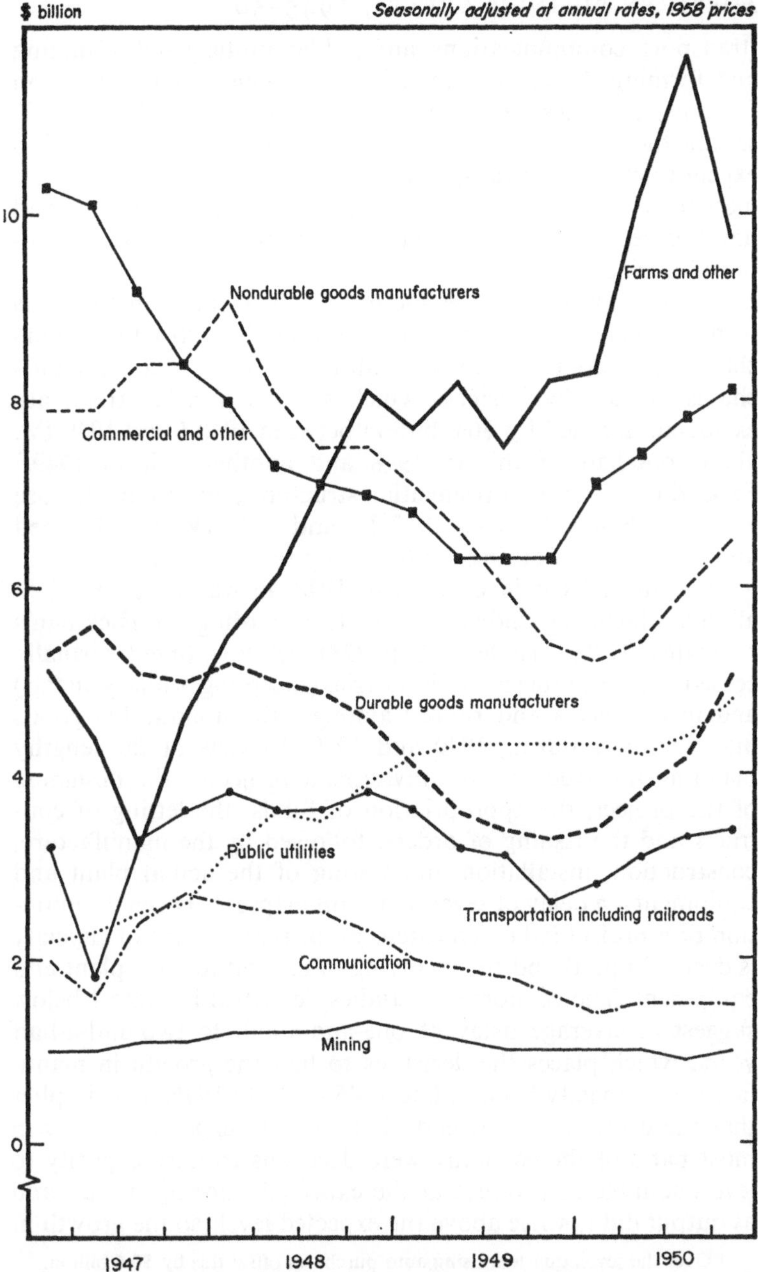

Fig. 4.3: Private fixed investment, 1947–50.

Source: SCB. New plant and equipment expenditures by business except for farms and other which is private fixed investment (non-residential) *minus* new plant and equipment expenditures (all industries). This residual includes mainly farm investment, but also investment by professionals, institutions such as private churches and schools, and real estate firms, and certain outlays charged to current account. All series deflated by PFI (non-residential) implicit price index.

(transport, communications, and public utilities) and of mining and farming, together with private non-business construction (schools, churches, etc.), rose throughout 1947 and 1948, offsetting the decline of the other sectors. After the end of 1948 expenditures by the transportation, communication and mining industries declined, although in public utilities, farming and non-business construction the rate of investment was maintained during 1949.

The main part of the decline in fixed investment in 1949 was in producers' durable equipment, rather than structures. Purchases of equipment tended to fall after 1948 I, and if the purchases of cars by business which showed a rising trend are excluded, declined by $6·0 billion between 1948 I and 1949 IV: about one-half of this in 1948 and another half in 1949.[1] Expenditures on non-residential structures, by contrast, rose about $1 billion between 1947 IV and 1948 IV, and declined about $1½ billion during the following twelve months.

The fall in fixed investment in 1948–49 was experienced in all manufacturing industries, while according to Hickman's estimates ([1965] Table B-3, p. 228) net investment virtually ceased in the durable goods industries (excepting primary metals) and in chemicals and rubber amongst the nondurable goods manufacturers during 1949 and 1950. In view of the lengthy planning involved in most investment projects—the designing of the project, the appropriation of funds, the letting of contracts and the issuing of orders, followed by the manufacture, construction, installation and testing of the actual plant and equipment—a delay of several months elapses between the initiation of a project (when an extension or replacement of capacity is decided upon) and the incurring of expenditure on plant and equipment. The econometric studies described in Note I below suggest an average delay of one-and-a-half to two-and-a-half years, which places the decisions to halt the growth in manufacturing capacity back in late 1945 or early 1946. This implies that the decisions at the end of the war to expand capacity in most parts of the economy were decisions to raise capacity to levels suitable to produce at the expected rates of output, and as output did not rise above the expected levels so the growth in

[1] Over the seven quarters rising auto purchases offset this by $0·6 billion.

capacity eventually ceased and net investment declined. There was in effect a once and for all decision to raise capacity and consequently the rate of investment after rising had to fall.

These changes are described in Hickman's model[1] and the figures are given in Table 2.5 on p. 74. Real business output increased between 1946 and 1948, and the desired stock of capital rose also. But the gap between actual and desired capital which had been 23 per cent of the latter at the end of 1945 had

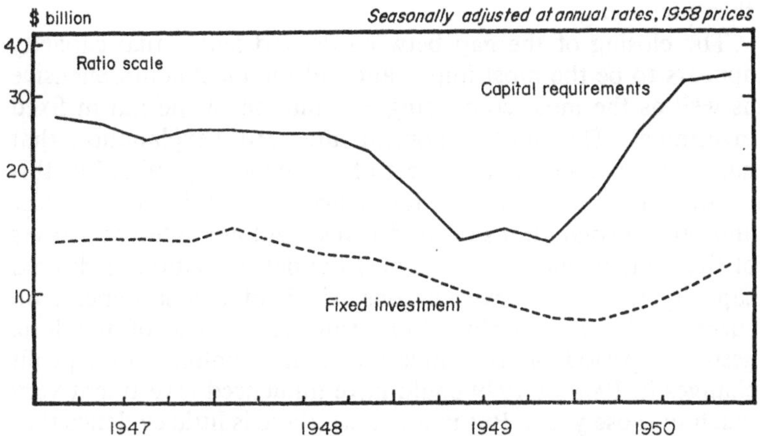

Fig. 4.4: Manufacturing fixed investment, 1947–50.

Source: SCB. Fixed investment is new plant and equipment expenditures by business, deflated by PFI (non-residential) implicit price index. Capital requirements are de Leeuw's estimates ([1962], data kindly supplied by Mr de Leeuw) converted to 1958 prices with the PFI index.

by the end of 1948 fallen to 13 per cent. In manufacturing industries the desired stock of capital increased rapidly, by 13 per cent, over the two years. Nevertheless while the gap between actual and desired stocks had been 23 per cent of the latter at the end of 1945, at the end of 1948 it had virtually vanished, being on Hickman's estimate under 4 per cent. For manufacturers, these conclusions are corroborated by de Leeuw's estimates of capital requirements shown in Fig. 4.4. These

[1] See pp. 73–5 above and Note E.

estimates are based on expected growth in sales, and take into account the desired degree of utilization of capacity and the time taken to expand capacity. They include both extensions to and replacements of capacity, and represent a stock of investment opportunities.[1] De Leeuw's quarterly figures begin in 1947 I and decline throughout 1947 and 1948, falling by 20 per cent between 1947 I and 1948 IV. By the second quarter of 1949 the stock of capital requirements was roughly equal to only eighteen months' replacement expenditures, whereas in 1947 I it had been equal to two years' gross investment at the levels then prevailing.

The closing of the gap between desired and actual capacity appears to be the most important and the most comprehensive as well as the most convincing explanation of the fall in fixed investment. The most important alternative explanation that has been suggested is the effect of a decline in profits, but this is not convincing. In Note I it is suggested that desired capacity and profit explanations of fixed investment are different aspects of the same phenomenon, namely the determination of desired capacity from sales expectations which of course depend on current sales and profits. Furthermore, in view of the long gestation period of fixed investment, it is unlikely that profit changes in 1948 or 1949 could have influenced investment very much in those years. But in any case, there is little evidence that the availability or the cost of finance in 1948 or 1949 had any significant part in the decline in investment expenditures. Internal sources of funds, which had been rising rapidly throughout 1947, continued to rise until the end of 1948, after which they ceased to rise, falling by some $3 billion in 1949 IV. In the first half of 1948 they rose because of the $5·6 billion increase in profits (excluding inventory profits, which were declining). In the second half of the year they continued to rise because while tax liabilities fell (because inventory profits dropped again) offsetting the rise in dividends, ordinary profits rose another $1 billion. In the first nine months of 1949 internal sources remained high because the decline in ordinary profits was offset

[1] See F. de Leeuw, 'The demand for capital goods by manufacturers: a study of quarterly time series', *Econometrica*, XXX, July, 1962, pp. 407–24, and the discussion in Note I below.

by inventory losses and a rapidly declining tax liability. The 1949 IV fall in internal sources was due to a $3·2 billion fall in ordinary profits while inventory losses were nil and the tax liability remained unchanged. This rapid growth in internal sources of funds apparently had no effect upon the rate of investment. Its effect was to reduce business dependence upon external sources: between 1947 and 1948 internal sources rose from $12·6 billions to $18·7 billions while external sources dropped from $14·6 billions to $8·5 billions; in the following year internal sources rose again, slightly, to $19·1 billions, while external borrowings were actually repaid on balance.[1] The main part of the decline in external sources was in reduced bank borrowing, trade debts and profits tax and other liabilities, and it was at the expense of a reduced growth of trade credit and other less liquid financial assets. On the other hand bond issues rose substantially in 1948.[2]

The switch to bonds followed the rise in short term rates and led in turn to a rise in bond yields.[3] Yields rose rapidly during the last four months of 1947, and formed a high level plateau during 1948, declining in January 1949 and again in the middle of the year. In view of the ease of finance in general, and the fact that decisions to spend in 1948 were taken over a year before, it seems unlikely that high costs of borrowing in early 1948 could have had anything but a very small influence upon the fall in fixed investment.

Manufacturing fixed investment continued to fall in 1950 I. Capital requirements (as defined above), however, had stopped falling after 1949 I and rose substantially in the first quarter of 1950 as sales rose. Gross investment consequently started to increase in 1950 II. In the other sectors of the economy—mining, transport, commerce (public utilities were the

[1] The figures of internal and external sources refer to non-farm, non-financial corporate business (*SCB*, November 1965, Table 1, p.10).

[2] Internal source figures for the individual industrial sectors are not available, but the profit figures suggest no conflict of evidence with the aggregate data. Profits of nondurable goods manufacturers rose until 1948 II, as did those of the trade and service sectors. Durable goods manufacturers' profits rose throughout 1948 into 1949. Profits of the regulated sectors fell only slightly in the second half of 1948 and maintained a high level during 1949. (These profits are before tax, plus inventory valuation adjustment: *SCB*, September 1965, Table 2, p. 52).

[3] See discussion on monetary policy, pp. 151–2 below.

exception)—the trough of investment had been reached in 1949 IV and expenditures were rising in 1950 I.[1]

HOUSING

After the middle of 1947, with few remaining controls and the disappearance of shortages of materials,[2] the construction of non-farm houses rose substantially, the volume of work done being nearly one-third greater in the final quarter of the year than at the beginning. The rapid rise in private starts which had recommenced in the final quarter of 1946 continued throughout 1947. Growth ceased after October, there being a slight decline from November 1947 to February 1948, followed by a return to high levels in March and April. After April a decline commenced which lasted until February 1949. Between 1947 IV and 1948 II starts fell by 4 per cent; between 1948 II and 1949 I they dropped by 20 per cent. The volume of non-farm construction reached a plateau at the end of 1947, being virtually unchanged from 1947 IV to 1948 III, after which it fell by about 12 per cent in the next six months.

Housing starts began to rise again after February 1949, and by September had passed the October 1947 peak. After November 1949 the rate of increase in starts tapered off, although at the peak in May 1950 starts were 31 per cent above the October 1947 level. The volume of construction started to rise again in 1949 III, by the final quarter of the year had surpassed the early

[1] I. Friend and J. Bronfenbrenner, 'Plant and equipment programs and their realisation', in *Short Term Economic Forecasting*, NBER Studies in Income and Wealth 17, Princeton University Press, 1955, after a study of the differences of actual and anticipated plant and equipment expenditures in 1949, reported that 'the special questionnaire sent to a sample of companies showing large percentage differences between actual and anticipated expenditures in 1949 indicates that for these firms changes in the sales and in the earnings outlook accounted for nearly half of the cases where actual expenditures in 1949 were lower than those anticipated (pp. 55–56).' Although the quantitative importance of the revision in anticipated expenditures is small—considerably less than the difference between actual expenditures in 1948 and anticipated in 1949—there is nevertheless some evidence of a short-run influence on investment. However, the hypothesis that I use in this study—that medium to long term influences predominate in fixed investment—is not affected by this evidence. I am indebted to Rendigs Fels for drawing my attention to the work of Friend and Bronfenbrenner.

[2] See pp. 90–1 above for the effect of shortages in curbing the expansion of building in early 1947.

1948 levels and in 1950 II was 27 per cent above the level two years previously.

The background to this brief and slight recession, and the revival, was the tightening of credit conditions and official anti-inflationary monetary policy, extending from late 1947 to late 1948, and the slackening of credit conditions and reversal of official policy throughout 1949. These monetary changes had their impact on housebuilding through changes in the supply of mortgage credit, and were partly reinforced by alterations in policy by the government housing agencies.[1] In late 1947 conditions in the mortgage market started to become tight as yields on mortgages rose and mortgage terms became more severe. During the first six months of 1948 the average yield on FHA home loans purchased in the secondary mortgage market rose by about one-quarter per cent, while between mid-1947 and early 1949 average cash downpayments required by lenders on VA home loans rose from under 10 per cent to nearly 18 per cent of the value of the house.[2] The Annual Report of the Housing and Home Finance Agency for 1947 remarked that mortgage terms began to stiffen towards the end of 1947 as lenders became more cautious and selective (p. 17). Interest rates had started to rise in the middle of 1947. Bond yields rose in September and the following three months, following the rise in short term interest rates allowed by the Federal Reserve System in July. Guttentag comments

'The banks appeared to be the only type of financial institution significantly affected by these moves, and their main response to rising short-term yields was to withdraw temporarily from the mortgage market. Between 1947 and 1949 net mortgage acquisitions by commercial banks fell by two-thirds. Since the banks had helped to create a climate of extreme ease in the mortgage market in 1946 and early 1947 by aggressively competing for mortgages, their sudden withdrawal from the market had a considerable impact.' ([1961] p. 296.)

[1] For an analysis of the economics of the housing market see Note J. Monetary policy is discussed below, pp. 152–3.

[2] Data from J. M. Guttentag, 'The Short Cycle in Residential Construction, 1946–59', *Amer. econ. R.*, LI, June 1961, Chart 3, p. 282.

The revival of construction was due to a reversal of these trends. Mortgage yields stopped rising after February 1949 and began a slow decline. Bond yields fell after November 1948. Downpayments on VA home loans were at a peak at the beginning of 1949 and declined rapidly thereafter. With the liberalization of terms, mortgage credit became more plentiful as the banks re-entered the market. The increasing availability of housing credit was maintained until mid-1950 and was matched by the continued growth in new starts.

Apart from its important role in following a permissive monetary policy—in allowing first the tightening and then the relaxing of the market for credit—the government played a minor part in the cycle in construction. Some of its actions in 1947–48 were depressive. The FNMA's authority to make a secondary market for VA-guaranteed and FHA-insured loans ended in mid-1947 (and was attributed by the Housing and Home Finance Agency to be a cause of the rise in VA home loan downpayments). Furthermore the FHA was without authority to insure mortgages for lower priced houses or multi-family rental units from April 30th (when authority expired) to August 10, 1948 (when new legislation was passed). Hickman suggests this hiatus caused some inhibiting uncertainty on the part of speculative builders.[1] Finally, as an anti-inflationary measure, on May 10, 1948, certain classes of federally insured borrowers were required to make a cash downpayment of 10 per cent of the cost of the work (this was discontinued from April 28, 1949).

Expansionary actions of government were more important than the repressive actions, although these actions were not taken as anti-recessionary measures. An Act signed by the President on July 1, 1948, re-established the authority of FNMA to provide a secondary market for federally insured mortgages. The Housing Act of 1948, signed on August 10th, restored the insurance programme for rental housing and liberalized the existing programme for low cost housing. These measures undoubtedly supported the mortgage market in late 1948, as well as stimulating some demand. The rapid growth of starts and mortgage lending from early 1949 is likely to have been assisted by the vigorous activity of the FNMA. The revival was re-

[1] B. G. Hickman [1960] p. 67.

inforced by the ending of the rapid rise in building costs. Construction costs, which had been rising more rapidly than the general level of prices, stopped rising after 1948 III and fell during the first three quarters of 1949. Not only did this benefit buyers of new homes, but with rents continuing their rise the profitability of speculative building increased throughout 1949.[1]

Thus largely through the medium of the credit market, residential building was first checked in early 1948, experienced a small recession, and revived strongly during 1949. These changes were only partly contra-cyclical in relation to the general level of activity, and to the reduced rate of building in late 1948 can be ascribed some part of the decline in purchases of household equipment and furnishings. But in so far as the contra-cyclical movement existed, in the sense of a retarding of building activity while the rest of the economy was booming, and an increase when the rest was in recession, the movement is due primarily to the contra-cyclical movement in the cost of credit and the availability of mortgages: the increased difficulty of borrowing at the top of the boom, and the greater ease of finance in recession.

THE FARM SITUATION

The stability in farm prices which had persisted through most of the first half of 1947 ended in the third quarter when first livestock product prices (in July) and then food grain prices (in September) started a rapid rise. This renewed burst of inflation occurred in a mixed marketing situation. The 1947 wheat crop was going to be the largest ever, but stocks were very low and the international demand was still great. On the other hand the 1947 corn harvest was below the average of the past decade, and prices of feed grains rose continuously through 1947. For cotton both the domestic and foreign demand slackened in 1947 with increases in U.S. and foreign crops and the recovery of textile production in other countries. Cotton prices rose until July and tended to decline thereafter.

Prices of most farm products reached a peak in January 1948 and fell sharply in late January and February. Wheat prices

[1] There is some evidence that the payment of the NSLI dividend in 1950 assisted house buying (see footnote[1], p. 110 above).

were in the forefront of the fall.[1] After February there was some recovery from the excess of the reaction from inflation, but by June the crop reports were confirming that the wheat harvest would be nearly as large as 1947, and that the corn crop also would be exceptionally large. Grain prices started to decline swiftly at mid-year, as did those of cotton and other crops. Prices of meat and dairy products, on the other hand, which had experienced the early 1948 decline, did not fall in the middle of the year probably because of reduced levels of production. Meat prices, however, started to fall in October.

Farm incomes, which had fallen sharply in 1947 II (see above, p. 85), started to rise again in the third quarter and continued to rise until the second quarter of 1948 when they reached the highest level they had ever reached and higher than they were to reach at any time in the future. In the third quarter they started to fall, but the substantial falls came in 1948 IV and 1949 I. Between 1948 II and 1949 III farm proprietors' income fell by \$6·7 billion or over one-third. Until the middle of 1948 the government programmes for stabilizing farm prices and incomes had played a minor part in stemming the decline in commodity prices as most prices in the first half of 1948 were substantially above the levels at which price-support schemes would come into operation. There was some support in the future markets for corn, wheat and cotton, but extensive support operations were applied only to potatoes, eggs, wool, peanuts and some types of tobacco—not to the major crops.

[1] After declining by 19 cents between January 16th and February 3rd, cash wheat prices at Kansas City fell 48 cents to \$2·30 per bushel between February 4th and February 13th. At the end of the month the price was back to \$2·38, the level of July 1947. Most observers attributed the decline to an improved outlook for U.S. and world supplies in the near-term and in the next crop year. The Southern Hemisphere wheat harvest had been excellent, Russia and Eastern Europe started to sell grains, early in the new year it had been announced that the success of the export goal for wheat would make more grain available for the domestic market and late in January it appeared that wheat feeding to animals was lower. The new crop outlook had been shaky in the autumn (because of dry soil) but improved steadily with news of rain in November and good protective snow cover. In a speculative and uncertain situation it is suggested that the cumulative reports of the improved supply situation eventually caused prices to break. (See *SCB*, March 1948, p. 3, and *National City Bank Monthly Letter*, March 1948, p. 28.) It is also likely that a series of government measures to restrict credit and announcements about inflation in January were influential in changing business opinion. (See below, p. 161.)

After July however the price fall was severe enough to initiate large and extensive supports. By the beginning of September one-tenth of the wheat crop was under loan or purchase option, as were smaller fractions of the other grain crops. During and immediately after the harvest the prices of corn, peanuts and wheat all fell below the support level and in the last six months of 1948 the CCC lent \$1·5 billion of which three-quarters went to cotton and wheat. There were signs that the support operations were contributing towards a firming of prices in November. The bulk of the support for the 1948 crop was given during the July–February period, and by February 1949, the CCC had laid out \$3·4 billion in loans and direct purchases. This was reduced by sales and repossessions and by June 30, 1949, total government investment in price support commodities amounted to nearly \$2·4 billion, of which half represented outstanding loans and half commodities in the CCC inventory. This support represents nearly 16 per cent of farm proprietors' income in year ended 1949 II.[1]

Between July 1948 and February 1949 the average level of farm prices declined by 15 per cent. After a slight recovery in March and April, for the remainder of 1949 the level continued to decline slowly, falling by 9 per cent between February 1949 and January 1950 when the decline ended. This slower decline throughout 1949 was experienced by all commodities. Substantially increased production of livestock and livestock products played some part in the fall in meat and dairy products, but grain prices fell despite the reduced harvests. Towards the end of 1949 stocks of corn were at an all-time record high level, while wheat stocks were rising. Price support for the 1949 crops, changed by legislation passed in 1948,[2] was more extensive than the 1948 support. Up to December 1949 purchases and loans were being made at about the same rate as a year earlier,

[1] An alternative measure of the size of price support is the cost of domestic acquisition by the CCC of agricultural commodities (purchases under price support and acquisitions in settlement of price support loans) which was \$2·545 billion in fiscal 1949 (*Statistical Abstract* 1965, p. 636). Sources for above paragraph are *SCB* August 1948, p. 2; October 1948, p. 5; December 1948, p. 2; February 1949, p. 18; and *Report of the Secretary for Agriculture*, 1949, pp. 15–18.

[2] The Hope-Aitken Act of 1948 froze support for basic crops at 90 per cent of parity for another year, after which a sliding scale was to be introduced. Under the Agricultural Act of 1949 support at 90 per cent was extended for another year.

and support for the 1949 crop as a whole was $2·7 billion—slightly greater than 1948, and representing 22 per cent of farm proprietors' incomes.[1] The end of the price decline and the beginning of a small rise in farm incomes in 1949 IV can be attributed to the strength of the price support operations.

The United States is not a closed economy, and in 1947 about 9 per cent of the value of gross farm output was exported in the form mainly of crude materials and processed foodstuffs.[2] Before the First World War, whenever the prices of materials and foodstuffs declined as domestic demand fell, foreign demand increased, and rising U.S. exports were associated with recessions in business activity.[3] Since the First World War this inverse relation between the domestic business cycle and exports

[1] Investment (outstanding loans and change in the inventory) was $2·68 billion; cost of domestic acquisition was $2·71 billion in fiscal 1950.

[2] In the 1947 interindustry study it is estimated that 9 per cent of the gross output of the agriculture and fisheries industry is ultimately disposed of as exports. This includes both direct disposals and indirect via, e.g., the food processing industry. This figure is similar to the average proportion of exports of goods and services to GNP in 1947 (8·5 per cent), but is substantially below the percentage for manufacturers like textile mills, chemical producers, and metal and machinery industries. See W. D. Evans and M. Hoffenberg, 'The interindustry study for 1947', *R. Econ. Statist.*, *34*, May 1952, Table 2, p. 123.

No breakup of the agriculture and fisheries figure for 1947 is available, but the 1958 study gives details as follows:

	Percentage of total output going to exports		*Total output $ million producers' prices*
	Direct	*Total*	
Livestock and livestock products	0·1	3·0	26,322
Other agricultural products	7·5	10·3	23,393
Forestry and fishery products	2·1	5·0	1,451
Agricultural, forestry and fishery services	0·2	7·3	1,564

Source: SCB, November 1964, Table B, p. 14; and September 1965, Table 1, p. 39.

The weighted average total percentage is 6·4, which compares with the average proportion of exports of goods and services to GNP in 1958 of 5·2 per cent.

In the *SCB* foreign trade statistics, the category Agricultural products includes crude materials such as unmanufactured cotton, and both crude and processed foodstuffs.

[3] 'Exports of crude materials . . . turned up almost every time domestic business fell back from a peak prior to World War I. That declining home demand contributed to the revival of exports in these instances is affirmed by a simultaneous softening of prices.' Ilse Mintz: *Cyclical Fluctuations in the Exports of the United States Since 1879*. NBER Studies in Business Cycles 16, NBER, New York, 1967, p. 272. This study provides a detailed analysis of the relation of U.S. exports to both U.S. and foreign business fluctuations.

of materials and foodstuffs has not been so evident, largely because of the greater synchronization of American and other countries' business fluctuations. In 1948 and 1949 the exports and overseas markets affected farm incomes in several different ways. First, the fall in agricultural prices throughout 1948 and 1949 was influenced by the gradual emergence in the recovering economies of Europe and Asia of better supplies of agricultural products. Partly this was due to the natural processes of rural rehabilitation; partly it was due to deliberate policies of raising agricultural output, of self-sufficiency in food production and of developing non-dollar area sources of supply. These changes in overseas markets made up a diffused phenomenon going on over a long period. At times specific factors had recognizable effects on commodity prices: the influence of foreign crop reports on the January 1948 drop in wheat prices has been referred to above.[1]

Secondly, the changed overseas supply conditions caused falls in the quantity of some agricultural exports. These falls came towards the end of the period we are concerned with, for example due to improved supplies, European wheat imports from the U.S. were sharply cut in the second half of 1949.

Finally, there were the offsetting factors in overseas markets. The pre-1914 price effect described above was almost certainly very weak. Falling prices of cotton and some other materials may have caused some stockpiling during the first half of 1949 in Europe: the effect, however, could not have been very strong or significant. More important was the European Recovery Programme, which accounts for most of the rise in the volume of exports in the first half of 1949.[2]

The conclusion is that agricultural prices were depressed by, amongst other things, increased agricultural output overseas, while any rise in exports due to falling prices was greatly swamped by the stimulus given by foreign aid. The direct effect of agricultural exports on farm incomes (i.e. excluding affects on domestic agricultural prices) in 1949 was stabilizing: the value of agricultural exports in 1949 was virtually the same as in 1948 because the large volume increase offset the price fall.

[1] Footnote 1, p. 128.

[2] For stockpiling and foreign aid see footnote 1, p. 134.

The immediate effect of these changes in the farm sector on the rest of the economy was substantial. The fall in farm incomes of over $6 billion between the second half of 1948 and the second half of 1949 was about one-half of the fall in personal income over the period (see Table 4.1). The decline in commodity prices led to an 8 per cent fall in retail food prices between July 1948 and February 1949 and up to December these were the only falling consumer prices.[1] But the effect on household spending and business activity is unlikely to have been anything like as depressing as the changes suggest at first glance. The short run marginal propensity of farmers to consume is likely to be considerably less than that of other households, and the $6 billion fall in farm incomes is unlikely to have led to more than a $4 or $5 billion fall in farm consumption expenditures, and this would have been offset by the $4 or $5 billion increase in disposable income represented by the fall in retail food prices. Furthermore, this argument is unaffected by considering farm investment, the volume of which was virtually unchanged between 1948 and 1949.[2] By and large, therefore, given the government price support policies and disregarding the effects of speculation about future changes in prices, the effects of changes in the farm situation on the economy in 1948–49 appear to have been self-cancelling or neutral.

[1] The fall in cotton prices led to no significant declines in retail clothing prices until early 1949, and only part of the fall in these prices during 1949 can be attributed to this source. The main retail food price falls were in dairy products, meats and poultry; cereal and bakery products barely falling (although wholesale prices did). The prices of dairy products, meat and poultry were influenced of course by the fall in the prices of feed grains which was the largest of all the commodity price falls.

[2] The following are the data ($ billion, 1958 prices):

	1948	*1949*
Producers' durable equipment:		
tractors	1·0	1·0
agricultural machinery	1·4	1·3
New construction	2·0	2·0
Total	4·4	4·3

Source: SCB.

TRADE AND THE BALANCE OF PAYMENTS

Exports

In the early months of 1947 exports of goods and services—particularly merchandise exports—increased rapidly. Partly this was due to increased U.S. government aid, particularly the use of the U.K. loan. The expansion was general, being experienced in most types of goods in most markets which were able to indulge in a restocking boom. During 1947 inventories were refilled and dollar balances and credits used up. For about eighteen months from 1947 I to 1948 II exports financed through normal channels maintained a high level. Total exports, however, after mid-1947 tended to fall as U.S. aid started to decline: between 1947 II and 1948 I the volume of exports of goods and services fell by $4·4 billion or 19 per cent.

The decline in aid-financed exports in late 1947 was reinforced by the imposition of controls over imports as countries found their dollar reserves dwindling (the U.K. autumn 1947 crisis and the ending of convertibility between the pound and the dollar was one of the more spectacular events), and also by the normal ending of restocking as backlogs were filled in cases such as cotton and cotton textiles. In 1948 the decline in U.S. exports became general (with the exceptions of West Germany and the Union of South Africa), the largest cuts arising in France, Britain, Canada and Brazil. All products—agricultural products, machinery, textiles and cars—fell.

During 1947 the realization that the recovery of the European economies was going to be more costly than had first appeared, and the fear of communist aggression in a number of countries, led to new plans for foreign aid. The major plan was sparked off by the Western European response to the offer of long term aid by the U.S. Secretary of State, George C. Marshall, on June 5th. By September 22nd a Committee of the Western European countries had reported on their needs and on December 19th President Truman asked Congress to authorize a four-year programme of assistance totalling $17 billion. (Interim aid of $540 million had been authorized on December 11th.) The European Recovery Programme as finally enacted in the Economic Co-operation Act of April 2, 1948, authorized first year appropriations of $4·3 billion together with increases in the Export-Import Bank's lending authority, subject to bilateral agreements with the recipient countries. Other aid appropriations in 1948 brought the total to over $6 billion.

From 1947 IV to 1948 II U.S. aid of all types had declined to an average annual rate of about $4·2 billion. Marshall Aid raised this to over $6·2 billion for the year 1948 III to 1949 II. As Fig. 4.5 shows, the level of aid-financed exports rose from a

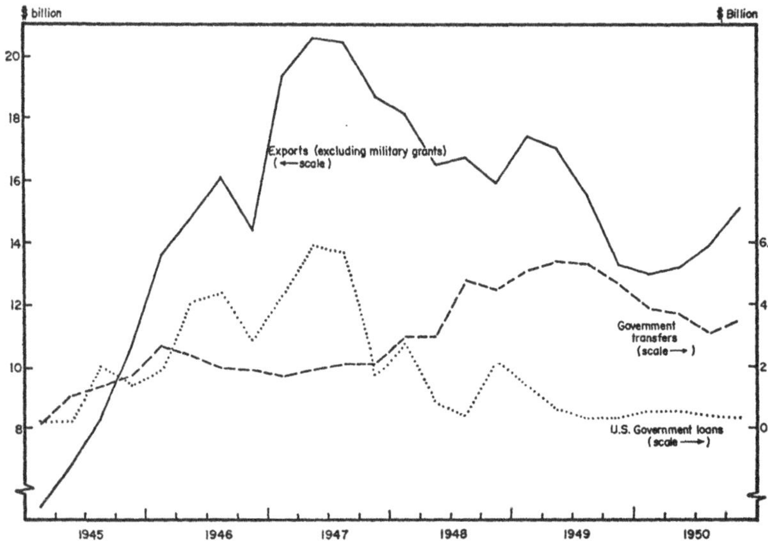

Fig. 4.5: Exports of goods and services, 1945–50.
Source: Table A.2.

low point in 1947 IV to a peak in 1949 I. While the declining trend in total exports of goods and services was not offset by this aid, the trend was temporarily arrested in the first half of 1949, the volume of total exports of goods and services rising between 1948 IV and 1949 I by 9 per cent. However after mid-1949 total exports resumed their decline, falling in volume by $1·2 billions in the third quarter and a further $2·4 billion in the final quarter. This decline ceased in the first half of 1950.[1]

[1] Due to changing supply conditions both in the United States and overseas, together with the impact of aid programmes and the measures of other countries

to control imports from dollar sources, the interpretation of changes in U.S. exports in the years 1948 and 1949 is difficult. The U.N. Department of Economic Affairs analysed the changes in U.S. commodity exports between the calendar year 1948 and the two halves of 1949 (at annual rates) as follows:

	All Commodities	*Foodstuffs*	*Crude materials*	*Semi-manufactures*	*Finished manufactures*
Current value ($ million, f.o.b.)					
1948	12,532	2,580	1,488	1,370	7,094
1949 First half	13,102	2,520	2,030	1,542	7,011
1949 Second half	10,669	1,933	1,531	1,166	6,039
Unit value index					
1948	100	100	100	100	100
1949 First half	96	89	96	99	97
1949 Second half	91	83	94	90	92
Quantum index					
1948	100	100	100	100	100
1949 First half	111	113	142	114	102
1949 Second half	93	92	110	94	90
Quantum index less foreign aid					
1948	100	100	100	—	100
1949 First half	100	95	105	—	97
1949 Second half	84	110	72	—	83

Source: World Economic Report 1949–50, UN, New York, March 1951, Table 52, p. 73.

This analysis shows clearly that between 1948 and the first half of 1949 all of the increased volume of exports was due to aid. Amongst normally financed exports, a small rise in materials and semi-manufactures was offset by falls in foodstuffs and finished manufactures. In the second half of 1949 the volume of normally financed exports declined by 16 per cent over the first half of the year, while aid prevented total exports falling by such a large amount.

Total exports declined during 1948, and hence it is likely that normally financed exports rose between the end of 1948 and early 1949. This is confirmed if government transfers and loans in Fig. 4.5 (see also Table A.2) are subtracted from total exports of goods and services to give a rough measure of normally financed exports—after a sharp fall in 1948 IV this measure rose in 1949 I and II. With conditions in so many importing countries being so varied, and with all U.S. exports in early 1949 increasing, it is not possible to identify with any certainty the sources of this increased normal demand in 1949, but material restocking (especially of cotton in Europe) seems the most likely source, and its timing may have depended on the fall in U.S. prices. Most commentators do not think that expectations of exchange rate adjustments were important influences (see for example *Economic Bulletin for Europe*, UN, Geneva, *10*, 1958, p. 56). The growing Japanese and German import demand, arising from the recovery of these two economies during 1949, was on the statistical evidence not strong enough to offset in 1949 the factors in other countries making for reduced normal imports.

In the later months of 1949 U.S. exports were affected by two foreign measures aimed at curbing the drain on the rest of the world's exchange reserves: the July sterling area cuts of approximately 25 per cent in dollar imports and the September 1949 international devaluation against the dollar. The former was probably effective over a period of time: U.S. exports of goods and services in the year up to 1949 II to the sterling area were $2·7 billion. In the following year they fell to $2·0 billion or by 26 per cent. At 1958 prices this fall was approximately $0·9 billion and accounts for half the fall in the volume of all U.S. exports in the second half of 1949. Devaluation is discussed below, pp. 138–41.

Imports

The marginal nature of imports in the U.S. economy suggests that the long run income elasticity of demand is above unity while the price elasticity is less than unity. Econometric studies tend to confirm these suppositions: the short run or 'impact' income elasticity since the war has been in the region of unity, the price elasticity in the region of —0·25, with long run, 'equilibrium' elasticities two to three times larger.[1] Furthermore a substantial part of U.S. imports—represented particularly by unfinished goods—is derived from the demand for manufactured goods and can be expected to change in the short run in accord with manufacturing production and manufacturers' inventory investment.

After the end of the war the volume of imports of goods and services had fallen as wartime demands were reduced, although as explained above on p. 97 the decline was not proportionate to that of output. With rising prices throughout 1946, however, the value of imports of goods and services rose. In the first half of 1947 the volume of imports (especially goods) rose a little as did prices. However the reduced rates of production in mid-1947 caused a slight drop in imports in 1947 III which coupled with a price decline starting in May and lasting until October caused the value of imports to fall by $0·6 billion or

[1] See Note K for reference to the studies and comments on the estimated elasticities.

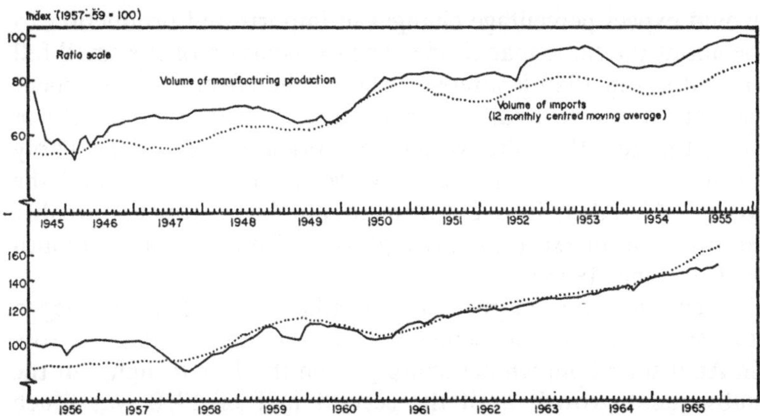

Fig. 4.6: Imports and manufacturing production.
Source: FRB and SCB.

7 per cent in 1947 III.[1] But by the final quarter of the year, output was rising again and until the third quarter of 1948 both industrial production and the volume of imports maintained high levels. Imports rose until 1948 IV, and with prices increasing steeply between October 1947 and May 1948 and showing no tendency to fall until February 1949 the value of imports rose by $2·9 billion or 36 per cent between 1947 III and 1948 III.

With declining production and incomes the volume of imports started to fall in the second half of 1948 and reached its trough in July 1949. The value of imports declined to an even greater extent because import prices fell continuously from February to November 1949. The extent of the decline in imports is difficult to measure because month to month changes in imports were very large during this period. Using a series smoothed with a moving average, it appears that the volume of imports declined from a peak in July 1948 by only 2½ per cent to a trough in July 1949. This compares with a fall in manufacturing production of 8½ per cent between July 1948 and May 1949. On the basis of the usual relationship between the volume of imports and manufacturing production in the recessions and expansions of the 1950s and 1960s which Fig. 4.6 suggests, one

[1] This fall contributed to the United Kingdom exchange crisis of the autumn of 1947 through its effect upon the earnings—especially from wool—of the overseas sterling area.

would expect percentage changes in imports and production to be about the same magnitude. The explanation of the small fall in imports in 1949 is almost certainly the effect of government purchases of commodities for its strategic stockpile, and it can be estimated that the volume of private imports probably declined by about 8 per cent between the year 1948 and the year 1949. Also, it is government purchases which probably account for an exceptionally high rate of imports in the month of December 1948.[1]

Manufacturing output stopped falling after May, and began to rise in August and September. The volume of imports rose in August and September sharply from the July trough, but the subsequent growth until the second half of 1950 was much slower.

The overall balance

The trend in the U.S. current balance of external payments from 1947 to 1950 is dominated by the large fall in exports interrupted only during early 1949. From mid-1947 to mid-1950 the current surplus declined as did the over-all surplus (taking capital transactions into account) or net change in official assets. However in mid-1949 a loss of confidence in sterling with a speculative attack on it caused a large inflow of short term capital and hot money into the United States which increased the U.S. overall surplus in 1949 III by over $1 billion. The next quarter, following the devaluation, there was a large outflow and—with the current surplus worsening—the overall balance fell from a surplus of $1 billion to a deficit of more than $1 billion.

The September 1949 *devaluation*

In the last quarter of 1949 the volume of U.S. exports fell by 13·3 per cent and showed no change in 1950 I. The volume of imports rose by 3·5 per cent in 1949 IV and by less than 1 per cent in the following quarter. These changes fit the broad patterns described in the previous paragraphs—a declining

[1] The *U.N. World Economic Report, 1953–54,* New York, 1955, p. 114, estimates that in the absence of government imports, imports of crude materials and semi-manufactures would have fallen in volume by 15 per cent between 1948 and 1949, from which it can be inferred that as the volume of other imports changed only slightly, total private imports declined by about 8 per cent.

trend in U.S. exports since mid-1947, and a demand for imported goods and services dependent on the level of income and output. However the interpretation of changes in U.S. trade and payments at the end of 1949 is complicated by the devaluation against the dollar in September. A large part of the world—most of the sterling area, most of Europe and Canada—devalued its currencies by amounts up to about 30 per cent, the average devaluation against the U.S. dollar being either 14 per cent or 12 per cent depending on weighting according to the country distribution of U.S. export or import trade.[1] The extent to which a devaluation is passed on in the form of lowered dollar prices for U.S. imports and exports depends on the nature of the markets for the goods and services and the prevailing state of business in both importing and exporting countries. MacDougall's analysis suggests that the 1949 devaluation might have led to an 8 or 9 per cent fall in dollar import prices and a 5 or 6 per cent fall in dollar export prices during the first year after the devaluation.[2] The actual falls in dollar prices were much less as can be seen from Table 4.4.

TABLE 4.4: *Percentage Changes in Imports and Exports after 1949 III*

	1949 III to 1949 IV	*1949 III to 1950 II*
Imports of goods and services at 1958 prices	3·5	10·4
Exports of goods and services at 1958 prices	−13·3	−11·0
Import prices	−1·6	3·8
Export prices	−1·4	−4·0
Disposable personal income at 1958 prices	0·7	6·8
Manufacturing production	−0·8	13·5

Source: SCB.

In 1949 IV both import and export prices fell by about 1½ per cent, and by 1950 II—before the Korean War had started—import prices had risen slightly while export prices had fallen by 4 per cent. Even if the devaluation was passed on by the

[1] See Donald MacDougall, *The World Dollar Problem*, Macmillan, London, 1957, p. 289.

[2] See MacDougall [1957] p. 310, n. 1, where the hypothetical consequences of a 10 per cent depreciation are summarized.

suggested amounts, other influences had swamped the price effects of the devaluation.

The effects of the actual price changes in 1949 IV were slight. Plausible short run price elasticities are −0·3 for imports and −0·6 for exports. These refer to deflated prices: deflated import prices fell by 1·6 per cent between 1949 III and IV; deflated export prices rose by 0·2 per cent.[1] Thus of the 3·5 per cent rise in the volume of imports of goods and services about 0·5 per cent rise was due to the price rise which incorporates the effect of the devaluation. Of the 13·3 per cent fall in the volume of exports of goods and services no part can be ascribed to the price change and hence the devaluation.

These results are in agreement with those of other investigators. Polak, for instance, concluded that the increase in U.S. imports from Europe in the year or so after the devaluation was due mainly to the recovery of U.S. production rather than to the devaluation. He also doubted whether there was much speculative holding back imports or speeding up exports before devaluation.[2] MacDougall lists the recovery from the U.S. recession, the outbreak of the Korean War, the July 1949 sterling area restrictions,[3] trade liberalization in Western Europe and the trend of European recovery as factors which might fully account for the post-devaluation fall in exports and rise in imports. And in his analysis of the effects of a devaluation on the overall external surplus or deficit of the rest of the world, he confirms both the econometric and the historical evidence by concluding that neither the quantity of U.S. imports, nor the quantity of U.S. exports, will be very responsive to a devaluation, at any rate during the first year after the event.[4] Nothing in the above argument is intended to deny that the devaluation

[1] Import prices are deflated by price of other goods consumed in U.S. represented by GNP goods deflator which did not change in 1949 IV. Export prices are deflated by price of rest of world's exports, represented by U.S. import price index. The elasticities are based on those in Table K.1 which are estimated from deflated indexes as described.

[2] J. J. Polak, 'Contribution of the September 1949 devaluations to the solution of Europe's dollar problem', *I.M.F. Staff Papers*, September 1951, pp. 1–32.

[3] See p. 136 above for an estimate of the importance of the sterling area dollar import cuts of July 1949. Devaluation may have made these cuts easier to enforce.

[4] MacDougall [1957] Chapter XIV, especially pp. 290–91, 302–03 and 306.

led to a substantial gain of reserves by the rest of the world. What is asserted is that the improvement in the rest of the world's current balance had little to do with devaluation. Devaluation had its main effect on the capital account, and the gain in reserves by the rest of the world which can be ascribed to devaluation was largely the recoupment of the previous loss through speculation in anticipation of devaluation.

CHAPTER 5

Inflation, Deflation and the Impact of Government

GOVERNMENT EXPENDITURES AND RECEIPTS

Government expenditures will be considered under the headings of defence, Federal civil purchases, state and local government purchases, transfers and foreign aid. Purchases of goods and services for national defence reached their postwar trough in mid-1947.[1] The 1947 defence budget (for fiscal 1948) was dominated by motives of economy, and appropriations were kept at low levels. There was however some provision for the re-equipment of the services—particularly the air force—and expenditures started to rise in the final quarter of 1947. The effect of this re-equipment on business was felt at the same time when military aircraft production started to rise from its very low levels.[2] The increase in expenditures continued in early 1948, and during the course of fiscal '48 the rise in defence purchases was substantial, there being an increase of about $1·7 billion (or 20 per cent) between 1947 III and 1948 II.[3] The 1948 budget accelerated this growth and purchases from 1948 II to 1949 II rose by $3·0 billion or 29 per cent. The bulk of the increase went to the armed forces, but increased expenditure on military assistance, atomic energy and other defence activities

[1] The category 'purchases of goods and services for national defence' in the national accounts includes budget expenditures on the military services, the military assistance portion of international security and foreign relations, civil defence, development and control of atomic energy, promotion of defence production and economic stabilization, and (before 1950) promotion of merchant marine. Non-military aid under international security programmes (such as ERP) is included under exports as a government transfer payment. See National Income Supplement to *SCB* (1954 ed.) p. 148 and *SCB*, August 1965, p. 10.

[2] For the rise in production of defence equipment in late 1947 and 1948 in relation to inventory investment see below pp. 176–7.

[3] The expenditures in this section are valued at current prices.

was significant. This rearmament reached its peak in the third quarter of 1949, the rise in defence equipment production having tapered off to a steady level at the end of 1948. In the 1949 defence budget the Administration deliberately sought to avoid increases for economy reasons—this policy had been announced as early as October 1948. In the controversy over the size of the Air Force in 1949 Congress eventually voted increased appropriations which President Truman said he would not spend. The curtailment of rearmament was effective, and expenditures dropped substantially in 1949 IV and 1950 I. By 1950 II defence purchases were some 6 per cent below the levels of a year previously.

Federal civil purchases, after their mid-1947 rise due partly to agricultural price support activities, receded in 1947 IV to the early 1947 levels. Increased spending was resumed in 1948 I and continued throughout the year.[1] Between 1948 I and IV civil purchases rose by $3·7 billion in current prices, doubling the amount. About four-fifths of the increase, concentrated mainly in the second half of the year, represented purchases of commodities and other operations of the CCC in its agricultural price support activities.[2] The other fifth was purchases for

[1] The 1948 budget message (for fiscal 1949) of the President proposed expenditures only slightly higher than those estimated for fiscal 1948. As approved by Congress, the budget expenditures were cut back to slightly less than 1948 levels, but as it turned out actual expenditures rose $6·5 billion.

[2] See above, pp. 128–30. The CCC purchases classified in the national accounts as 'stabilization of farm prices and income' and measured as change in loans outstanding plus change in inventory were:

Federal Government purchases: civilian
$ billion quarterly totals (not seasonally adjusted)

	Total	*CCC purchases*
1948 I	0·6	−0·228
II	1·1	−0·154
III	1·5	0·269
IV	2·5	1·343
1949 I	1·6	0·330
II	1·3	0·080
III	1·8	0·502
IV	2·2	0·739
1950 I	1·6	0·385
II	0·7	−0·485
III	0·9	−0·518
IV	1·1	−0·133

Source: CCC purchases: Office of Business Economics, Department of Commerce. Total: *SCB.*

a wide range of functions, including water conservation, highways, postal services and housing. These increases were greater than the normal trend of increase, and tended to decline slightly during 1949 when the price support purchases were maintained. Total civil purchases fluctuated during 1949 about the late 1948 level. State and local government purchases of goods and services continued their climb, rising by $1·3 billion in the first half of 1949. In real terms this was twice as rapid as usual, and a large part of the increase was for public works and probably represents a speeding up of expenditures because of the decline in business activity.

Personal transfer payments tended to decline throughout 1948 due to the steady fall after 1947 III in veterans benefits. This decline was reversed in 1949, when unemployment benefits rose steadily throughout the year, increasing between 1948 III and 1949 IV (their peak) by $1·5 billion. Over this eighteen-month period other personal transfer payments increased by $0·3 billions.[1] The foreign aid programme has been described earlier.[2] After the early postwar aid had fallen away from its mid-1947 peak level, the European Recovery Programme increased government transfers in cash and kind, and official loans, by some $2 billion in the second half of 1948. The peak was in the first quarter of 1949, after which aid expenditures—transfers and loans—declined. The fall was quite sharp in the last quarter of 1949 when the amount of aid returned to its mid-1948 levels.

Rising government expenditures in 1948 made a substantial change in the overall Federal, state and local government budgetary situation as Fig. 5.1 shows. After the end of the war the combination of rising receipts (despite tax cuts) and falling Federal expenditures had changed the 1945 total deficit of $39·5 billions to a surplus of $16·1 billion in the first quarter of 1947.[3] The stability of both revenues and expenditures during 1947 kept the surplus at this unusually high level. State and local government receipts and expenditures both rose, and their

[1] The NSLI dividend paid in 1950 I and II has been discussed above, pp. 109–10.

[2] Pp. 133–5.

[3] This is the combined Federal, state and local government surplus on income and product account as in the national income and expenditure accounts. It is seasonally adjusted and at an annual rate.

small surplus declined slightly, while federal government receipts and expenditures tended to be unchanged. In early 1948, however, the surplus started to decline. While Federal revenues tended to fall following the reduction in individual tax rates effective in 1948 II, expenditures as we have seen rose rapidly. State and local government receipts and expenditures continued their steady growth, their small surplus disappearing. The overall result was that between 1947 IV and 1948 IV the total

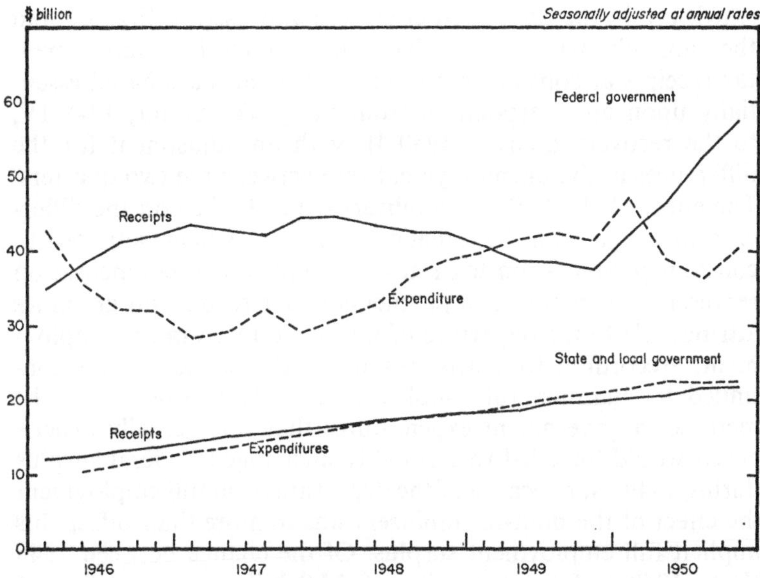

Fig. 5.1: Government revenue and expenditure, 1946–50.
Source: SCB.

surplus declined from $16·0 billion to $3·5, and of the $12·5 billion fall in the surplus about $5·3 billion was due to the reduction in personal taxes.[1] The recession in incomes and business activity accentuated this decline. Federal expenditures continued to rise until 1949 IV while revenues declined by $3 billion during the course of the year. A state and local government deficit appeared as expenditures rose more rapidly than

[1] See below Table 5.2.

revenues. From an overall surplus of \$3·5 billion in 1948 IV a deficit of \$5·0 billion had emerged in 1949 IV.

This swing from surplus to deficit was largely the result of the so-called built-in, or automatic, stabilizers, i.e. the fiscal results of changes of income and employment upon given tax and benefit rates. The most important of these are corporate profits and unemployment compensation. In Table 5.1 are summarized the results of the estimates made by W. Lewis. These estimates are based on data which do not incorporate revisions which are in the data cited elsewhere and used in Fig. 5.1, but they are otherwise comparable.[1] In the table full employment tax receipts at constant pre-recession tax rates are based essentially upon an interpolation from the peak quarter, 1948 IV, to the recovery quarter, 1950 II, with an adjustment for the differences in the unemployment rate between the two quarters. The effect of the built-in stabilizers depends thus on the difference of actual from hypothetical full employment, adjusted to constant pre-recession tax rates. Unemployment compensation represents the increase in payments under regular programmes attributable to the departure of the economy from full employment. According to Lewis' results, if the economy had continued to maintain full employment (at late 1948 rates), the increase in government expenditures that was actually experienced would have led to a roughly unchanged Federal surplus during 1949. But because of the departure from full employment the effect of the built-in stabilizers was to more than offset this implicit full employment surplus. Of the change between 1948 IV to 1949 II from a surplus of \$3·8 billions to a deficit of \$3·9 billion, a total change of \$7·7 billion, \$2·8 billion was due to the fall in profits tax, \$0·9 billion to unemployment compensation and \$1·2 to the fall in other taxes: a total of \$4·9 billion or nearly three quarters of the change. In the Federal sphere there were no budgetary changes in 1949–50 which can be regarded as deliberately discretionary anti-recessionary measures, except possibly the NSLI dividend of 1950.[2]

[1] See W. Lewis, Jr. [1962]. Lewis gives the federal surplus in 1948 IV as \$3·8 billion while the national accounts revision of 1965 gives \$3·4 billion.

[2] For the dividend see the footnote on p. 110 above. The speeding up of state and local government construction in early 1949 was referred to above, p. 144.

TABLE 5.1: *Factors Affecting the Federal Surplus 1948–50*

	1948 IV	1949 I	1949 II	1949 III	1949 IV	1950 I	1950 II
	$ billion, seasonally adjusted at annual rates, current prices						
Surplus at pre-recession peak	3·8	3·8	3·8	3·8	3·8	—	—
Factors not due to recession:							
Increase in receipts at full employment, constant tax rates	—	0·6	1·2	1·8	2·4	3·9‡	4·5‡
Purchases of goods and services							
National defence	—	1·4	1·6	2·0	0·9	0·5	−0·1
Other	—	−1·4	−1·8	−1·9	−1·8	3·5	4·8
Transfers to persons	—	0·5	0·6	0·7	0·6	9·0§	2·5§
Transfers abroad	—	0·8	1·8	0·9	0·7	0·7	1·2
Other*	—	—	0·1	0·5	0·5	0·8	1·0
Subtotal: implicit full employment surplus	3·8	3·1	2·7	3·4	5·3	0·2	8·5
Less effect of built-in stabilizers:							
Corporate profit tax accruals	—	−1·3	−2·8	−2·5	−2·9	−2·2	0·1
Excise taxes	—	−0·4	−0·3	−0·1	−0·6	−0·9	−0·2
Employment taxes	—	−0·1	−0·2	−0·2	−0·3	−0·2	−0·1
Individual income tax accruals	—	−0·3	−0·7	−0·8	−1·3	−0·2	−0·3
Unemployment compensation	—	−0·6	−0·9	−0·9	−0·7	−0·8	−0·4
Other adjustments†	—	−1·8	−1·7	−1·7	−1·6	0·3	0·7
Total: actual surplus	3·8	−1·4	−3·9	−2·8	−2·1	−3·8	8·3

NOTES: * Grants to state and local governments, net interest paid and net subsidies.

† Exclusion of capital gains tax from individual income tax accruals; differences in timing between full accrual basis of individual income tax and national income account basis; and exclusion of $2.5 billion corporate profit tax accrual in 1950 I on account of late 1950 tax increase.

‡ Includes OASI payroll tax increase $0.9 billion.

§ Includes NSLI dividend $8.4 billion in 1950 I and $2.0 billion in 1950 II.

Source: W. Lewis Jr. [1962], Table 20, p. 128.

The relative importance of the main changes in Federal revenue and expenditure in 1948 and 1949 are summarized in Table 5.2. (The table does not disclose the continued rise in foreign aid until 1949 II and its subsequent fall. Furthermore the effect of the 1948 Revenue Act tax reductions are estimated as a decline in liabilities in 1948: the reduction in net tax payments began in 1948 II and as has been pointed out above (p. 108) refunds were made during the first half of 1949.) From the point of view of accounting for the surplus, it is clear that in 1948 both rising purchases and the tax cut were important, the former being quantitatively the largest influence. In 1949 the effect of the built-in stabilizers was the only important factor.

It is useful to make a distinction between those influences which would have an immediate impact on output and business activity, and those having at most a delayed effect. In the first group are purchases and foreign transfers (purchases by definition directly affect output; foreign aid was the financial counterpart of exports) and some transfers to persons such as unemployment benefits which are likely to be spent immediately.[1] By contrast, increases in DPI arising from falls in taxes would, according to the presumed shape of the consumption function, have an effect on PCE only with a considerable delay, the exception to this being that if consumers wished to purchase consumer durables such as cars, windfall income gains—such as occurred from tax refunds in the first half of 1949—would help to finance the purchase. Similarly, reductions in profits tax liability would have a delayed effect—if any—on business investment. It thus appears that purchases and foreign transfers provided an immediate expansionary impact in 1948. The effect of the tax changes was lagged as far as change in DPI was concerned, while it has been pointed out above that in any

[1] Because of the government payment and budgetary system, money items of government expenditure are recorded on a delivery or a cash basis, instead of on an accrual basis. The difference is significant for military hardware such as ships and aeroplanes, and for civilian items of a fixed capital nature (see J. Scherer, 'The report of the President's commission on budget concepts: a review', *Federal Reserve Bank of N.Y. Monthly Review*, *49*, December 1967, pp. 231–38). Consequently the impact of changes in Federal purchases is likely to have been *before* the changes recorded in the national income statistics.

TABLE 5.2: *Factors affecting the Change in the Federal Surplus or Deficit 1948 and 1949*

$ billion, current prices, based on seasonally adjusted data at annual rates

	i	*ii*	*iii*	*iv*	*v*	*vi*
	Purchases of goods and services	*Transfer payments to foreigners (net)*	*Effect of built-in stabilizers*	*Effect of 1948 tax change*	*Other (net)*	*Total (decline in surplus or increase in deficit)*
Change:						
1947 IV to 1948 IV	7·1	2·4	0·0	5·3	−3·0	11·8
1948 IV to 1949 IV	0·6	0·7	5·8	0·0	0·2	7·3

Source: i, ii, vi. As in national accounts.
iii. Table 5.1.
iv. The Treasury estimated that for personal incomes of $200 billion the 1948 Revenue Act would reduce income tax by $4.7 billion. Between 1947 IV and 1948 IV personal income rose from $197.4 billion to $214.5 billion, and allowing for this rise the effect of the reduction in rates between these quarters is estimated to be about $5.3 billion.
v. Residual (includes effect of income growth on tax receipts in 1948, transfers to persons [except unemployment benefits], grants-in-aid and net interest).

case the change in taxes in 1948 was not the major factor in the change in DPI and hence in PCE.[1]

In 1949, the situation is less clear. Leaving aside personal tax changes, change in unemployment benefits ($0·7 billion), purchases and foreign transfers had a direct expansionary effect on output in 1949, but this effect was small in total. (As has been mentioned, an annual analysis at this point is misleading: purchases and foreign aid rose in the first half of 1949 and declined in the second half. The impact on output and business activity was strongly expansionary at first; depressing in the second half of the year.) The unusually large tax refunds in the first half of 1949 undoubtedly assisted the financing of rising automobile purchases, but all the evidence points to the independence of this car boom of short run financial factors. The more difficult problem concerns the effect of the fall in net personal tax payments in 1949 upon PCE as a whole. As incomes fell the marginal propensity to consume rose to maintain consumption. It is impossible to say for certain whether consumption would have been maintained in the absence of the 1948 tax cut and the operation of the built-in stabilizers. If the 1949 recession is looked at in isolation, one is tempted to say that these factors, by preventing DPI from falling further, helped to sustain consumption.[2] If, however, consumption behaviour over the entire postwar period is taken into account, one of the striking features is the short run stability of expenditures on nondurables and services, and there is no evidence to refute the view that the marginal propensity to consume would have risen, in the absence of 1948 tax cut and built-in stabilizers in 1949, as far as was necessary to sustain consumption. The conflict of views cannot be settled, but to place the tax falls in perspective it must be remembered that the decline in prices largely offset the fall in farm income, and that the fall

[1] Holmans [1962], p. 99, suggests that the 1948 tax cuts 'kept consumption demand [in 1948] rising at something close to the previous rate until the fourth quarter, instead of levelling off at a rate somewhat below that reached in the second quarter.' However Holmans does not consider the other influences upon either DPI and PCE.

[2] Lewis [1962], p. 127, says that 'the effect of the tax cut on personal savings and consumer assets was undoubtedly a factor in the extremely shallow decline in consumption expenditures once the recession started.'

in household equipment purchases was probably the result of the combined effect of fall in housebuilding and the imposition of instalment credit controls. Between 1948 III and 1949 III DPI fell by \$6·5 billion, and during this time the volume of PCE on nondurables and services was virtually unchanged. The \$1·9 billion fall in net personal taxes at the time was a small influence.

MONETARY AND CREDIT POLICIES

Beginning in mid-1947 interest rates started to rise and the ease of obtaining credit declined. The wartime policy of the Federal Reserve System of maintaining low, fixed interest rates on long term securities was continued through 1946 and early 1947 at the cost of continuous expansion of the money stock. However on July 10, 1947, a series of measures to raise short term rates was started. The posted $\frac{3}{8}$ per cent buying rate on Treasury bills and the repurchase option granted to sellers of bills were ended. On August 8th, the Federal Open Market Committee discontinued the $\frac{7}{8}$ per cent buying rate on certificates. The Treasury gradually raised the rate on newly issued certificates to $1\frac{1}{8}$ per cent in December, 1947, and the bill rate moved up to 1 per cent. At the same time the Treasury increased the amount of long term debt relative to short with the result that long term yields rose slightly in October and November. On December 24th the Open Market Committee established a new low support level for the price of government bonds and yields rose to 2·45 per cent which was the level they were maintained at during 1948.[1] What had happened was that the sharp narrowing of the differential between long and short rates made short term securities relatively more attractive and caused lenders to alter their portfolios. A reverse shift thus occurred in the Federal Reserve's portfolio. From November 1947 to March 1948 \$5 billion of bonds were purchased and \$6 billion of short term securities sold, so that Federal Reserve credit outstanding declined by about \$1 billion over the period. In the words of Friedman and Schwartz,

[1] Details of policy changes from M. Friedman and A. J. Schwartz [1963], pp. 578–9.

'the announced pattern of rates taken as a whole, therefore, continued to be above rather than below the level consistent with no change in the money stock. Since the pattern was then made effective, whereas before that actual rates had been below the announced rates, monetary contraction was . . . actually produced during calendar 1948.'[1]

At the same time as these deflationary effects were enforced, the Federal Reserve System was imposing other anti-inflationary policies. When Congress ended the authority of the Board of Governors to regulate consumer credit on November 1, 1947, the System urged banks to avoid making non-essential loans. In January 1948 discount rates at all Reserve Banks were raised, although the new rates being below market rates (the Treasury bill rate was permitted to rise again in mid-1948) the changes were ineffective. Another ineffective increase occurred in August. More important were increases in reserve requirements in February, June and September 1948.[2]

Thus the actions of the authorities in late 1947 and early 1948 were pointed in a deflationary direction, first curbing the growth and later causing a decline in the money supply. But as well as this general monetary effect, there was a specific effect on the credit markets by way of the rise in interest rates. As has been pointed out above, business expenditures on plant and equipment were unlikely to have been affected to any significant degree by tighter money in 1948, but the housing market was.[3]

Corporate bond yields had followed the yield on government securities by rising quite sharply from September to December 1947. They had sagged a little in the second quarter of 1948 with the renewed rise in commodity prices and prospects of inflation, but had returned to their February level by November. At the end of 1948 and beginning of 1949 they fell sharply.

[1] [1963], p. 580. Using Friedman and Schwartz's figures (Table A-1, p. 718), currency held by the public plus commercial bank demand deposits reached a peak in January 1948 and by December had fallen by nearly $2 billion.

[2] To acquire the added reserves, banks sold securities which, under the support programme, the System had to buy. These purchases caused an increase in Reserve credit outstanding but this was a reaction to the change in reserve requirements rather than a source of monetary expansion.

[3] Pp. 124–5 and 159–60.

Mortgage yields followed bond yields with a delay, and it was the rise in bond yields which caused banks—heavily invested in mortgages—to shift out into bonds substantially and rapidly, reducing the supply of credit for housing. This factor is regarded as the main cause of the ensuing fall in housing starts. No other market for goods and services was affected in this way, although there is some evidence that the renewed instalment credit controls later in 1948 curbed household buying to some extent.[1]

In adopting anti-deflationary measures the Federal Reserve System responded slowly to the decline in business activity and prices. In March and again in April 1949 the instalment credit controls were relaxed. Between May and September there were six reductions in reserve requirements. As we have seen, corporate bond yields fell at the beginning of 1949. However, the System had actually sold government securities to prevent yields from declining and corporate bond yields were stable from February to June. Then the policy of pegging was discontinued and both bond yields and yields on short term securities declined, bond yields for over six months. With the decline in bond yields in early 1949 mortgage funds again became plentiful and mortgage yields started to decline in February when housing starts were rising once again.

Changes in the supply of money

Following Friedman and Schwartz's analysis,[2] the change in the money stock can be attributed to three 'proximate' determinants: the change in high powered money (Federal Reserve notes, gold certificates and Treasury currency in circulation, and deposits at Federal Reserve banks), the change in the ratio of commercial bank deposits to bank reserves, and the change in the ratio of commercial bank deposits to currency held by the public. The latter ratio, after falling during the war years, has tended to rise continuously since 1945 with slight slackenings in the rate of growth in the periods of downturn in business activity. The deposit-reserve ratio has also tended to rise since the war, more rapidly but more erratically than the deposit-

[1] See above, p. 112.

[2] [1963], pp. 50–53, and Appendix B. I have also relied to a large extent upon their analysis of the 1947–49 period, pp. 574–85 and 604–10.

currency ratio, with most of the changes being attributable to changes in the System's reserve requirements. Changes in high powered money in the period we are concerned with have arisen firstly because of changes in the American gold stock due primarily to the surplus on the U.S. balance of external payments, secondly because of the Treasury surplus and the associated debt-management policies, and finally because of the effects of the Federal Reserve System's policies.

During the first half of 1947 the money stock rose quite rapidly, as high powered money increased and the deposit-currency ratio continued its postwar rise. After mid-year, however, the rise in the money stock slowed down markedly, and was virtually unchanged between September and January 1948. After January it tended to decline for a year.[1] The change in the second half of 1947 can be attributed to changes in all three proximate determinants: a fall in the deposit-reserve ratio from mid-1947 to early 1948 (probably due to changes in the distribution of reserves between banks), a constant level of high powered money from September 1947 to June 1948 due to the end of growth in bank reserves over the same period, and a marked slowing down of the growth in the deposit-currency ratio in the last quarter of 1947 and first quarter of 1948. I shall first consider the change in high powered money during the year as a whole, and then return to the situation at the end of the year. The relative importance of the factors accounting for this change is summarized in Table 5.3 which consolidates the financial operations of the Treasury and the FR System. The data are organized in the form of a sources and uses of capital funds table, the balance of the various operations measuring the change in high powered money. The table draws attention to the fact that in 1947 most of the gross saving of $10·1 billions due to budgetary and other surpluses was offset by the purchases of securities by the authorities from the public and the banks. In other words the policy of supporting the prices of government securities inevitably nullified any deflationary effect the Federal surplus might have had. Additional inflationary influences were government lending abroad and the

[1] This description applies whether or not time and savings bank deposits are included.

inflow of gold, although part of these inflationary influences was offset by the fall in government deposits outside the FR (these are mainly special loan and tax accounts with commercial and savings banks). The net effect was the small rise in high powered money in the form of a rise in the reserves of the member banks of the FR system.

Now return to the changed situation at the end of the year. Although the statistical picture is not entirely clear, it appears that in 1947 IV the direction of several of the influences described above altered. First, the federal surplus temporarily increased as Federal current expenditures declined slightly. Second, the balance of payments surplus fell (as it had done the previous quarter with reduced lending abroad and gold inflow). These two factors, tending to depress bank reserves, made effective the rise in interest rates initiated by the authorities after the middle of the year. The fall in security prices—although held in control by the Federal Reserve—checked the desire of banks to buy increased reserves to offset the effects of Federal finance and the balance of payments. It appears that the various influences which combined to produce the squeeze on liquidity were independent and their coincidence accidental. The squeeze was unsought, but was a prelude to the deliberate measures of early 1948.

The impact of this liquidity squeeze at the end of 1947 and in early 1948 on bank lending was marked and noticed. Commenting on the change in interest rates at the end of 1947 the National City Bank said that

'Banks [are] very much more cautious in making intermediate-term capital loans. Many banks feel they have all the term loans they want. Insurance companies are being more 'choosy' . . . loans to marginal borrowers are likely to be pushed back. Ratios of debt to equity are being scrutinized more closely. Borrowers are being asked more often to pare down their requirements, and some programmes for capital outlays have been held in abeyance.'[1]

A month later in January, 'bank lending has slowed up, reflecting seasonal influences as well as caution induced by the drop

[1] *National City Bank Monthly Letter*, January 1948, p. 9.

TABLE 5.3: *Summary Consolidated Sources and Uses of Funds of Federal Government and Federal Reserve System 1947 to 1949*

	1947		1948 $ billion		1949	
Sources:						
1. Government gross saving		10·1		7·8		−1·3
2. Government domestic borrowing		2·8		2·9		2·3
3. Increase in member bank reserves at FR	1·8		2·6		−3·9	
4. Increase in FR notes, etc.[1]	−0·9		−0·2		−0·4	
5. Increase in high powered money		0·9		2·4		−4·3
TOTAL		13·8		13·1		−3·3
Uses:						
6. Purchase of securities from public and banks		8·6		8·5		−5·5
7. Government domestic lending		0·3		0·4		0·9
8. Government net lending abroad		3·5		1·5		0·7
9. Change in gold holdings		2·2		1·5		0·2
10. Government currency and deposits outside the FR		−1·0		0·9		0·6
11. Other net assets and statistical discrepancy		0·2		0·3		−0·2
TOTAL		13·8		13·1		−3·3

[1] Federal reserve notes, gold certificates and Treasury currency in circulation, plus other Federal Reserve deposits.

Source: *FRB*, August 1959, pp. 1059–60 and Friedman and Schwartz [1963], Table B-3, p. 806, as follows (sources and uses are derived from year to year changes in assets and liabilities):

line 1: *FRB* p. 1059. Total financial assets less total liabilities.
2: *FRB* p. 1059. Fixed value redeemable claims, consumer savings, trade debit, other loans and miscellaneous liabilities (except IMF demand notes).
3: *FRB* p. 1060. Member bank reserves.
4: line 5 minus line 3.
5: Friedman and Schwartz [1963] p. 806, column (1).
6: *FRB* p. 1060. Federal obligations of monetary authorities less p. 1059. Federal obligations.
7: *FRB* p. 1059. Credit market instruments (except loans to rest of world) plus trade credit.
8: *FRB* p. 1059. Loans to rest of world, plus miscellaneous assets less IMF demand notes.
9: *FRB* p. 1060. Gold.
10: *FRB* p. 1059. Tax and loan accounts plus currency and other deposits.
11: Total sources less lines 6 to 10.

in the bond market and by ever-widening recognition of the dangers in the present inflationary situation.' The significance of the federal surplus was recognized, and although seasonal, the 'vast tax collections' in January were described as 'highly deflationary'.[1] And commenting on the events of February the Bank said that 'since the turn of the year bank loans have been extended at a rate which evidently has little more than offset repayments of old loans. . . . It thus appears that bank lending has not been actively inflationary in this period. Treasury surplus revenues have been effective in reducing the supply of money in the hands of individuals and the business community even though offset in part through the selling of government bonds by bank customers and the public in general.'[2]

In 1948, as has been pointed out, the money stock declined. The deposit-currency ratio continued its slow rise, but the deposit-reserve ratio fell substantially after February because of the rises in reserve requirements. It was the rises in reserve requirements during the year which account for part of the large increase of $2·6 billion in high powered money and which offset the effects of this increase. Commercial banks, in order to get the necessary quantity of reserves, sold about $3 billions of government securities during the course of 1948—about $1 billion due to the rises in requirements in February and June, and $2 billion in September.[3] The Treasury surpluses of course fell in 1948, gross savings for the year as a whole being $7·8 billion or over $2 billion less than in 1947. The effects of this change on the money supply were, however, more than offset by the other financial changes. In the first place, if we exclude the $3 billion of bonds purchased by the FR to increase bank reserves, net purchases of securities from public and banks fell between 1947 and 1948 by about $3 billion. Secondly, net lending abroad declined and the gold inflow dropped, totalling between 1947 and 1948 just over $2 billion. Finally, there was a

[1] *National City Bank Monthly Letter*, February 1948, p. 17.

[2] Ibid., March 1948, p. 29. Friedman and Schwartz [1963], p. 580, comment that 'the situation was not recognized at the time', presumably referring to official recognition of official actions. These authors do not discuss the influence of the fiscal changes, nor do they make it clear when they think the rise in interest rates was made effective.

[3] Friedman and Schwartz [1963], p. 576.

swing of nearly $2 billion in government deposits outside the FR from a fall of $1 billion in 1947 to an increase of $1 billion in 1948.

The money stock was fairly constant over 1949, a large rise in the deposit-reserve ratio in the middle of the year—in response to the reduction in reserve requirements between May and September releasing $4 billion of bank funds—being offset by a decline in high powered money. In the early part of the year the action of the FR in selling over $3 billion of bonds to peg their price more than offset the small rise in gold holdings. Later in the year there were further falls in bank reserves when commercial banks responded to the lowering of reserve ratios by buying government securities. All told banks increased their holdings of government securities by $4·4 billions during the year whilst their reserve requirements were reduced by about the same amount. Superficially the actions of the authorities in 1949 were overall deflationary. A purchase of securities from banks and public of $8·5 billions in 1948 changed in 1949 to a sale of $5·5 billion to produce a swing of $14 billion. Net lendings and increases in gold stock fell. These events offset the swing of about $9 billion in the Federal balance from surplus to deficit, but the offset was equal to the fall in bank reserves which we know was used to buy securities. It is necessary however, to distinguish between the clearly deflationary attempt to prevent the rise in bond prices in early 1949, and the subsequent purchase of bonds by banks because the demand for loans had fallen.[1]

THE TOTAL IMPACT

During the first nine months of 1947 government expenditures and receipts were relatively stable, and business activity was not significantly affected by changes in government fiscal or monetary policy. The effects of the large Federal budgetary surplus were largely offset by official willingness to purchase securities at stable prices and by other expansionary financial operations. During the second half of 1947 the authorities allowed interest rates to rise, and at the end of 1947 the budgetary surplus

[1] Bank loans (excluding consumer credit and mortgages) declined by $1·7 billion during 1949.

temporarily ceased to be offset with the result that liquidity was squeezed with several effects on activity. The most important effect was the drying up of the residential mortgage market, leading to a fall in housing starts and eventually a decline in construction by $2·2 billion between 1948 II and 1949 II. This decline in housebuilding led also to a small fall in household purchases of furniture and equipment. The second important effect of the liquidity squeeze was to confirm businessmen in their opinion that agricultural commodity markets in particular were returning to normal and that inflationary pressures were subsiding. In this way the squeeze played a part in the fall in farm prices in early 1948. Beyond these two effects the influence of the monetary and fiscal changes were diffused and cannot be isolated from other changes. In particular there does not appear to have been any strong or distinct effects on business fixed investment or inventory accumulation, either directly or through speculative buying arising from price changes.

During 1948 monetary policy continued to be restrictive while instalment credit controls went into effect in September. However, throughout the year and also during the first half of 1949 government fiscal actions had an expansionary effect on incomes and expenditure—government purchases rose, foreign aid supported exports and taxes were reduced. Between 1948 II and 1949 II the total government surplus declined by $14·5 billion; of this fall $7·3 billion was due to the rise in purchases and foreign transfers which probably had a direct and immediate effect on output. Compared with this the changes induced by monetary policy and credit contraction could only have been small: as stated above, residential construction fell by only $2·2 billion between 1948 II and 1949 II. Even allowing for the changes in consumer durables it is clear that the depressing effects of monetary changes in 1948 were more than offset by expansionary fiscal changes.

The fiscal and monetary policies of 1948 continued into the first quarter of 1949. By the second quarter monetary policy had ceased being restrictive, and instalment credit controls had been discarded. Housing starts had started to rise again after February, but this is to be attributed more to the general emergence of easier credit rather than to official actions. Fiscal changes continued to be expansionary in the first half of the year. After mid-1949 the balance of forces changed: the government deficit ceased to grow as purchases of goods and services and foreign transfers declined, offset by an increase in the effect of the built-in stabilizers. Allowing for the likely more immediate effect on output of purchases and foreign aid, fiscal changes on balance were probably slightly depressing. If the housing revival is treated as independent of government policy and the monetary changes as expansionary but relatively unimportant, then the impact of government in the second half of 1949 was neutral, tending to be depressing.

The most important conclusions to emerge from this review of the effects of government actions are, firstly that there was a combined and partly accidental depressing monetary and fiscal change at the end of 1947, producing the recession in housebuilding. Secondly, that the fiscal changes in 1948 and early 1949 had strongly expansionary effects which offset the depressing monetary changes and probably delayed the onset of the upper turning point of the business cycle. Finally, that a slightly depressing or at best neutral overall effect emerged in mid-1949, despite the built-in stabilizers and the change in monetary policy.

PRICES AND WAGES

After rising only slowly during the first six months of 1947, the price level started to rise again rapidly after the middle of the year. Between January and June the consumer price index rose by 2·5 per cent (mainly due to the large rise in farm prices in March); between June and January 1948 the rise was 7·6 per cent and was experienced by most goods and services, especially food and housing. The wholesale price index of non-food and non-farm commodities rose by 8·6 per cent between June and January. This penultimate burst of inflation was preceded by the main impact of the 1947 round of negotiated wages increases which pushed up the rate of growth of hourly earnings sharply in May and June, 1947. These wage increases undoubtedly provided the opportunity for increases in some prices. But the burst of inflation occurred at the time when the shortage of labour was at its postwar peak—with maximum weekly hours worked and minimum unemployed—and when pressure of excess demand in several other markets was at what was subsequently recognized as a peak. It is difficult to avoid the conclusion that excess demand was the main factor in the price increases in late 1947.

There were, however, some speculative elements in this price rise, especially in the rise in farm prices, and those of grains in particular. The fall in wheat prices in January-February 1948 marked the end of this speculative rise.[1] The ending of fears of continued grain shortages was one factor; possibly of importance in the uncertain general business situation were a number of official anti-inflationary measures and statements appearing in January,[2] and the deflationary monetary policy existing at the time.[3] Certainly in the months from November to February bank loans became more difficult to obtain and more expensive, and these pressures together with the warnings and fears of deflation were sufficient to make traders and others prepared to reduce prices. Most food prices fell in February 1948 (see Fig. 5.2). The largest fall was in grain, livestock and livestock products prices, pulling down the wholesale and retail price levels of foods. Because of this the consumer price index ceased to rise, falling slightly. Prices of some related goods (such as hides, leather and shoes) fell also, but prices of most non-farm

[1] For details of the rise and fall, and the factors influencing expectations, see above, pp. 127–8.

[2] At the time public concern with inflation was intense. On October 23, 1947, President Truman had called a special session of Congress to deal with inflation (as well as with interim aid for Europe). The President proposed a comprehensive programme including restoring consumer credit controls, regulating commodity speculation, allocating and rationing scarce commodities, strengthening rent control and imposing price and wage ceilings. The final Anti-Inflation Act, signed on December 28th, gave the President few of the powers requested, authorizing only voluntary agreements to allocate commodities and to regulate commodity trading. On January 5, 1948, the President endorsed a voluntary programme launched by the American Banking Association to discourage excessive or inflationary uses of bank credit. Then on January 7th, in his annual message to Congress, he warned that 'inflation holds the threat of another depression'. The Economic Report submitted to Congress on the 14th reinforced these views and recommended further anti-inflationary measures. At the same time there were clear warnings that credit controls would become tighter: on January 10th nine out of twelve Federal Reserve Banks raised their discount rates (the other three following later), and on 23rd it was announced that reserve requirements in New York and Chicago would be raised as from February 27th.

[3] For monetary policy, see above pp. 151–2.

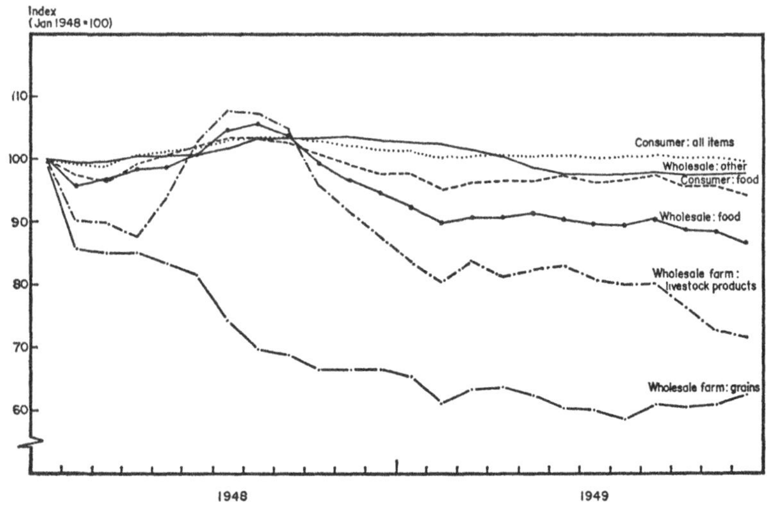

Fig. 5.2: Price changes 1948 and 1949.

Source: SCB.

goods tended to remain unchanged. Textile prices continued to rise but at a slower rate. The wholesale price index for non-farm, non-food commodities was virtually unchanged from January to April.

After February, divergent movements appeared. Farm grain prices continued to decline, but livestock and livestock product prices rose sharply in the second quarter because of reduced livestock slaughtering. Food prices—both wholesale and retail—consequently started to rise again, the food component of the consumer price index increasing by 7·2 per cent between March and July, the index itself rising by 4·1 per cent. This renewed surge of prices revived the earlier fears of inflation. After some resistance to claims for higher wages during the first few months of the year, there was a more rapid rise in rates of pay in May and the following three months (between April and August hourly earnings rose by 4 per cent), initiated and possibly guided by a substantial increase given by General Motors in May. The inflationary expectations were reinforced by the provisions for automatic quarterly cost of living adjustments in the

GM contract.[1] Non-farm and food prices rose rapidly in July and August, the increases in steel prices being substantial. While this final surge of inflation in the industrial sector was spending itself, in the farm sector prices were falling again. Grain prices fell very steeply in July and August as the plentiful 1948 harvest became apparent, and with the fall in the price of animal feedstuffs meat prices stopped their rise in August and in September started a substantial decline. The effect of these changes was that the wholesale and retail food price indexes reached a peak in August and declined thereafter. The peak in the all items consumer price index was a month later. Industrial prices on average continued to rise until December when the first small fall in the wholesale index occurred. Clothing prices had been falling since August (retail apparel since November) following the substantial drop in cotton prices in July and August. Metal and metal product prices, however, were rising at the end of 1948 and continued to rise in 1949 I.

For food and retail prices in general, the main part of the fall was over by February 1949. Wholesale prices of non-farm, non-food products however continued to fall throughout the first half of 1949, mainly due to the fall in metal prices in 1949 II. Increases in hourly earnings continued until January 1949, after which the wage level remained remarkably unchanged until the end of the year.

The final burst of inflation in mid-1948 was partly due to the peculiarities of the farm situation, partly to the attainment of high levels of output and demand for some products—especially steel and cars—just before the recession. It is unlikely that steel prices would have been raised or that GM would have granted such a generous wage increase if the demand for these industries' products had not been high and rising. Similarly, the fall in price levels at the end of the year was partly due to the farm situation, and partly due to the gradual emergence of declining demand and reduced output. It is significant that in building, textiles and furniture and furnishings, where the pressure of demand abated early in 1948 and where output levelled off or started to fall around the middle of the year, prices of materials and output rose only slightly during the second half of the year

[1] For details see *National City Bank Monthly Letter*, June 1948, pp. 62–64.

or else started to decline. In metals, where the demand remained strong for longer, price increases continued into 1949. In attributing the fall in industrial prices to the decline in excess demand, and the fall in farm prices also to primarily a changed balance of supply and demand, I am explicitly rejecting explanations of the changes in the price level due to general monetary deflation (although I have recognized the effect of increased interest rates on the rate of house building). I am also explicitly rejecting an explanation of the price level changes as due to speculation and the revision of erroneous expectations, although the role of speculation and revised expectations was significant in the case of some markets, especially for grain in January 1948. In mid-1948 when fears of inflation again began to be voiced, and when President Truman attempted to make political capital out of Congress's refusal to adopt his anti-inflationary programme,[1] some elements of speculation may have been again present. The talk of danger, and the popular belief that inflation would be followed by severe deflation may have been instrumental in the timing of some price reductions in August and September. But this sort of influence, while discussed at length in the popular press and the serious financial journals, must have been slight: there is no evidence of unusual inventory speculation and the actual price changes—even after it was clear that prices were falling—were small. The scope for panic was slight. By and large the price changes from late 1947 on represented changes in the long run balance of market forces.

[1] The President called a special session of Congress between the Presidential nominating conventions and the elections, and on July 27th put forward his proposals which were virtually the same as those of 1947 (see above, p. 161, n. 2). Eventually on August 16th, a small part of the plan was enacted: authority was given to the Federal Reserve Board to reimpose controls over consumer credit and to raise the maximum reserve requirements for member banks (PL 80–905). The authority was to lapse on June 30, 1949. In his election campaign Truman criticized Congress for not adopting his proposals, and said that a Republican victory would lead to 'runaway prices'.

CHAPTER 6

Output and Inventory Investment, 1947 to 1950

Unlike the period from the end of World War II to mid-1947, with its readily discernible sequence of demobilization and recovery to high levels of activity, the period from the second half of 1947 to the end of 1949 contains conflicting tendencies, changes in the levels of activity in some parts of the economy being offset by changes in others. Judged by final sales to households, business and government (excluding change in inventories), the 1947–49 period is one of slow but steady growth. Judged by final sales of goods alone, as shown in Table 6.1, the period is one of no growth from the second quarter of 1947 to the third quarter of 1948, but some growth thereafter. In contrast to final sales, output rose during 1947 and 1948 after which it fell substantially in the first half of 1949. Inventories consequently accumulated at an increasing rate from late 1947, and the fall in output in 1949 matched a large fall in inventories. After output started to rise again in the second half of 1949 the inventory decline tapered off, although the renewed growth in inventories of durable goods was seriously upset by the steel strike in the final quarter of 1949. By 1950 I the recovery in output was strong and general, and both final sales and inventory accumulation were rising. In the overall picture the special position of inventories is clear: without the rise and fall in inventories in 1948–49 (and disregarding multiplier effects on final sales) output would have grown at a rate of about 3½ per cent per annum throughout 1948 and early 1949 and there would have been no recession. Interest must centre on the cause or causes of the cycle in inventory accumulation.

TABLE 6.1: *Gross National Product and Selected Components, 1947 to 1950*

(1958 price, seasonally adjusted at annual rates)

$ billion

	Non-residential fixed investment (excl. autos)	*Residential construction*	*Exports of goods and services*	*Automobile purchases*	*PCE durables (excl. autos)*	*PCE non-durables and services*	*Government purchases military*	*Government purchases civil*	*CBI nonfarm*	*Goods output*	*Goods final sales*	*GNP output*	*GNP final sales*
1947 I	34·2	14·3	23·3	9·0	17·3	179·8	14·2	24·4	1·1	170·1	170·1	306·4	306·3
II	33·2	13·5	23·7	9·7	17·5	182·6	13·4	26·4	1·6	172·6	173·3	309·0	309·8
III	32·8	15·5	22·9	8·9	18·3	182·9	13·6	27·1	−0·2	171·4	173·8	309·6	311·9
IV	33·3	18·4	20·5	10·3	19·0	181·2	14·1	26·2	3·1	174·8	172·5	314·5	312·3
1948 I	35·3	17·9	19·3	11·1	18·2	182·5	14·0	27·1	2·8	175·6	172·3	317·1	313·7
II	34·7	18·7	17·7	10·0[1]	19·0	184·5	15·2	30·3	3·5	177·4	172·8	322·9	318·2
III	34·6	18·0	18·0	10·5	19·0	184·5	15·4	32·4	4·6	179·4	173·6	325·8	320·0
IV	35·6	16·8	17·4	11·2	18·0	186·6	16·9	33·8	3·5	180·9	176·5	328·7	324·3
1949 I	33·6	16·0	19·4	11·7	17·1	187·5	17·7	33·6	0·0	176·5	177·0	324·5	325·0
II	31·2	16·2	19·3	14·8	17·1	188·2	18·4	35·4	−5·2	173·0	179·3	322·5	328·8
III	29·5	17·7	18·1	15·2	18·1	187·4	18·9	35·3	−1·5	175·5	178·0	326·1	328·6
IV	28·9	19·8	15·7	15·2	19·1	189·3	17·7	36·1	−6·0	171·8	178·3	323·3	329·8
1950 I	29·5	22·0	15·7	16·5	19·3	191·8	17·9	35·5	3·2	183·6	180·1	339·6	336·1
II	32·3	23·7	16·1	17·2	19·1	195·5	17·5	33·8	5·4	187·8	181·7	348·5	342·5
III	35·0	24·8	16·5	20·7	24·2	198·7	19·2	32·5	5·0	197·0	191·0	362·8	356·8
IV	35·5	23·5	16·8	19·3	20·3	197·1	22·5	32·3	16·4	202·0	184·4	370·1	352·5

[1] The fall in automobile purchases (and output) in 1948 II was due to a strike at Chrysler in May.

Source: SCB and Department of Commerce. *Automobile purchases:* automobile expenditure components of PDE and PCE. *Government purchases:* national defence deflated with Federal purchases implicit price index; civilian (Federal other plus state and local) deflated with government purchases implicit index. GNP final sales equals the first nine columns *less* imports of goods and services (not shown). GNP output equals GNP final sales *plus* CBI nonfarm and CBI farm (see Table 6.2).

At this point it is necessary to stress the care required to use inventory data. Care is necessary for several reasons. In the first place, statistics of book values of inventories for the years of our period of interest are available under only an industrial, not a market classification. It is not possible, for instance, to distinguish the inventories of firms producing predominantly defence goods from those producing consumer durables. Second, and more important, the reliability of estimates of the inventory change component in GNP (CBI) is regarded as lower than that of other components. Primarily this is due to the difficulties of adjusting reported book values to conform with national income definitions, i.e. the valuation of the volume change over a period at average prices of the period.[1] It is reflected in the size of some of the periodic revisions made in the published figures. For instance, the 1965 national income revision resulted in substantial alterations in the previously published figures of changes in durable goods industries in 1947.

A breakdown of the CBI estimates into manufacturing, trading and other sectors is necessary for the analysis that follows. The Office of Business Economics does not publish an industrial breakdown of CBI on the grounds that the detail is not as reliable as the industry breakdowns for most other types of national income data. They do however allow their unpublished estimates to be used, and these together with the published figures for farm and auto dealers' CBI form the basis of Table 6.2 and Fig. 6.1. The trends in inventory investment disclosed by the table and the figure are not in conflict with other information, and provided undue attention is not given to isolated quarter to quarter changes the estimates appear sufficiently reliable for our purposes. A breakdown of manufacturers' inventory change by stage of fabrication has been prepared and published by Stanback, and with some alterations this is shown in Fig. 6.2.[2]

[1] See National Income Supplement to *SCB*, 1954 edition, pp. 135–38.

[2] Stanback, T. M., *Postwar Cycles in Manufacturers' Inventories*, NBER Studies in Business Cycles No. 11, NBER, Washington, D.C., 1962. The Stanback breakdown is based on a detailed deflation of the raw data, taking into account the average length of time inventories have been held. Stanback says (p. 128) that these estimates are 'roughly comparable' to those provided by the OBE: 'they differ only in that coverage and procedures used in deflation were not identical'.

TABLE 6.2: *Change in Business Inventories by Industry*
(1958 prices, seasonally adjusted at annual rates)
$ billion

	Durable goods					Nondurable goods			
	Total	*Manu-facturers*	*Traders excluding auto dealers*	*Auto dealers*	*Other*	*Total*	*Farm*	*Manu-facturers*	***Traders***
1947 I	0·9	−0·7	2·3	0·1	−0·8	−0·8	−1·0	1·7	−1·6
II	1·6	0·7	0·6	0·0	0·3	−2·4	−2·3	−0·7	0·6
III	3·4	1·4	1·0	0·1	0·9	−5·7	−2·2	−0·3	−3·3
IV	−0·1	−0·9	−0·4	0·3	0·9	2·3	−0·9	0·8	2·3
1948 I	0·8	−1·7	3·2	−0·1	−0·6	2·5	0·5	1·1	0·9
II	1·0	0·0	1·4	−0·2	−0·2	3·6	1·2	2·3	0·1
III	1·4	0·4	0·6	0·4	0·0	4·3	1·2	1·8	1·3
IV	1·6	0·1	0·6	0·7	0·2	2·8	0·9	0·6	1·3
1949 I	0·1	0·6	−0·9	0·3	0·1	−0·6	−0·5	0·5	−0·5
II	−5·4	−2·8	−2·4	0·4	−0·6	−0·9	−1·0	−0·6	0·8
III	−0·9	−3·2	1·9	1·3	−0·9	−1·6	−1·0	−0·3	−0·3
IV	−5·8	−2·4	−0·9	−1·5	−1·0	−0·7	−0·5	−0·5	0·4
1950 I	−0·5	−0·1	−0·3	−0·3	0·2	4·0	0·3	0·7	3·0
II	4·6	1·9	1·4	1·1	0·2	1·4	0·6	−0·5	1·3

Source: Totals, Auto dealers and Farm from *SCB*.
Manufacturers and Traders (retailers and wholesalers) unpublished data from Office of Business Economics.
Other is residual.

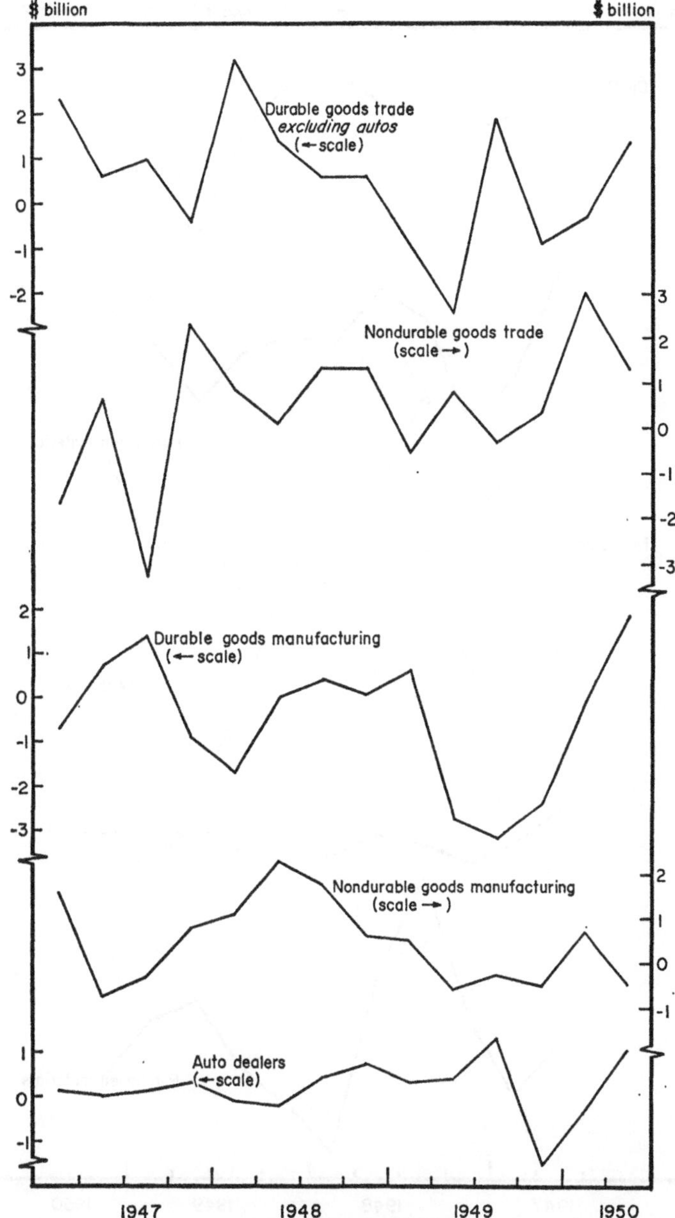

Fig. 6.1: Change in business inventories by industry, 1947–50.
Source: Table 6.2.

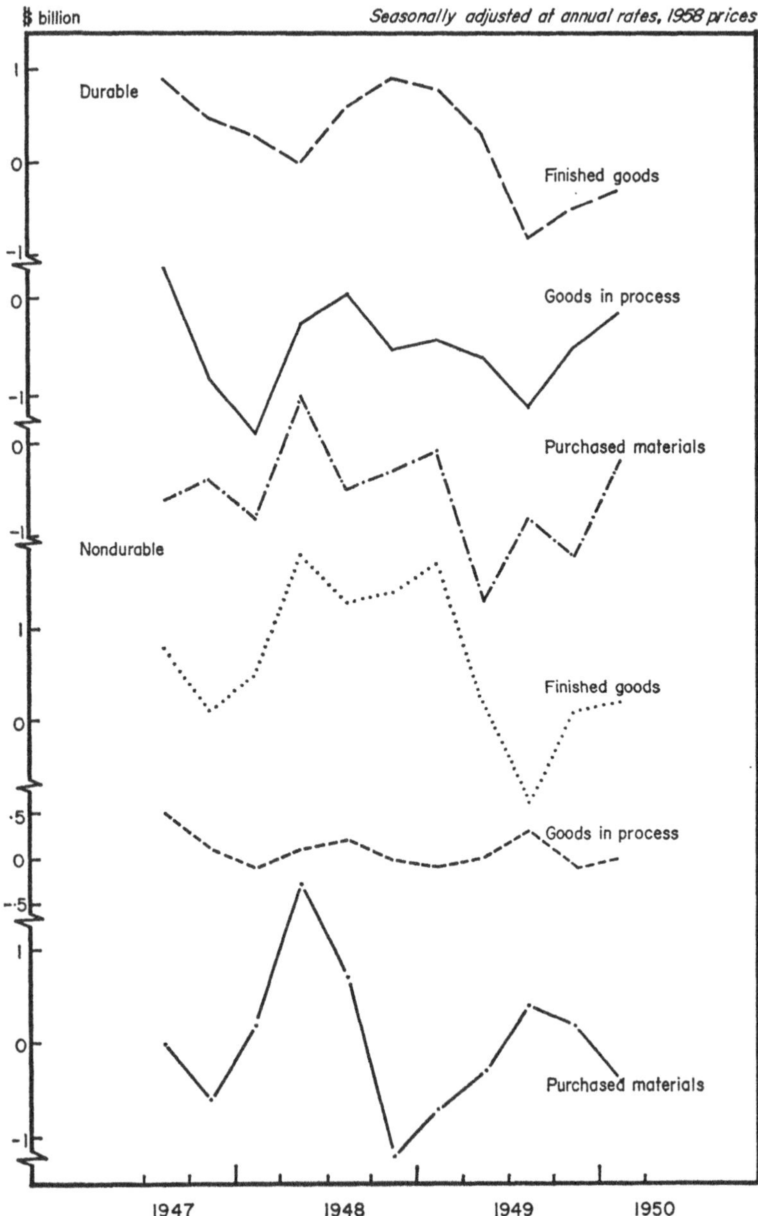

Fig. 6.2: Change in manufacturing inventories by stage of fabrication, 1947–50. *Source:* Stanback (1962), Table B-5, pp. 140–43, converted to 1958 prices with national income implicit goods price indexes (durable series multiplied by 1·307; nondurable by 1·198).

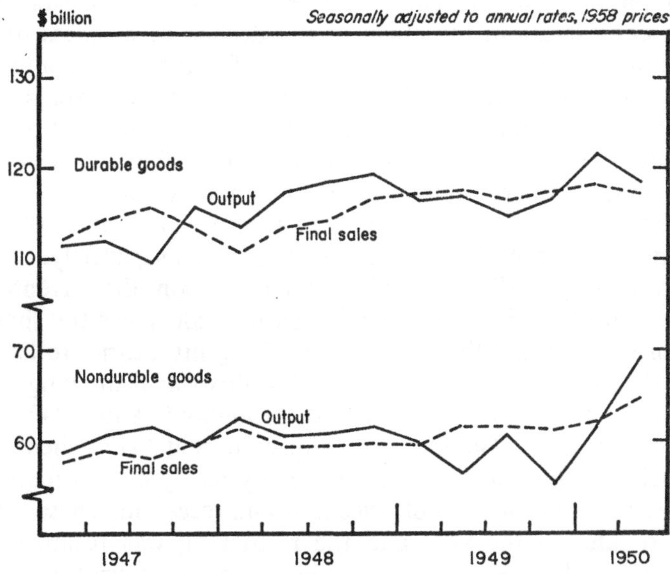

Fig. 6.3: Output and final sales of durable and nondurable goods, 1947–50. *Source:* SCB.

DURABLE GOODS[1]

As Fig. 6.3 shows, total final sales of durable goods, after reaching a peak in 1948 I, declined the following quarter to a level which was maintained for a year. After a rise in 1949 II back to the 1948 I peak level, sales were again steady until growth was resumed in early 1950. As has been shown in the previous chapters, the relative stability in total final sales during 1948 and 1949 hides different movements in different markets. During 1948 new cars were still in short supply and sales rose rapidly during the first half of 1949. Business investment in machinery and equipment fell steadily from early 1948 through 1949, as did exports (except for the small rise in early 1949). Consumers' expenditure on household equipment and furniture declined at the end of 1948 but had recovered by the end of 1949. Government purchases rose sharply, civilian from early

[1] Coal mining is considered along with the other fuel industries in the nondurable goods section below.

1948, military from the end of the year. If car sales are excluded from consideration, the effect of the decline in business fixed investment on the remaining final sales of durables is seen to be dominant: sales after 1948 I declined at a rate of over 4 per cent per annum up to mid-1949. In the following account of the inventory changes in businesses dealing in durable goods I consider firstly traders—retailers and merchant wholesalers—and secondly manufacturers. Because of the special position of the car market, automobile dealers are considered separately.

Until early 1948 the main influence upon the inventory behaviour of retailers and merchant wholesalers was the shortage of supplies and the difficulty of raising inventories to levels considered normal in relation to sales. Postwar restocking was a lengthy process which continued throughout 1946, 1947 and into early 1948. There was a pause in mid-1947 when the restocking temporarily ceased, probably partly due to fears in some sectors of business of price falls and recession. These fears passed later in the year and the restocking was resumed in 1947 IV and 1948 I.[1] On the evidence of the inventory-sales ratio shown in Fig. 6.4 the postwar restocking boom was over by 1948 I. The durable goods retailers' inventory-sales ratio (excluding auto dealers) reached 0·81 in 1948 I and was only slightly higher two quarters later. The rise in 1948 IV, due to the fall in sales, does not conflict with the conclusion that by 1948 I durable goods retailers had at last achieved a stock–sales ratio which was to be normal until the Korean War. Although the monthly inventory–sales ratio series shown in Fig. 3.3 has more erratic movements than the quarterly ratio, it shows the same changes: a rise in early 1948 to a high level, until September fluctuations about a level similar to that of late 1949 and early 1950, with a large rise in September and October 1948 in which the large fall in sales was the main factor. During 1947 and up to the middle of 1948 the general trend of rising inventories was interrupted by fluctuations in the rate of accumulation mainly because of the changes in household purchases. When traders'

[1] One reason for the pause may have been uncertainty about the future of controls over consumer credit. After lengthy discussion, Congress on July 25th voted to end all existing controls on November 1st. The August and September statistics record substantial increases in new orders placed with manufacturers of durable goods.

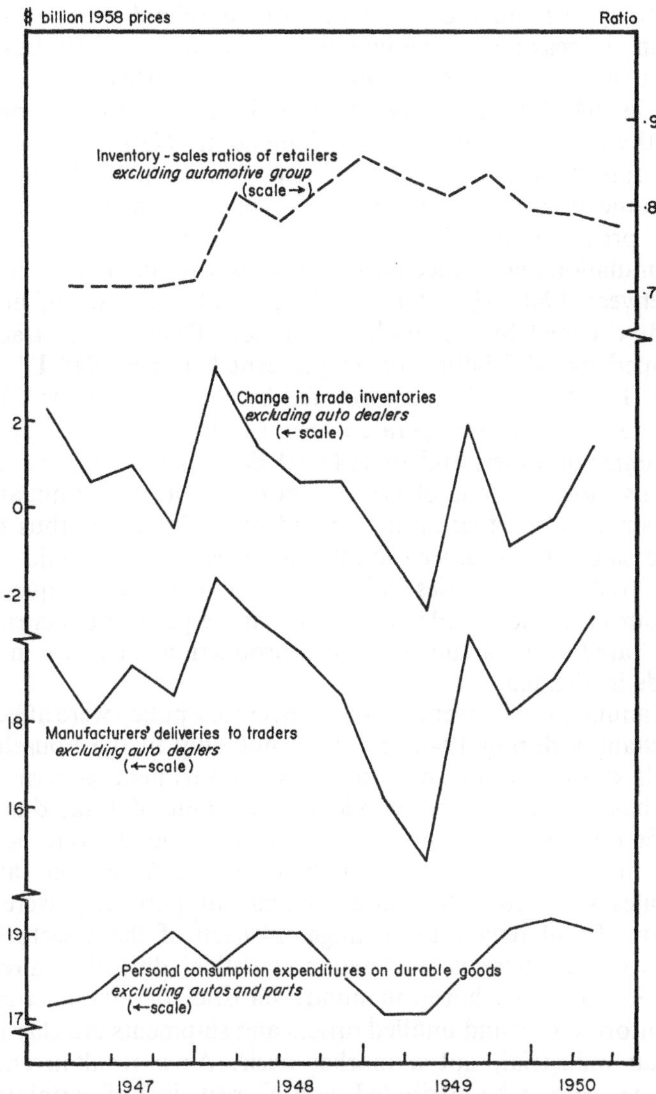

Fig. 6.4: Sales and inventory change in the durable goods sector, 1947–50.
Source: Inventory-sales ratio and PCE: SCB.
Inventory change: Table 6.2.
Manufacturers' deliveries to traders: CBI durable goods traders *plus* PCE durable excluding automobiles.

inventory accumulation is added to household purchases to obtain a measure of manufacturers' deliveries to traders as shown in Fig. 6.4, the figures reveal a fairly steady rise to a peak in 1948 I, followed by a rapid fall. I interpret this to mean that the ending of the restocking demand in 1948 I was followed by a fall in orders to and purchases from manufacturers. At the same time the levelling out of consumer demand during 1948 provided an additional reason for a fall in inventory accumulation and reduced orders placed with manufacturers.

Between 1948 III and 1949 I household purchases of home goods declined by just under $2 billion. Deliveries to traders dropped by $4·7 billion or 25 per cent between 1948 IV and 1949 II and traders' inventories fell by some $4 billions.[1] This was obviously an exaggerated response to the fall in sales of consumer durables, and in 1949 III deliveries to traders rose. Because household purchases rose also, inventory accumulation was small. The situation at the end of 1949 III was thus that while sales of consumer durables were back at their mid-1948 level, traders' inventories had fallen substantially. Consequently, the output of household furnishings and equipment was rising very rapidly, as is shown by the production index for home goods in Fig. 6.5.

Manufacturers' inventories and inventory policy were affected by changes during 1948 and 1949 not only in the household goods sector but also in business fixed investment, government purchases and the automobile market. Out of total durable goods output in 1948 of $61 billion, home goods were nearly $20 million, producers' equipment was $26 million, automobiles were $8 billion and government purchases were $4 billion. I will review the changes in each of these sectors of activity, but there is one major statistical difficulty, already mentioned, to be borne in mind: statistics of manufacturers' inventories, new and unfilled orders and shipments are classified on an industrial, not a market basis. As a result inventory changes cannot be attributed with a great deal of certainty to happenings in particular markets.

[1] The main exception to these trends was the production and sales of television sets which in late 1948—early 1949 were entering the early stage of their first boom.

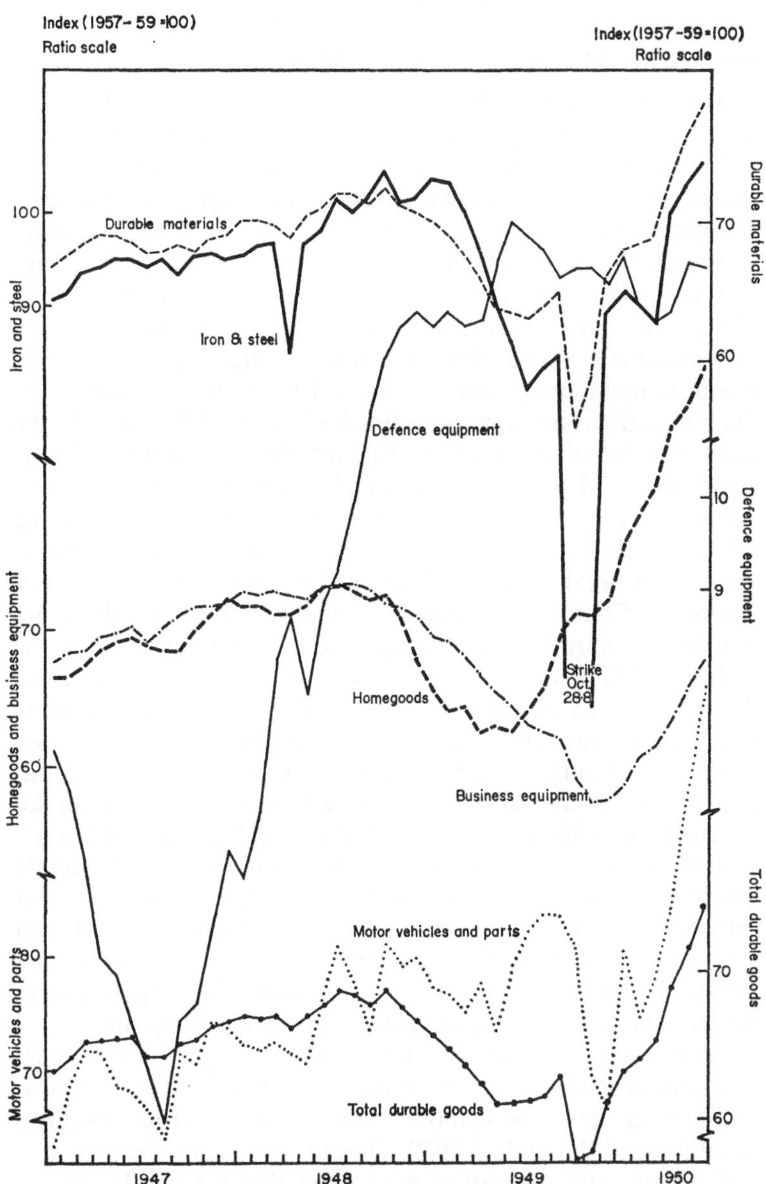

Fig. 6.5: Durable goods manufacturing output, 1947–50.

Source: FRB. Home goods includes domestic appliances, furniture and floor coverings and miscellaneous hardware. Defence equipment is derived from the indexes of total equipment and business equipment, using the published weights for 1957–59.

Although home goods were only one-third of durable goods output, they are likely to have been a larger part of manufacturers' inventories of finished goods and of investment in those goods, because only a small part of the output of producers equipment and defence goods would have been held in stock. Consequently it is reasonable to interpret changes in manufacturers inventory investment in finished goods as mainly changes in home goods. The mid-1947 slowdown in traders' restocking (see above) thus probably resulted in an unintended rise in manufacturers' inventories in 1947 II and III, shown by the high rate of investment in finished goods in Fig. 6.2. In the third quarter of the year, as Fig. 6.5 shows, output of home goods declined and manufacturers' inventory investment was reduced. From the fall in output of home goods it can be inferred that manufacturers' stocks of finished home goods were in general at desired levels, i.e. amongst most manufacturers of home goods the early postwar inventory shortages had been repaired.[1] With the increase in traders' demand at the end of 1947 manufacturers' inventory investment declined despite the rise in output. After 1948 I deliveries to traders declined, as stagnation descended on the home goods market. However, although output stopped rising in July, finished goods inventories of manufacturers began to accumulate at an increasing rate which was aggravated by the big fall in deliveries to traders in 1948 IV and 1949 I. Manufacturers consequently cut output between November 1948 and April 1949 by 13 per cent and eventually in the second quarter of 1949 reduced their rate of accumulation. The big drop in stocks in the third quarter came—as has been suggested above—from rising deliveries to traders due to increasing consumer sales and restocking.

Production of business equipment as Fig. 6.5 shows rose throughout 1947 to reach a level in early 1948 which was maintained until September, after which output declined steadily until the end of 1949. Output of defence equipment—which was only a small part of total durable goods output, probably no more than 5 per cent—doubled during the course

[1] Manufacturers' inventory-sales ratio for durable finished goods, shown in Fig. 3.3, rose to August 1947 after which it was virtually unchanged until January 1949.

of 1948 as the armed forces were increased and rearmed. Aircraft production in particular increased during the second half of 1948 and maintained its new level throughout the first half of 1949. Automobile production tended to rise rapidly from 1947 on, although the rise was erratic, with frequent drops in output, due to supply shortages and strikes. Nevertheless there was a rapid and relatively sustained rise in output from the third quarter of 1948 until November 1949 when the effects of the steel strike were felt. During the period 1948 III to 1949 II, output of automobiles rose by about $4·3 billion, offsetting nearly half of the decline in output of all other durable goods.

The effect of these changes in output of durable goods upon the production of materials differed in different circumstances. Whereas output of durable goods materials as a whole declined after October 1948 and fell continuously through the first half of 1949, iron and steel production was slightly higher in the first quarter of 1949 than in the last quarter of 1948. Output of consumer durable steel—in particular sheet steel for automobiles—rose in 1948 IV and again in 1949 I and stayed at this high level until affected by the steel strikes in October and November. During the first half of 1949 the high demand for steel by the automobile makers more than offset the falling demand for steel mill products for equipment, construction, cans and other uses. By the third quarter of 1949 the falling demand for castings, forgings and mill products in general had resulted in a drop in pig iron and ingot output, such that total iron and steel production was in July nearly 20 per cent below the January–February levels (with allowance for seasonal influences) although output rose in August and September.

The steel industry was the major exception to the trends during the first half of 1949. Output of non ferrous metals and products reached a peak in July 1948, and declined thereafter until mid-1949, output of fabricated metal products reached a peak in 1948 I, maintaining a fairly steady level of production until the end of the year and falling during the first half of 1949, while production of structural metal parts fell from November. Output of glass, bricks, cement and other building materials, and lumber products declined during 1948 IV.

In the preceding paragraphs I have reviewed the main influences upon changes in the inventories of durable goods manufacturers; I will now summarize by interpreting these changes from the viewpoint of manufacturers' inventory policy. The analysis that follows is based on the simplest theory of inventory policy which is that manufacturers' inventory purchases vary in the same direction as changes in unfilled orders and expected sales. The change in unfilled orders is relevant to firms producing to order and applies particularly to goods in process and purchased materials. The change in expected sales—which is taken to be indicated by the change in recent and current sales—is relevant to firms which undertake their own selling or sell from stock; it applies to finished goods as well as the other types of inventory. As well as inventory changes arising from planned changes in purchases, inventory change can be unplanned due to unexpected changes in sales or unexpected changes in supply conditions due, for instance, to strikes. The precise way in which desired inventory change is related to changes in orders and sales is a difficult fact to establish: here I am concerned primarily to draw attention to the more obvious coincidences of direction of change.[1]

As Fig. 6.6 shows, unfilled orders tended to fall throughout 1947 and 1948 as first rising output and later falling orders reduced the postwar backlog. This decline was checked temporarily during the period 1947 IV to 1948 III by a large rise in orders. In 1947 IV, the rise in orders was due to the traders' restocking referred to above; later in 1948 II the rise was sustained by the rearmament embodied in the fiscal 1949 defence budget (passed by Congress in May and June) which as has been pointed out amongst other things authorized the ordering of new aeroplanes as part of the expansion of the air force.

Final sales of durable goods rose in 1947 IV and 1948 I, but the rise ceased during the remainder of 1948. At first, in 1947 IV and 1948 I, the increase in orders and sales did not result in a rise in inventories: investment in finished goods fell, while stocks of goods in process and materials declined. But in the

[1] A survey of the quantitative relationships disclosed in the econometric literature is given in Note L.

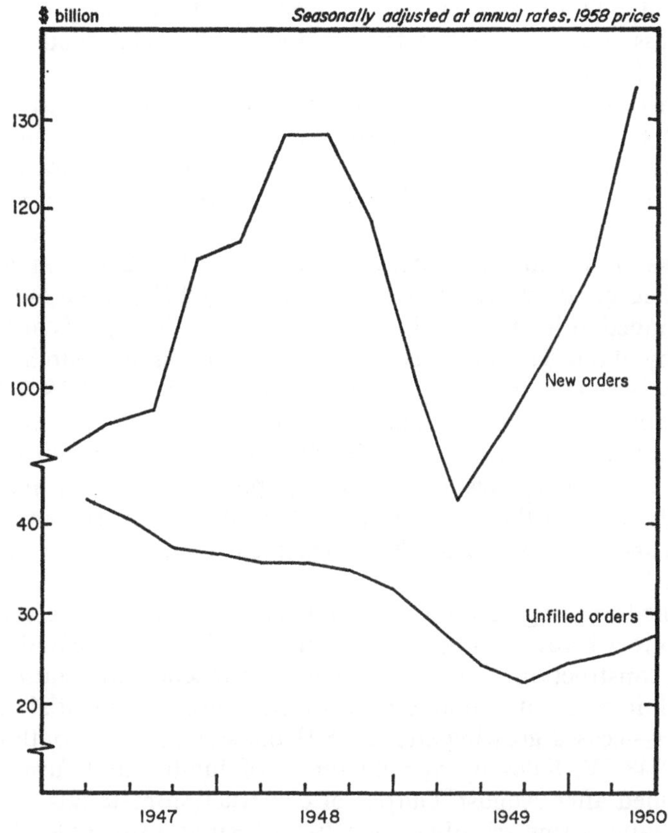

Fig. 6.6: Durable goods manufacturing new and unfilled orders, 1947–50.
Source: SCB. Deflated with national income durable goods implicit price index.

second quarter of 1948 stocks of purchased materials rose in response to the increase in orders and goods in process stopped falling as fast as before.

This rearmament-induced stockpiling was however not strong enough to withstand the effects of falling orders and sales in other parts of the economy. As traders successfully avoided any increase in their stocks, and as sales of producer goods fell, manufacturers started to accumulate stocks of finished goods, and despite lowered rates of output (excluding autos) in the second half of 1948 which reduced inventories of goods in process and purchased materials, stocks of finished goods rose by $1·5 billion in 1948 III and IV.

This unsuccessful attempt to cut inventories continued into 1949 I, when stocks of finished goods continued to rise as purchased materials and goods in process fell. It was not until the second quarter of 1949, when the production of durable goods had been cut by 11 per cent of its 1948 III level, that stocks of purchased materials fell by nearly $2 billion and finished goods started to stop rising. In 1949 III, while output continued at its depressed level, stocks of finished goods at last fell by about $1 billion, as did goods in process and purchased materials. This inventory decline during 1949 II and 1949 III was concentrated predominantly amongst the machinery manufacturers, where nearly half the decline occurred. About one-fifth arose in the transportation equipment industries, and is attributable to the declining rate of production in the aircraft industry after 1949 I as the rearmament contracts were completed.

The foregoing account of the influences upon manufacturers' inventory investment has not specifically referred to the building and construction industries except in connection with business fixed investment. Total output of structures—residential and other—ceased growing after 1948 II and started a six month fall in 1948 IV. Sales by manufacturers of lumber and furniture declined after August. Output of construction materials which had (after rising rapidly during 1947) been at a steady level for the first half of 1948, increased slightly in 1948 III, but declined in the final quarter. Inventories of manufacturers of lumber, furniture and stone, clay and glass products rose throughout 1948 and during the first quarter of 1949. In view of the pressures on the building industry up to early 1948 it is likely that the construction materials industry was one group of manufacturers who until 1948 were unable to build up stocks to satisfactory levels but who did so during the second half of that year. Later in 1949 II and III while business continued to decline—especially as business fixed investment fell—output of materials was cut back more severely as inventories reached or surpassed desired levels.

For the period's boom industry—automobile manufacture—inventory changes at the manufacturing level cannot be isolated in the statistics. On the evidence of the production statistics, however, new orders by auto makers for materials and components, and hence the makers' inventories of purchased materials and goods in process, must have risen throughout 1948 and early 1949. At the trade level, auto dealers' inventories tended to rise slowly during 1947 and 1948, small fluctuations reflecting the fluctuations in output. In the second half of 1948 as output started to rise rapidly there was a substantial rise in inventories which tapered off in early 1949 as sales rose.

By the third quarter of 1949 the situation in the durable goods industries was that final sales of durables (excluding automobiles) were $2·7 billion below the level of a year before, inventories of all types (excluding dealers' automobiles) had dropped by $7·3 billion of which $5 billion was in manufacturing. Traders' inventories had fallen by over $2 billion although in 1949 III consumer home goods purchases were rising and only $1 billion below the 1948 III level. In so far as traders' inventories in mid-1948 were normal, and manufacturers' inventories were not excessive,[1] it is obvious that business as a whole had reduced inventories to the point where the actual level was well below the desired level. On a conservative estimate, at the end of 1949 III durable goods inventories were about $3 billion (at an annual rate) below the desired level.[2] With most of the fall in fixed investment and exports offset by rising sales of home goods,[3] the stage was set for some restocking, and new orders placed with durable goods manufacturers started to rise for the first time in over a year in August and September 1949. Total durable manufacturing

[1] In fact some in the metal industries were still abnormally low, judged by the historical trend.

[2] Between the end of 1948 I, when I judge traders' stockpiling to have ceased, and the end of 1949 III durable goods inventories declined by $2·2 billion at an annual rate. During most of this period final sales were unchanged, rising slightly in the middle of 1949. Automobile inventories were probably still below desired levels, and in 1949 III as described below there was inventory accumulation in anticipation of the steel strike. $3 billion appears a very conservative estimate of the difference between desired and actual inventories.

[3] Durable goods final sales, excluding automobiles, were $45·9 billion in 1949 III and declined slightly to $45·3 billion in 1950 I.

production which had been unchanged from May until July, showed a small rise in August and a substantial increase in September. The rise came almost entirely from the home goods and materials industries.

At this stage in the 1949 recovery, business behaviour in all parts of the economy was influenced by the steel strike of October and November. This strike not only caused the fall in durable goods output and GNP recorded in the final quarter of the year, it also resulted in a large rundown of inventories not only of steel but of a wide range of manufactured products such as cars.[1] The precise effect is difficult to judge, partly because one has to guess what normal inventory behaviour is, partly because the lengthy preliminaries to the strike allowed businessmen to accumulate inventories in anticipation of shortages. A reasonable guess of the strike-induced rundown of inventories in 1949 IV and 1950 I would be in the region of $4 billion (expressed at an annual rate) or just over 5 per cent of durable goods inventories. This guess is made up as follows. It is likely that auto dealers increased their inventories in 1949 III in anticipation of the strike, but by only a small fraction of the rundown of $2 billion in 1949 IV. Their inventories fell further in 1950 I and rose by less than $1 billion in 1950 II, and are likely to have been still in deficit from the strike by at least $1 billion at mid-1950. Durable goods manufacturers were still reducing stocks substantially in 1949 III but I judge that with output rising the desired level of inventories was rising also. Their deficit due to the strike would be in the region of $2 billion, but as they managed to invest in inventories in the first half of 1950 $1·8 billion it is likely that their strike deficit in mid-year would have been cancelled. Durable goods traders —mainly retail stores—ran down inventories by about $1·5 billion in 1949 IV although this was partly due to the continued rise in sales of home goods. While they did not increase their inventories in the following quarter, the $2 billion rise in 1950 II suggests that they had repaired any strike-induced deficits by the middle of the year. Thus of a total rundown of durable goods inventories of about $4 billion, it is likely that at least

[1] For the influence of the strike on the automobile industry see Note H.

$1 billion (of auto dealers' stock) had still to be replaced when the Korean War started.[1]

The main forces behind durable goods output and inventory change in the nine months before the Korean War were thus, first, a gap between desired and actual inventories of some $3 billion at the end of 1949 III; second, a rundown of inventories because of the strike of some $4 billion of which about $3 billion had been replenished by the end of 1950 II; and finally no increase in the final sales of durables (excluding autos) until 1950 II when fixed investment started to rise again. The upshot was that of the increase in output between 1949 III and 1950 II of $8·3 billion, $1·7 billion was increased auto output, and the main part of the remainder—$4·9 billion—went into manufacturers' and traders' inventories. Nevertheless by the middle of 1950 these inventories were probably still some $4 billion below their desired level—and with sales and orders rising the desired level was rising also.

NONDURABLE GOODS

The main part of final sales of nondurable goods—personal consumption expenditures—grew at a slow rate from early 1947 into 1950. As has been pointed out above, consumption per head of population of foodstuffs, apparel and other nondurables during this period was virtually unchanged, and the growth was due primarily to growth of population. Of the remaining small part of nondurable sales, exports declined from mid-1947 for a year, and government purchases rose steadily from early 1948 to mid-1949. The main changes in total sales were a sharp fall

[1] The arithmetical outline of these estimates is as follows (though it must be stressed that the figures are no more reliable than the impressionistic statements in the text):

Change in business inventories
$ billion

Seasonally adjusted at annual rates.

Quarter	*No Strike*	*Strike*	*With Strike*
1949 II	−5	—	−5
III	−2	1	−1
IV	−1	−4	−5
1950 I	0	−1	−1
II	2	3	5

CBI 'with strike' are actual figures rounded.

of nearly $5 billion between 1947 III and 1948 I due mainly to the fall in exports while other expenditures were unchanged, followed by a large rise in 1948 II which continued for another year and which reflected the rise in government purchases as the rearmament programme was increased at the same time as Federal civil expenditures rose.[1] In interpreting the inventory and production movements, it is necessary to distinguish the absence of growth, after 1947 III, in consumer expenditures and exports—which were directly related to traders' and manufacturers' inventories—from the rising government expenditures after 1948 I which bore no strong relationship to non-farm inventory changes.

As was noticed above, p. 93, retail restocking had probably been nearly completed in the last few months of 1946. As Fig. 3.3 shows the inventory–sales ratio at that time was only slightly below the level it maintained during 1948 and 1949. Also, in the first quarter of 1947 wholesalers of nondurable goods also raised their inventory–sales ratio to a level which was normal in the light of subsequent behaviour. This raising of inventories to desired—or close to desired—levels led to a cessation of inventory investment during the first half of 1947. Businessmen probably did not expect retail sales to continue to rise as they did,[2] and traders' inventory–sales ratios consequently declined in the second and third quarters. In the third quarter the large fall in traders' inventories shown in Fig. 6.7, at a time when PCE on nondurables was still rising, suggests that businessmen seriously misjudged the general business situation in attempting to trim inventories.

Inventory levels were restored in 1947 IV with a high rate of investment which declined in 1948 I. For the first three quarters of 1948 producers' deliveries to traders (measured by the sum of inventory change and PCE on nondurables in Fig. 6.7) was at a steady level, changes in PCE being offset by changes in

[1] As has been explained, the most important rise in Federal civil expenditures in the second half of 1948 was due to purchases of farm output under farm income stabilization schemes. Exports under the Marshall Aid plan are included in the export statistics and had the effect of slowing the decline in exports in the second half of 1948.

[2] There were expectations of an end of the postwar boom in early 1947: see p. 103 above.

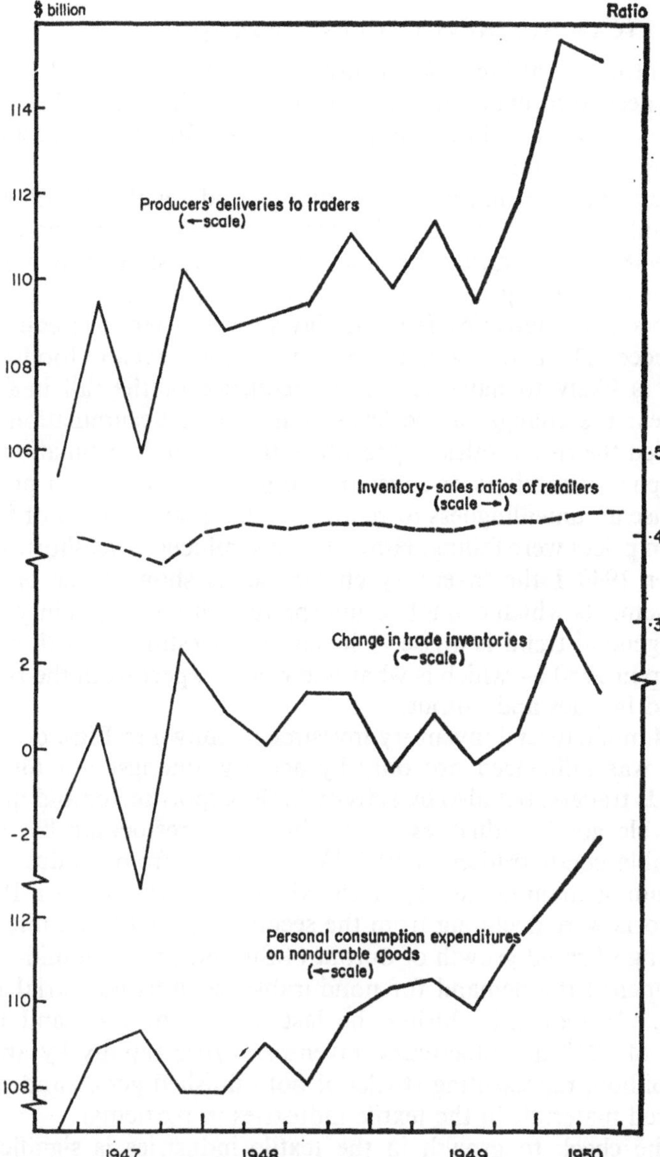

Fig. 6.7: Sales and inventory change in the nondurable goods sector, 1947–50.
Source: Inventory-sales ratio and PCE: SCB.
Inventory change: Table 6.2.
Producers' deliveries to traders: CBI nondurable goods traders *plus* PCE nondurable.

inventories. During 1948 an inventory rise of about $1 billion was needed to maintain steady inventory–sales ratios. The bulk of the rise occurred in retailing, with about $0·5 billion accumulating in apparel shops.[1]

Personal consumption expenditures and retail sales of nondurable goods after a lengthy period of little change increased in 1948 IV and during the first half of 1949. Merchants' inventories rose in response to this in 1948 IV but not in 1949 I when orders and deliveries fell and inventories were consequently reduced. The main reduction appears to have been in foodstuffs and is likely to have been a consequence of the fall in food prices: the change in the level of inventory accumulation exceeded the rise in sales, suggesting either an underestimation on the part of retailers of consumer response to the fall in prices, or else an unwillingness of retailers to hold large stocks of food when prices were falling. However, this influence was shortlived. After 1949 I the inventory change series shows some erratic movements which cannot be interpreted with any certainty, but the general trend is a rise in inventory investment—with a big jump in 1950 I—which is what one would expect from the rising trend in sales and output.

Manufacturers' inventory investment, shown in Figs. 6.1 and 6.2, was influenced not only by activity amongst nondurable goods traders, but also by activity in the export sector and in the durable goods industries. After the heavy restocking by nondurable goods traders in 1947 IV, purchases from producers—including manufacturers—declined in the early part of 1948. Exports were declining from the second half of 1947, while the ending of rapid growth of output of durable goods in mid-1947 dampened the demand for nondurables such as industrial textiles. Consequently during the last quarter of 1947 and first half of 1948 manufacturers' inventories rose rapidly by about $1 billion, representing stocks of both finished goods and purchased materials in the textile industries in particular.

The check to growth in the textile industries is significant because inventory accumulation by traders at the same time was predominantly in textiles. Apart from the lack of growth in household expenditures on clothing, after 1947 II exports of

[1] These are rough estimates at 1958 prices from book values.

textiles started to fall and although these exports were a small (less than 5 per cent) part of the total textile market, by 1948 III they had declined by about one-third. Output of apparel reached a peak as early as January 1948 (see Fig. 6.8), running at a high but steady rate until June after which output declined. Textile mill production reached a peak in May and declined rapidly in the second half of the year. Manufacturers of leather goods had been cutting back their output since November 1947.

The fuel industries were affected by the general mid-year slowdown in activity: output of petroleum products stopped increasing after May 1948, and declined during the first half of 1949; in coal mining output reached a peak in May and began a rapid fall in August; while gas production grew slowly until October, and then declined slightly until the end of the first quarter of 1949. Outside fuel and textiles, other producers were affected by the slowdown in activity: manufacturers of containers (output of paper and paper products declined after June), of chemicals (after July), and of rubber and plastic products (after October). Total output of materials for nondurable manufacturers reached a peak in June. The major group of industries which were unaffected by the decline were food, beverage and tobacco manufacturers whose output remained at a steady level throughout 1948. From June 1948 until April 1949 output of nondurable manufactures fell by 6 per cent. The major fall was in textile mill production, which between June and April fell by 21 per cent. Coal mining was disrupted by strikes, and its changes are difficult to measure, but between July 1948 and May 1949 output dropped by about 16 per cent. Crude oil output was not reduced until the second quarter of 1949.

The decline in output during the second half of 1948 led to a fall in investment in purchased materials in 1948 III, and substantial disinvestment from 1948 IV to 1949 II.[1] Accumulation of finished goods—which must have been unintended—

[1] The fall in wholesale prices in the second half of 1948 is not regarded as an independent or important factor initiating inventory liquidation, except possibly in the case of cotton whose large harvest in 1948 was an important factor behind the fall in cotton prices in June. The possible small effect on retail food inventories in 1949 I was referred to above p. 186.

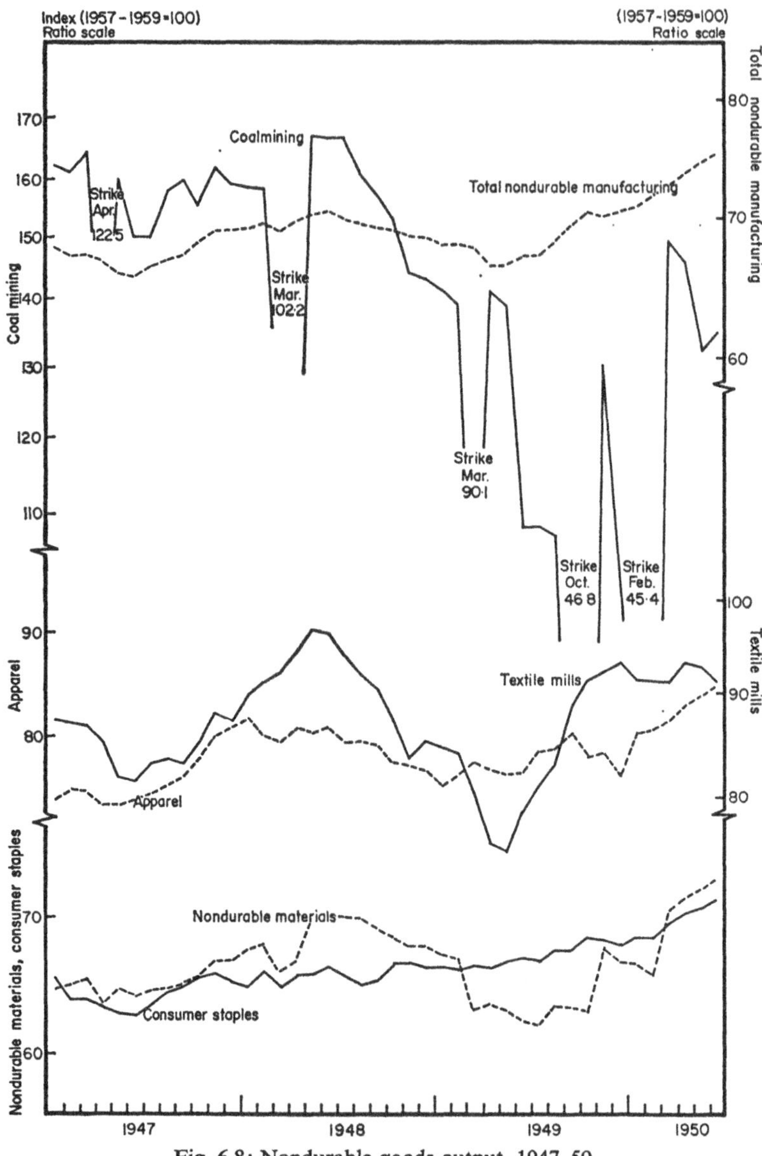

Fig. 6.8: Nondurable goods output, 1947–50.

Source: FRB. Consumer staples include processed goods; beverages and tobacco; drugs, soap and toiletries; newspapers, magazines and books; consumer fuel and lighting; sanitary paper products.

continued until the second quarter of 1949 when investment ceased. In the third quarter these stocks fell substantially. Even more than in the upswing in inventory investment, in this downswing the main part was played by the textile industries whose inventories actually fell from August 1948 until September 1949. In fact the dominant feature of the whole sequence of changes in the nondurable goods industries is the cycle in inventory investment by textile manufacturers.

Retail sales of nondurables rose strongly throughout 1949 (with the exception of a dip in 1949 III) and even more rapidly in the first half of 1950. As has been pointed out, traders tended to increase their inventories from 1949 II on. Manufacturers' inventories, which after a $1 billion rise from end-1947 III to mid-1948, and another $¾ billion rise to end-1949 I, fell by about $⅓ billion during the rest of 1949 and did not start to rise again until 1950 I. The relatively slow growth of nondurable output up to mid-1950 contrasts with the rapid rise in durable output and stems from the if anything high level of inventories in mid-1949 in the former industries compared with the severely reduced inventories in the latter. Textile mill output started to rise again in June 1949 but did not surpass its previous peak until August 1950. Apparel output reached the bottom of its decline in May 1949 but remained virtually unchanged until early 1950. The leather industry's output fell throughout 1949, starting to pick up in 1950 I. Nondurable materials as a whole reached their trough in July 1949 and made a slow recovery until November. Consumer staples, including food, in contrast paused in their growth from December 1948 to April 1949 and then resumed their steady rise. The mining sector reached its trough in October 1949, due partly to the fall in crude oil output until July with only a slow revival thereafter and partly to the severe coal strike in September. It was not until March 1950 that coal output reached its late 1948 level again, and coal stocks consequently declined substantially.[1] However, by 1950 II the pace of growth of consumer demand was such that neither manufacturers' nor traders' nondurable inventories were rising

[1] The large decline in Other CBI shown in Table 6.2 during the second half of 1949 is due to the fall in coal and other fuel stocks arising from the cutbacks in output and strikes.

fast enough, and the growth of output of most consumer non-durables was accelerating.

The farm sector

The situation in farming during 1948–49 has been discussed above on pp. 127–132. Farm output rose in 1948 because of the very good harvests of feed grains and cotton. A substantial part of the crops were stockpiled. Poor harvests in 1947 had resulted in farm inventories declining. During 1948 these inventories rose, the total inventory change for the year being nearly 5 per cent of gross farm output at current prices. Farm inventories would have risen further and prices fallen lower but for the government's income and price stabilization scheme; during 1948 CCC net purchases were $1·2 billions. Thus 8 per cent of farm output was stockpiled in 1948. In 1949 total farm output declined slightly, a decline in crop production offsetting a rise in livestock output. The CCC continued its operations on an increasing scale and by the end of the year had purchased another $1·7 billions, enabling farm inventories to fall by about $0·9 billions at current prices.[1]

EMPLOYMENT

By early 1947 the effect of demobilization on the total labour force was being offset by net new entrants, and during the course of 1947 as a whole the labour force grew by 1·3 per cent per annum. The effective end of demobilization meant, however, that the civilian labour force's growth declined sharply. Whereas it had risen by 5·3 million between December 1945 and December 1946 (or 10 per cent), in the next twelve months it rose by only 1·2 million (or 2 per cent). The pressure in the labour market was severe throughout the year, unemployment being at a low level during 1947 I, and after a small rise accompanying the mid-year sag in output, declined again towards the end of the year. In the last two months of the year the unemployment rate had dropped to the very low level of 3·4 per cent. The changes in the average workweek[2] reflected these trends, falling

[1] CCC purchases are from footnote [2], p. 143 above.

[2] Average hours worked per week by production workers in manufacturing establishments.

in the middle of the year, and rising to a high level in November and December. The growth in the total labour force continued at a slow rate in early 1948 and after the middle of the year virtually stopped, there being little increase between mid-1948 and mid-1949. In the absence of any significant demographic changes, the reason for the absence of growth was presumably the increase in retirements and reduced school leaving following the decline in the demand for labour. The armed forces in the second quarter of 1948 started to increase in numbers, increasing by about 0·2 million between mid-1948 and mid-1949. The civilian labour force consequently declined slightly over the period. After mid-1949 all these tendencies were reversed: the total labour force started to rise, the size of the armed forces declined slightly and the civilian labour force again grew.

The peak pressure in the labour market was probably felt November 1947 to January 1948. The unemployment rate reached a trough during these months and hours worked reached a peak. After January the average workweek began a fairly steady decline which lasted until October 1949. The unemployment rate after rising to just over 4 per cent in March and April maintained a fairly steady level at around 3·7 per cent until December. Total employment continued to rise until July, thereafter falling to a trough the following July. The changes from July 1948 to July 1949 are summarized in the table:

TABLE 6.3: *Change in Labour Force, July 1948 to July 1949*

	million
Total labour force	+0·090
Armed forces	+0·170
Civilian labour force	−0·080
Employed—agriculture	+0·418
Employed—non agricultural industries	−2·350
Unemployed	+1·852

Source: Monthly Report on the Labour Force.

The impact of the declining demand for non-agricultural labour after mid-1948 was reduced by the unusually large rise in agricultural employment due to the very large 1948 harvest, together with the rise in size of the armed forces and the reduced rate of growth in the total labour force (the effect of which on the employment situation would have been at least 0·5 millions). The unemployment rate started to rise in December 1948 and in August 1949 was 6·8 per cent.

Recovery after July 1949 in the non-agricultural sector was rapid despite the resumption of the increase in the growth of the total labour force and a drop in the numbers of the armed forces. In the twelve months after July, non-agricultural employment increased by 2·7 million, and the average workweek which had reached its low level in April 1949, by July 1950 had risen by 6 per cent (over two hours) and equalled the level at the peak before the recession. The rate of unemployment fell only slowly however, and in July 1950 was still 5·1 per cent compared with the 3·6 per cent two years previously. The explanation of this is the strong and persistent decline in farm employment after mid-1949, the result of the fall in farm incomes and the beginning of a long-term trend which between 1949 and 1964 caused farm employment to decline from 8 millions to 4·8 millions. The changes in the twelve months after July 1949 are summarized in the table:

TABLE 6.4: *Change in Labour Force, July 1949 to July 1950*

	million
Total labour force	+0·707
Armed Forces	−0·148
Civilian labour force	+0·855
Employed—agriculture	−0·962
Employed—non-agricultural industries	+2·746
Unemployed	−0·929

Source: Monthly Report on the Labour Force.

The fall in farm employment exactly accounts for the difference between the 1950 and 1948 unemployment rates; in other words, the expansion of the non-agricultural employment absorbed the industrial unemployed, the growth in the labour force and the decline in the armed forces, leaving the fall in agricultural employment as a substantial labour reserve in mid-1950.

CHAPTER 7

A Model of the 1948-49 Recession and Revival

SECTORS OF A SIMPLIFIED MODEL

The purpose of this chapter is to distinguish the main factors influencing the downturn and upturn in business activity, and to consider the relation of these factors to the end of inflation. The NBER's turning points are November 1948 and October 1949, and in the following model the downturn, when the forces of recession became predominant, is placed in the final quarter of 1948, and the upturn, when the forces of recovery became predominant, is put in the later part of 1949 III and early part of 1949 IV. The ending of inflation and beginning of deflation is placed at the end of 1947 IV and early part of 1948 I.

The approach is essentially multisectoral: an aggregative approach to 1948–49 is very misleading because so many different trends were in evidence in different sectors of the economy at the same time. The turning points in aggregate activity and the end of aggregate excess demand were determined by the balancing of different forces arising in different sectors. The sectors of the economy which have been distinguished in the chapters above are fixed capital formation, residential construction and the furnishing and equipping of houses, government, the foreign sector, farming, the automobile industry, households in their capacity as buyers of nondurable goods and services, manufacturers, nondurable goods traders, and durable goods traders with the exception of auto dealers. These sectors in the simplified model are reduced to five, grouped according to the characteristics and determinants of components of GNP.

The first group consists of the first five activities above:

broadly speaking, fixed investment with the government, foreign and farming sectors. The final expenditures of this group—gross private domestic investment (less automobiles), government purchases of goods and services, net exports and the change in farm inventories—have the characteristic that they were largely uninfluenced by the changes in aggregate income and output in 1948–49. In this sense in Chapter 1 I have called them autonomous expenditures and this is a convenient term. The influence of government pervades this group: monetary and fiscal policy alters residential construction, foreign aid affects net exports, and farm policy influences both government purchases and the change in farm inventories. The group is however by no means dependent on influences exogenous to the U.S. domestic economy: business investment depends on sales, profits and costs; residential construction is influenced by changes in the ease and cost of obtaining mortgages some of which are independent of changes in official policy; and the import component of net exports is closely dependent on income and output. The truly exogenous factors in the short run are defence expenditures and exports. Nevertheless it is assumed as a first approximation that during 1948 and 1949 the changes in these expenditures can be taken as given and uninfluenced by the changes in aggregate output and income. This assumption has to be relaxed in 1949 to allow for the response of residential construction to cheap money arising from the recession. The changes in these autonomous expenditures are shown in Fig. 7.1. Between the first half of 1947 and 1948 II they rose by about $9 billion or 8 per cent. During the next eighteen months they remained more or less unchanged. Thus from having a very rapid rate of growth in late 1947 and early 1948 they changed in a short space of time to no growth.[1]

The second sector in the simplified model is the automobile industry. Production was released from material shortages at the end of 1948 and, as Fig. 7.1 shows, expanded during 1949 to offset the absence of growth in the first sector. Consumers,

[1] In this calculation the change in farm inventories and government purchases of farm products under the farm stabilization programmes are included in autonomous expenditures. Their exclusion would produce a decline in autonomous expenditures in the second half of 1948 and early 1949.

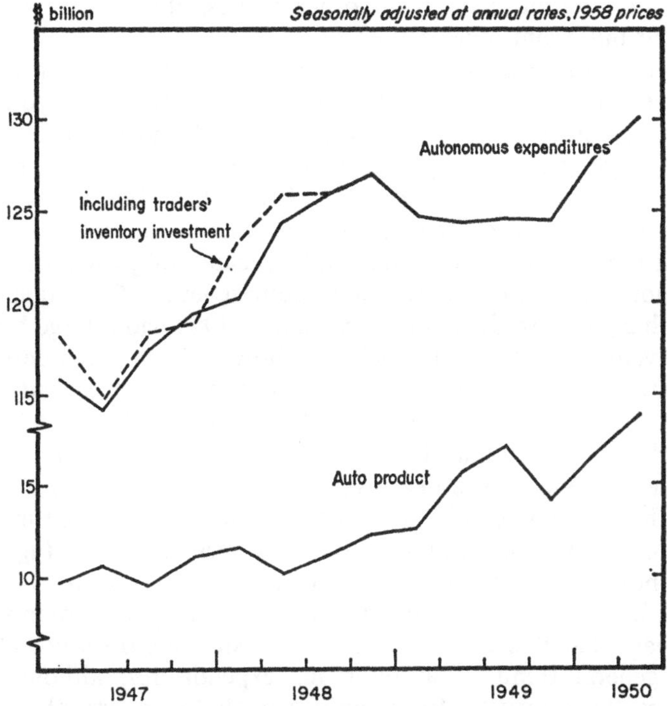

Fig. 7.1: Autonomous expenditures and auto product.

Sources: SCB. Autonomous expenditures consist of GNP *less* PCE nondurables and services, CBI (but not farm and auto dealers) and auto product. Durable goods traders' inventory investment from Table 6.2.

business and auto dealers were prepared to absorb the rising output to replenish their depleted stocks.

The third sector is households in their capacity as buyers of nondurables and services. They maintained their purchases at the high level reached in late 1947, despite increases in income in 1948 and falls in income in early 1949. It is supposed that the short run marginal propensity to consume declined in 1948 and rose in early 1949. This normal response to short run changes in income was stabilizing both before and after the downturn. It can be interpreted, for a given constant multiplier, in terms of first a fall and later a rise in autonomous expenditures, the fall offsetting output rises from other causes, the rise offsetting output falls from other causes.[1]

The fourth sector is durable goods traders (except auto dealers). The reason for treating them separately is the nature of their inventory investment. Excess demand and shortages for durable goods, especially household furnishings and equipment, persisted until the end of 1947. Until then, businesses had voluntarily reduced their inventories below equilibrium levels. With the ending of excess demand—because of growth of production—inventories were below desired levels. Consequently durable goods traders in the first half of 1948 had a large burst of inventory investment which did allow them to reach desired inventory–sales ratios. Once the desired ratio was reached, the rate of inventory accumulation fell to a normal level, i.e. that which would maintain the normal inventory–sales ratio.

The burst of inventory investment by these traders in the first half of 1948 can be regarded as equivalent to a rise in the autonomous expenditures of the first sector, and in Fig. 7.1 autonomous expenditures are shown from 1947 I to 1948 II including the inventory investment of durable goods traders. It appears that this burst of inventory restocking does not alter the general trend of autonomous expenditures, although it makes the transition from rapid growth to no growth more pronounced.

The final sector includes both manufacturers (excluding car makers) and nondurable goods traders. In general this sector passively responded to changes in the other sectors. Its postwar restocking by and large was over by the end of 1947 and its inventory–sales ratios were normal in early 1948 (the exceptions included the important case of steel, which should perhaps for the purposes of this model be grouped with the auto industry). An ending of the rate of growth of most sales of the products of these businesses in 1948 led to a decline in inventory accumulation and a corresponding fall in output. In Fig. 7.2 the experience of manufacturers in 1948 and early 1949 are summarized in a simplified way. In 1948 for various reasons the rate of

[1] The interpretation in terms of changes in the value of the income multiplier—falling before the turning point; rising after—gives a misleading analysis of the stability of output in the recession.

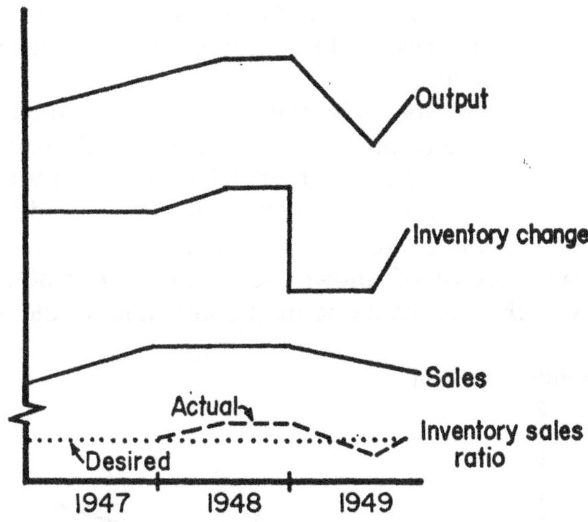

Fig. 7.2: Model of inventory change of manufacturers.

growth of sales declined (in some cases the level of sales fell): amongst consumer durable makers shipments to distributors and merchants fell in mid-1948 as the latter's restocking boom ended; other machinery makers, especially of business equipment, had experienced falling orders since early 1948; while sales of consumer goods had ceased growing after late-1947. Manufacturers responded by reducing their rate of output increase; in some cases by cutting levels of production. But because of lags in recognizing changes and taking decisions their inventories of finished goods and purchased materials rose. Later in 1948 when the output cuts and falls in sales became general the inventory situation became worse and in early 1949 severe reductions in production were required to trim inventories. This simple model of manufacturing inventory behaviour does not apply to automobile makers, nor does it describe the activity of some armament firms such as aircraft manufacturers, who increased their inventories in 1948 as rearmament increased, and reduced them in the first half of 1949 as their contracts neared completion. Some manufacturers and nondurable goods traders responded to the recession when it came by anticipating greater falls in sales than actually eventuated and consequently reducing inventories by unnecessarily large amounts. As the small extent of the recession became apparent these inventories were rapidly restored.

I shall now describe how the sectors contributed to the determination of the turning points. One approach would be to set out econometrically an interdependent multisectoral model which attached appropriate importance to regular and irregular features of economic life. Such an approach presupposes a much greater degree of knowledge and certainty of form of relationships than is available at present, and would be pre-

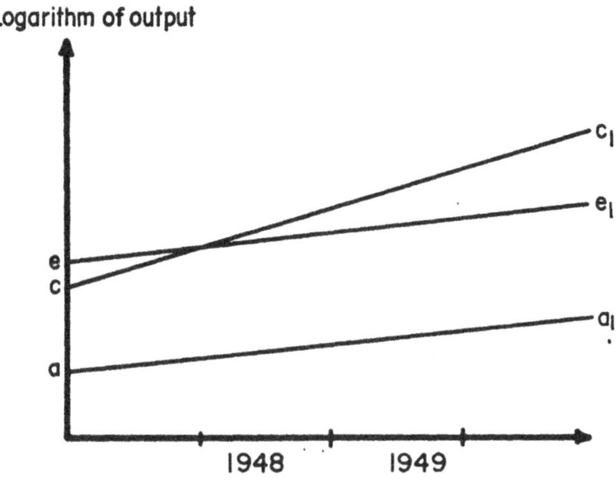

Fig. 7.3: Equilibrium output model with growth of capacity.

mature and misleading. Instead I attempt something much more modest: the effects of the changes in the sectors upon the whole economy are examined by modifying in appropriate ways the aggregate equilibrium output model described in Chapter 1.

THE EQUILIBRIUM OUTPUT MODEL[1]

Purchases of GNP are divided into two categories. In the first are autonomous expenditures: net exports, fixed investment,

[1] The general features of the equilibrium output model have been briefly described in Chapter 1, pp. 41–5. To assist the reader some parts of that description are repeated here, although students unfamiliar with economic theory are advised to refer first to Chapter 1.

automobile output, government purchases, residential construction, expenditures on household equipment and change in farm inventories. In Fig. 7.3 they are represented by the curve aa_1. In the second category of purchases are consumer expenditures on nondurables and services, and non-farm inventory accumulation. Consumer expenditures depend on income and can be represented by some simple function of GNP (a consumption function). Inventory accumulation depends on the change in aggregate sales of goods and can be represented by another simple function of change in GNP (an inventory accelerator, or induced investment function). Given the level of autonomous expenditures, the definitions of the consumption and inventory accelerator functions determine a level of output where desired saving and investment, and actual savings and investment, are all equal. This is equilibrium output, and in the figure it is shown by the line ee_1. ee_1 is derived from aa_1 by the multiplication of autonomous expenditures by a given parameter (the Hicksian supermultiplier).

The next element of the model is capacity output. This is defined as that level of output produced from existing plant and equipment at normal rates of profit. During the period we are concerned with, 1947–50, it is assumed that as a matter of fact capacity output equals full employment output, i.e. output produced from existing plant and equipment when the labour force is fully employed at normal hours of work. Capacity output can also during the period be defined as the level of output above which inflationary pressures develop. When demand for goods and services exceeds capacity output, prices rise, shortages and waiting lists appear, profits rise above normal, and with the number of hours worked per week increasing and with unemployment falling labour costs and wage rates rise more rapidly than usual. The line cc_1 in the chart describes the growth of capacity output.

Equilibrium output had exceeded capacity output from the end of the war until the first months of 1947, and again in the second half of 1947 and early months of 1948. The price stability of the first half of 1947 was a pause in the lengthy period of excess demand extending from the war years until early 1948 when capacity output rose above equilibrium output.

The first quarter of 1948 marks the end of inflation, indicated by the fall in farm prices and reduced pressure on the labour market. Supply conditions had been easing gradually ever since the end of the war, and while in 1948 there were still important shortages, by the early part of the year capacity had risen in a sufficiently large part of the economy to mark the end of general excess demand.

Let us now consider the instability of inventory investment. In Hicks' explanation of the persistence of the trade cycle, the instability of induced investment—Hicks is concerned primarily with fixed investment—is the cause of the cycle.[1] In the present model of the 1948 downturn a similar role is played by inventory investment: fixed investment is placed in the autonomous category. In a purely Hicksian situation, the inventory accelerator would work as follows. An initial displacement from an equilibrium output, say, by a fall in autonomous expenditures, would through the multiplier lead to a lower level of output. This in turn through the accelerator would lead to a fall in inventory investment, which would generate further falls in output. The path of output generated in this way depends on the values of the parameters of the model. I have given reasons above in Chapter 1, pp. 45–8, for thinking that output would take a relatively steady path to the new equilibrium position. In other words, the response of the system to the initial displacement would be stable. Oscillations about the new equilibrium level caused by over- and under-investment in inventories, if they occurred at all, would be heavily damped. The typical response to a displacement from equilibrium—caused by, say, a decline in the rate of growth of autonomous expenditures—would be a fall in inventory investment which would probably overshoot the new equilibrium mark, followed by a rise to the new equilibrium level which might involve a small overshooting above the level, but the amount of which would be negligible. The parameters of the model are not expected to lead to inventory investment doing more than amplifying upswings or downturns: I do not expect it to produce a sequence of cycles. The 1948 downturn is not to be explained as part of a persisting inventory cycle. Rather, what

[1] J. R. Hicks [1950].

have to be emphasized are the unique features of a situation which resulted in a fall in inventory investment.

In Hicks' cycle theory the concept of the floor plays a crucial role. The floor level of output is the multiplied level of autonomous investment, and as gross fixed investment cannot fall below zero, output cannot fall below the floor level. Output, because of the explosive nature of investment arising from the size of the fixed investment accelerator, 'bounces' from ceiling (set by capacity output) to floor. In the present version there is no floor.[1] The limit to inventory disinvestment is set only by the speed at which production can be cut back. However, no floor is needed to prevent a descent into bottomless depression. The passage from a higher equilibrium output to a lower equilibrium output is—as has been emphasized above—a stable phenomenon: either a smooth or a heavily damped path. After a once and for all fall in equilibrium output, actual output falls to a new level and, in the absence of any further change in equilibrium output, will stay at the new level. Only a rise in equilibrium output can bring about a lower turning point and a recovery from recession. I am explicitly ruling out a recovery arising from a rebound of inventory investment from a high rate of disinvestment, although such a rebound can contribute to the strength of a recovery in its early stages. The lower turning point, i.e. the end of recession and beginning of recovery, depends upon either a rise in autonomous expenditures or changes in the consumption or inventory investment functions which have the same effect as a rise in autonomous expenditures.

THE DOWNTURN

I first consider the inventory policy of durable goods traders. Fels has treated their behaviour as typical of business in general and provides a general theory of the 1948 turning point.[2] As was described above, businesses voluntarily reduced their inventories below equilibrium levels during the period of excess demand, and hence when excess demand disappeared

[1] Compare this with the discussion of the role of inventories in Hicks' theory by G. L. S. Shackle, *A Scheme of Economic Theory*, Cambridge University Press, 1965, pp. 148–49.

[2] R. Fels, 'The U.S. downturn of 1948', *Amer. econ. R.*, LV, December 1965, pp. 1059–76.

inventories were below desired levels. Thus on the basis of this hypothesis it would be argued that with the ending of the inflation in early 1948 inventory accumulation would rise as businesses brought their inventories up to desired levels. Fels argues that once the inventories reached the desired levels accumulation ceased and output declined. Fels also explicitly chooses low values of his inventory accelerator coefficient which allow a rise in output and then a fall which overshoots the equilibrium level. He is not concerned with the lower turning point.[1]

The evidence reviewed in Chapter 6 does not suggest that Fels' hypothesis is generally true for business, although it clearly applies to durable goods traders. The effect of the inventory policy of these traders is illustrated in Fig. 7.4. The end of excess demand and inflation is marked by point d, when capacity output rose above equilibrium output at the end of 1947. Inventory investment at that point rises to restore inventories to desired levels and actual output—whose path is marked $odp_1p_2o_1$—increases to p_1. At p_1 inventories are at the desired level, and inventory investment declines. Output falls to the equilibrium level, possibly overshooting the level to fall to p_2, but eventually settling down at o_1. If autonomous expenditures[2] were not growing, the new equilibrium output o_1 would be below that of the upper turning point, p_1. An increase in autonomous expenditures is required to provide an upturn. If on the other hand autonomous expenditures grow throughout,

[1] 'The desired amount of inventories is assumed to grow with real output though less than proportionately (loc. cit., p. 1067).' Fels chooses $c = 0{\cdot}6$ for the marginal propensity to consume out of GNP, and $w = 0{\cdot}2$ for the inventory accelerator coefficient. He has no lags, and hence if we write y_t as deviation from equilibrium output at t, his first order difference equation is:

$$y_t = cy_t + w(y_t - y_{t-1})$$

whose solution is $y_t = Ar^t$

where A depends on initial conditions and $r = -\left(1 \frac{w}{1-c-w}\right) = -1.0$. Thus after excess demand is removed and inventories rise by the amount of the desired increase, A, output will forever after oscillate about the equilibrium level, one period above it by A, the next below it by A, and so on. This is an unusual output path and shows the danger of divorcing the problem of the lower turning point from that of the upper point. The logic and usefulness, however, of the hypothesis are not in dispute.

[2] Autonomous expenditures in Fig. 7.4 exclude traders' inventory restocking. It would be possible to include the restocking in autonomous expenditures and to conduct the analysis above in terms of first an increase, then a fall, in autonomous investment.

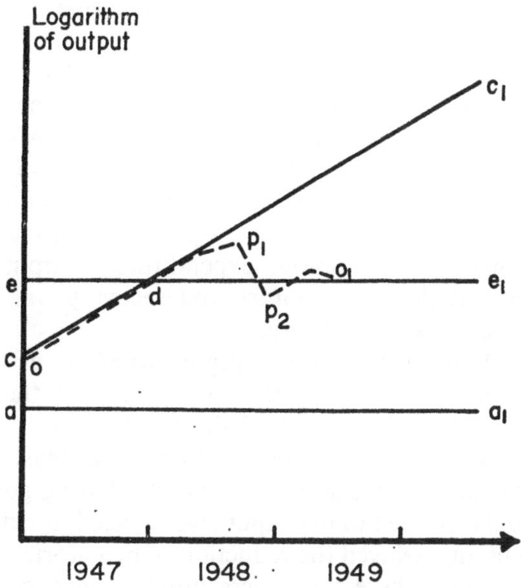

Fig. 7.4: Equilibrium output model: durable goods traders and the downturn.

at some point the fall in output arising from the end of restocking will be offset by the rise in output due to the autonomous expenditure growth.

The sector whose expenditures are autonomous is the next to be considered. These expenditures virtually ceased to grow after 1948 II, and represented the declining demand for fixed investment goods and exports, offset by rising defence purchases and government and private holdings of farm products. Apart from rising defence purchases and the fall in residential construction the other changes were related indirectly to the ending of excess demand. The growth of capacity was a consequence of a high rate of investment and a cause of a fall in that rate. The prospect of good harvests in early 1948 led to the first fall in farm prices. And falling exports were partly a sign that some of the international shortages were disappearing. The effect of the ending of excess demand was delayed by rising government purchases for some three months, and was considerably reduced in magnitude. The rise in government purchases in 1948 more than offset the fall in residential construction which I have attributed largely to government monetary and fiscal policy at the end of 1947.

Fig. 1.4, p. 43, illustrates the consequence of the end of growth in autonomous expenditures, shown by its change from aa_1 to a_1a_2 at time t, representing 1948 II.[1] Equilibrium output at t falls to the level e_2e_4 and actual output and inventories must fall. Output will probably overshoot the mark, falling to e_3, subsequently rising to the level e_2e_4. In the absence of any further change in autonomous expenditures, output will not change from this level; an upturn and recovery will require a rise in autonomous expenditures.

This fall in inventories and output, which is essentially a transition phenomenon, was the main cause of the 1948–49 recession. The restocking boom following the end of inflation, described above, reinforced the transition by increasing growth in early 1948 and stopping it subsequently. Rising government purchases delayed the fall in output and reduced its extent. Lags in decision taking delayed the reduction of inventories especially in manufacturing where there were unintended rises in inventories towards the end of the year, the main fall in manufacturing output consequently coming in 1949.

The remaining influences upon the turning point and the recession are minor. They are both related to the ending of excess demand. Household consumption remained steady during 1948 and had the effect of reducing the rate of growth of equilibrium output. This tended to bring forward the date of the turning point. The growth of car output during 1948 tended to delay the turning point, and provided a ready market for steel products when other demands were flagging. The fall in the marginal propensity to consume from its abnormally high 1947 level, and the subsequent stability of consumption, was one factor in the decline of excess demand. The growth of car output was a consequence of the greater availability of steel which in turn depended upon the expansion of steel making capacity and the decline in other demands for steel.

[1] Reduced growth of orders for some goods would have been felt by business before 1948 II, and in some industries the consequential changes would have started earlier in the year.

THE UPTURN

The analysis of the previous section has implied that the recession needed an independent force to bring about recovery. This did not come from aggregate autonomous expenditures as defined above. After falling in 1949 I they remained roughly unchanged during the rest of that year. Within this aggregate there were several offsetting movements. During the first half of 1949 rising government purchases offset falling fixed investment. During the second half of the year rising residential construction, induced by cheaper mortgages as easier credit conditions developed early in the year, offset declines in most other expenditures.

The factors encouraging recovery and bringing an early upturn were the great boom in car sales, the sustained consumption during the recession, and the related unnecessarily large reduction in inventories in some parts of the nondurable goods industries in early 1949 which led to a need to restock later in the year. I shall comment briefly on these factors, together with the peculiar influence of the steel strike. Automobiles were the last remaining goods to be in short supply in 1948, and the strength of demand was shown in the abnormally high prices of second hand cars, and inflated dealers' margins, even in early 1949. The fall in demand in other sectors of the economy and in particular the easing supply position for sheet steel allowed car output to rise in 1948 IV and 1949 I sufficient to almost offset the fall in autonomous expenditures in 1949 I. In 1949 II a very big rise in auto output began and this continued into the third quarter of the year. If autonomous expenditures are added to auto output, the aggregate rose by 3½ per cent between 1949 I and III, compared with hardly any rise during the previous year. The effect of rising auto production was of course most pronounced in durable goods production: between 1949 I and 1949 III auto product rose by \$4·4 billion (seasonally adjusted at annual rate, 1958 prices) while the rest of durable goods output fell by \$3·5 billion (it fell in 1949 II and recovered to some extent in the following quarter). Thus the rise in car output and sales more than offset the decline in other durable goods production and when added to autonomous expenditures provided the strong growth factor which the economy needed to cause equilibrium output to resume growing in the third quarter.

Household purchases of nondurable goods and services did not fall as incomes fell in early 1949.[1] As has been discussed above, the effect of the automatic fiscal stabilizers, the 1948 tax cut, the farm stabilization programme, and the fall in retail prices offset a large part of the fall in incomes, and what remained was more than offset by the short run rise in the marginal propensity to consume. In terms of the equilibrium output model, this stability of consumption can be interpreted as a rise in autonomous expenditures, with a constant multiplier, offsetting falls in income from other sources. Thus stable consumption limited the fall in output and the fall in desired inventories. Without this stability in consumption the growing force of automobile output would have been unable to produce a turning point as early as it did.

Stable consumption affected the turning point in another way. It is likely that some businessmen misjudged the extent of the recession once it had started. Fed by economists, publicists and politicians on a diet of cautionary tales of the big slump which must follow a postwar inflation, they mistakenly forecasted falls in consumption. Both for this reason and for precautionary reasons, some businesses—particularly in textiles and clothing—reduced inventories more than was necessary. As time showed that the forecasts were wrong and that their inventories were becoming excessively low there was a reversal of policy and an attempt to stockpile inventories. The effect of this inventory behaviour was first to aggravate the extent of the recession, and later to hasten the appearance of the upturn. This behaviour—mainly on the part of nondurable goods businesses—appears to have played a minor role in all the post-1945 recessions and recoveries.

The final factor in the upswing to be mentioned was the steel strike in October and November 1949. The turning point was in evidence and recovery was on its way before the strike. But inventories of steel and other durable goods were accumulated in anticipation of the strike in the weeks before it started, and

[1] Taking the year 1948 IV to 1949 IV there was a slow growth of about 2 per cent, consumption per head being constant.

this inventory accumulation was another minor factor in hastening the appearance of the turning point. Later, when the strike ended, the effort to replenish inventories was an important factor in the strength of expansion in the first half of 1950.

* * *

The downturn of 1948 and the upturn in 1949 were each the result of a number of influences pulling in different directions. In 1948, however, there was one strong general influence acting on most parts of the economy: this was the ending of excess demand early in the year which stopped inflation and was linked to declining demand in several sectors. But for the stimulating effect of rearmament, the 1948 downturn might have occurred much earlier in the year. But for the expansion of automobile output, the recession would have been more severe and the upturn delayed. However, the expansion of automobile output was endogenous in the sense that rearmament obviously was not.

Epilogue: The Situation In The Middle of 1950

In the second quarter of 1949, both total GNP and durable goods output reached the lowest levels in their decline, rising the following quarter. Building and construction output rose strongly in 1949 II after its previous standstill and the output of nondurable goods rose again after their brief recession. Between 1949 II and 1950 II GNP rose by $26 billions or 8·1 per cent, interrupted only in 1949 IV by the steel strike which affected output of durable goods. The composition of this GNP increase is as follows:

TABLE 8.1: *Change in GNP and Components 1949 II to 1950 II*
(1958 prices)

(based on seasonally adjusted, quarterly totals at annual rates)

	$ billion
PCE (excluding autos)	9·2
Non-residential fixed investment (excluding autos)	1·1
Residential construction	7·5
Exports	−3·2
Imports	0·9
Government purchases	−2·5
Auto output	3·1
CBI (non farm; excluding autos)	9·9
Durable goods:	
Output	13·1
Final sales	3·1
CBI	10·0
Nondurable goods:	
Output	1·6
Final sales	−0·7
CBI	2·3
GNP	26·0

Source: SCB.

Three factors dominated the revival: the rise in household expenditures, residential construction and the replenishment of inventories. The last two represent to some extent a rebound from the underspending in early 1949: housing starts had been reduced despite the shortages of accommodation; and inventories had been reduced too much because of lags and misjudgement of the extent of the recession, and because of the strike.

The American economy in mid-1950 was still expanding. Disposable personal income was rising and the boom in personal consumption showed no signs of faltering (although the car market was approaching normal). Housing starts had risen to their highest postwar level. Manufacturers' inventories, despite the heavy investment of the past year, were probably still below desired levels. The Joint Economic Committee of Congress, reporting in June (before the Korean War had broken out) was cautiously optimistic:

'So far as 1950 is concerned [economic forecasts] remain optimistic. . . . Low inventories, backlogs of demand for steel accumulated during the strike, continued high levels of auto sales, an unusually high rate of construction contract awards and heavy Government outlays in State and local as well as Federal jurisdictions . . . are counted upon . . . to maintain a high level of purchasing power throughout the year. . . . The May 1950 Survey of Business Expectations made by Dun and Bradstreet Inc. showed that more businessmen expect increases in sales and net profits than at any time since July 1949. These signs point to a renewed upsurge in the economy. . . . Most observers reserve judgement as far as 1951 is concerned, inasmuch as a measure of tapering off in the automobile, steel and construction industries seems highly probable.'[1]

The prospects for some stability in costs and prices and the avoidance of renewed inflation were good. Although the average work week in manufacturing was rising and in June had almost reached the very high levels of late 1947, unemployment was still over 5 per cent of the labour force. Labour cost per unit of output of manufacturing industry was still falling in the

[1] *Senate Report 1843*, 81st Congress, p. 4.

middle of the year and profit margins were rising. On prices the main pressure came from farm products which rose slowly but steadily from January. Other wholesale prices and also the consumer price index were quite steady during the first half of the year. Thus in mid-June the prospects were for steady and stable growth and a continued absence of inflation.

NOTE A

GNP in 1945 and 1946 at 1958 Prices

Constant price estimates of quarterly GNP and its components for 1945 and 1946 are not published by the Department of Commerce, and to provide an indication of quarterly changes in real output and expenditure in those years the published current price estimates have been deflated by various price indexes based on 1958. The estimates are shown in Fig. 2.1 above, together with the later official data, and in Table A.1.

The price deflators and details of adjustments are as follows:

Personal consumption expenditure
Series [A] 1946: implicit national income price index for DPI at 1958 prices from *SCB*. 1945: CPI.
Series [B] as for [A] but adjusted as explained below.

New construction (nonresidential): ENR Construction Cost Index.

New construction (residential): ENR Building Cost Index.

Change in business inventories (farm): Wholesale price index, farm products.

Change in business inventories (non-farm): Wholesale price index other than farm products and foods.

Government purchases (Federal national defence): As for PCE, adjusted by ratio to annual GP (Federal) implicit index in 1945 and 1946. The 1947 I estimate in Table A.1, and those for later quarters in Fig. 2.1, are deflated with the GP (Federal) implicit price index.

Government purchases (Federal other and State and local): As for PCE, adjusted by ratio to annual GP (State and local) implicit index in 1945 and 1946. The 1947 I estimate in Table A.1, and

TABLE A.1: *GNP at 1958 Prices in 1945 and 1946 $ billion. Seasonally adjusted at annual rates*

	Gross National Product [A]	*Personal Consumption Expenditures* [A]	*Non Residential Construction*	*Residential Construction*	*Change in Business Inventories (farm)*	*Change in Business Inventories (nonfarm)*	*Government Purchases of Goods and Services (Federal National Defence)*	*Government Purchases of Goods and Services (Federal Other and State and Local)*	*Exports of Goods and Services*	*Imports of Goods and Services*	*Producers' Durable Equipment*	*Gross National Product* [B]	*Personal Consumption Expenditures* [B]
1945 I	372·8	178·8	4·3	2·0	−1·0	−3·9	167·1	20·4	6·4	13·7	12·4	356·6	162·6
II	377·9	179·1	5·3	2·2	−1·0	1·8	163·8	19·9	8·2	14·2	12·8	361·7	162·9
III	348·3	182·7	5·7	2·9	−1·0	−4·6	133·5	16·4	10·8	13·9	15·8	331·7	166·1
IV	321·8	191·4	7·4	4·2	−0·6	−1·7	88·7	15·6	15·3	13·9	15·4	304·4	174·0
1946 I	315·9	204·4	11·1	9·9	−0·3	10·2	37·2	21·4	19·1	11·3	14·2	297·4	185·9
II	320·4	208·4	12·6	11·9	−0·2	14·5	25·8	22·4	20·2	11·5	16·3	301·5	189·5
III	311·1	203·0	13·1	13·1	−0·1	9·2	19·5	23·6	21·1	11·1	19·7	305·0	196·9
IV	302·4	198·3	12·8	13·4	−0·2	6·9	19·2	24·4	17·8	10·8	20·7	302·5	198·3
1947 I	306·4	203·4	11·8	14·3	−1·0	1·1	14·2	24·2	23·3	10·2	25·1	306·4	203·4

those for later quarters in Fig. 2.1, are total government purchases less defence purchases.

Exports: Unit value index.

Imports: Unit value index.

Producers' durable equipment: Wholesale price index, metals and metal products.

Linking: except where otherwise stated, indexes for 1945 linked with annual 1945 implicit deflator, and for 1946 with annual 1946 implicit deflator.

Gross national product [A] is the sum of the deflated expenditures (less imports) including PCE [A]. GNP [B] is the sum including PCE [B].

National income sources do not provide separate estimates of 1945 quarterly exports and imports of goods and services. The balance of payments sources were adjusted to conform with national income definitions as is shown in Table A.2.

The outstanding feature of the [A] estimates in Table A.1 is the fall in personal consumption by $10 billions in the second half of 1946, contributing one-half of the fall in GNP during that period. These estimates are almost certainly wrong.

To deflate PCE in 1946 I have used the implicit quarterly price index used in the official national income and product estimates to deflate disposable personal income. It is the same as the index used to deflate annual PCE, and thus the estimate of annual deflated PCE is the same as the official estimate (except for rounding errors). The interpretation and reliability of the price indexes is affected by price controls and their removal in the second half of 1946. Under price control, the decline in quality and the legal avoidance and illegal evasion of controls caused prices to rise by more than price indexes during the period of controls. Consequently, as Friedman and Schwartz point out 'the jump in the price index on the elimination of price control in 1946 did not involve any corresponding jump in 'prices', rather, it reflected largely the unveiling of price increases that had occurred earlier'.[1] Thus the decline in PCE estimated in the second half of 1946 is likely to be an overestimate because both consumption under price controls and the price rise after the removal of price controls are overestimated by the conventional measures.

[1] Friedman and Schwartz, [1963], p. 558.

TABLE A.2: *Exports and Imports of Goods and Services 1945–46*
$ billion. Seasonally adjusted at annual rates

	(1) Exports of goods and services excluding military grants	(2) Government nonmilitary transfers total	(3) Military grants gross	(4) Military receipts (Reverse Lend Lease)	(5) Imports of goods and services less military	(6) U.S. government loans
1945 I	5·4	0·1	11·7	5·6	7·2	0·2
II	6·7	1·0	12·5	4·0	7·6	0·2
III	8·3	1·3	7·1	1·6	7·4	2·0
IV	10·7	1·7	2·7	0·2	7·4	1·4
1946 I	13·6	2·7	—	—	6·8	1·9
II	14·8	2·4	—	—	7·2	4·1
III	16·1	2·0	—	—	7·3	4·4
IV	14·4	1·9	—	—	7·6	2·9

Note: [1] Income on investment is included in exports of goods and services.
[2] Net government income is included in net transfer by government.

Sources: (1) 1946: *SCB*, 1966 National Income Supplement, Table 4.1, line 2.
1945: Exports of goods and services including military (*U.S. Balance of Payments Supplement* 1963, Table 2, line 1, p. 6) *less* (3). *N.B.* not s.a.
(2) 1946: *SCB*, 1966 National Income Supplement, Table 4.1, line 7.
1945: Government payments *less* lend lease and civilian supplies distributed by the armed forces. (*The Balance of International Payments 1946–48*, Table D, p. 196).
(3) 1945: Lend lease payments and civilian supplies distributed by the armed forces. (*The Balance of International Payments 1946–48*, Table D, p. 196).
(4) 1945: Total government receipts (gross) (*U.S. Balance of Payments 1946–48*, Table D, p. 196).
(5) 1946: *SCB*, 1966 National Income Supplement, Table 4.1, line 4.
1945: Imports of goods and services including military (*U.S. Balance of Payments Supplement, 1963*, Table 2, line 3, p. 6) *less* (4). *N.B.* not s.a.
(6) *U.S. Balance of Payments Supplement, 1963*, Table 2, line 38, p. 6. *N.B.* not s.a.

A further difficulty is that sales and production data used to estimate consumption expenditures at current prices may have been unreliable under price control: they may underestimate expenditures by failing to record black market sales. This factor might go some way to offset the effect of the difference between actual and nominal prices. But the importance of the factor cannot be estimated and in the estimates I have adjusted prices and left the official expenditure data unaltered.

A breakdown of the fall in PCE in the second half of 1946, deflated by the component indexes of the CPI, shows that the fall was due to a large fall in purchases of food and beverages, a small fall in clothing purchases being offset by rises in the other groups. This is corroborated by the official deflated annual PCE estimates in which food and beverages declined by \$2·1 billions (1958 prices) between 1946 and 1947 while the rest of PCE rose by \$4·9 billions. There is also an independent estimate of food consumption per capita, a weighted average of quantities of foods, which after rising by 3 per cent between 1945 and 1946, declined by 2 per cent between 1946 and 1947.[1] But the quantities in this index are measured by weight, and thus the index may fail to record important quality changes such as probably occurred during and after the removal of controls. However, in so far as there was a fall in consumption at the end of 1946, it is certain that it was mainly due to a fall in purchases of food. The supposed fall of \$10 billions (1958 prices) represents a decline in total PCE of about 5 per cent, but it represents a fall of about 13 per cent of PCE on food and beverages. There is no evidence, as Fig. A.1 shows, of any change of this magnitude in farm marketing or food manufacturing in the second half of 1946 or early 1947; the graph shows marketings and production at relatively steady levels with a small recovery in food production in 1946 IV following a small decline in the middle of the year.

There was an increase in the last quarter of 1946 in the inventories of retail food stores by over one-third in book value. During the quarter nominal retail food prices rose by about 7 per cent so the rise in value must represent a large increase in volume. However, this inventory accumulation allowed these retailers to raise their inventory–sales ratio from 0·19 in 1946 III to 0·22 in 1947 I which

[1] U.S. Bureau of the Census, *Historical Statistics of the United States, Colonial Times to 1957*, Washington D.C., 1960, Series G 545.

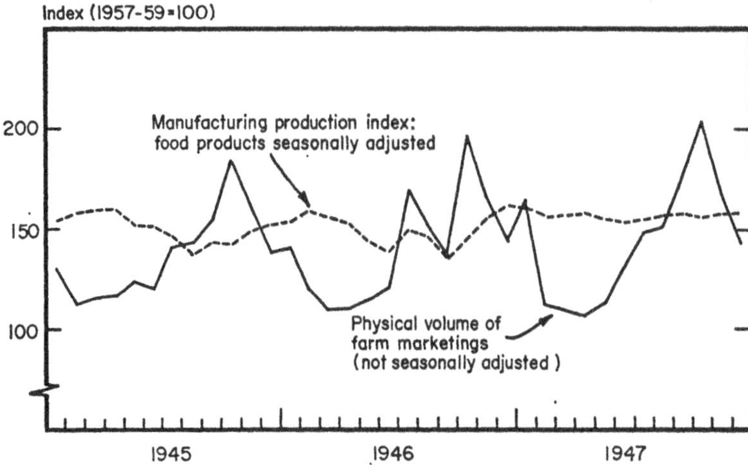

Fig. A.1: Food output, 1945–47.
Source: SCB.

was the level it was kept at during the next two years. This rise in retailers' inventories at the end of 1946 therefore must have been a planned rise, not an unintended increase due to a fall in sales. On the other hand, the reason why retailers were able to restock just when they did may have been due to reduced excess demand, but not necessarily falling demand.

The position is thus that the direct evidence of a 5 per cent fall in PCE in the second half of 1946 is unreliable, and there is no supporting evidence—in fact all the evidence suggests that a fall in consumption is extremely unlikely. In Chapter 3 above[1] two alternative hypotheses about the change in PCE in the second half of 1946 are considered, and set out in Table 3.1. Estimate [B] which assumes that consumption rose by 4 per cent in 1946 III, and again by smaller amounts in the two following quarters, is selected as that which most likely describes the actual changes in 1946. This estimate provides the figures for PCE from 1946 II to 1946 IV in the [B] series in Table A.1 and is the one used throughout this study.

The PCE [A] estimates show a 16 per cent rise in consumption between 1945 II and 1946 II. An analysis of the components of PCE does not suggest that this is unlikely. The 10 per cent increase in

[1] Pp. 80–2.

civilian population during the period would have led to at least a 10 per cent increase in private expenditures on food and beverages (even though total food production did not change). Clothing production rose by 16 per cent between 1945 II and 1946 II and thus the deflated expenditure increase of 5 per cent appears to be an underestimate. Deflated durable goods purchases doubled from their very low level and production figures do not disprove this rise. Expenditures on other nondurable goods and services, deflated with the 'miscellaneous' subgroup of the CPI show a 13 per cent rise. Deflated housing expenditures rose 9 per cent. If the food increase is set at 15 per cent, this rough figuring set out in Table A.3 gives an increase in consumption virtually the same as the PCE [A] estimate derived from an aggregate deflator. Consequently I have no reason to reject the PCE [A] estimates up to 1946 II, and they have been linked to the [B] estimate for 1946 II to give the early [B] series.

TABLE A.3: *Personal Consumption Expenditure, 1945 to 1946*

	1945 II *$ billion*	*Per cent increase between 1945 II and 1946 II at constant prices*
Durable goods	7·4	100
Clothing and shoes	15·9	5
Food and alcoholic beverages	40·8	15
Housing	12·3	9
Other	42·4	10
TOTAL PCE	118·8	17

NOTE B

Recent Theories of Consumption[1]

Utility analysis and consumption

Following Modigliani and Brumberg and Ando and Modigliani we can derive a consumption (or savings) function as follows.[2] Assume an individual receives utility only from present and prospective consumption; he neither expects to receive nor desires to leave any inheritance; and the proportion of his total resources that he plans to spend on consumption at any date is determined by his tastes and not by the size of his resources. The inheritance assumption can be relaxed without affecting the results if specific assumptions about the timing of the bequests and the shape of the utility function are made. For an individual of age t the utility function is

$$U = U(c_t^t, c_{t+1}^t, \ldots, c_L^t), \tag{i}$$

where c_t^t is consumption at age t, and L is age at death. This function is maximized subject to a budget constraint:

$$a_t^t + \sum_{i=t}^{N} \frac{y_i^t}{(1+r)^{i+1-t}} = \sum_{i=t}^{L} \frac{c_i^t}{(1+r)^{i+1-t}}, \tag{ii}$$

[1] For recent general reviews and bibliographies see D. B. Suits, 'The determinants of consumer expenditure: a review of present knowledge', in *Impacts of Monetary Policy*, a research study prepared for the commission on money and credit, Prentice-Hall, Englewood Cliffs, N.J., 1963, pp. 1–57, and R. Ferber, 'Research on household behaviour', in the American Economic Association and the Royal Economic Society *Surveys of Economic Theory*, III, Macmillan, London, 1966.

[2] F. Modigliani and R. Brumberg, 'Utility analysis and the consumption function: an interpretation of cross-section data', in *Post-Keynesian Economics*, ed. K. K. Kurihara, Rutgers University Press, New Brunswick N.J., 1954, A. Ando and F. Modigliani, 'The life cycle hypothesis of saving: aggregate implications and tests', *Amer. econ. R.*, LIII, March, 1963, reprinted in *Readings in Business Cycles*, the American Economic Association's series of republished articles on economics, X, Irwin, Homewood, Ill., Irwin, 1965, Allen & Unwin, London.

where a_t^t is assets at beginning of age t

y_t is expected income (excluding interest) in t-th year

r is the rate of interest

N is the age at retirement.

(If assets are bequeathed at death, a_{L+1} enters into both the utility function and the budget constraint.) From the first order maximization condition it can be shown that consumption of an individual of age t is proportional to the present value of resources accruing to him over the rest of his life:

$$c_t^t = k_t^t w_t^t, \tag{iii}$$

where w_t^t is the present value of resources and equals the l.h.s. of eq. (ii)

$$w_t^t = a_t^t + \sum_{i=t}^{N} \frac{y_i^t}{(1 + r)^{i+1-t}}, \tag{iv}$$

i.e. assets (or net worth) plus the present value of non-property income the individual expects to earn over the remainder of his earning life. For given t, k_t^t depends only on the particular form of the utility function U and the rate of interest r.

This derivation of a consumption (or savings) function implies the following motives for savings:

a. The desire to accumulate assets to bequeath to heirs. Consideration of this is neglected here.

b. The desire to maintain a given consumption flow which differs from an expected income flow.

For both these reasons there need be no close and simple relation between consumption in a given short period and income in the same period.

The above derivation has neglected uncertainty which introduces two additional motives for saving:

c. The precautionary motive: the desire to accumulate assets to meet emergencies.

d. The desire or necessity to have an equity in certain types of assets, the services of which the individual desires to consume, i.e. consumer durable goods such as houses.

Any possession which can be turned into cash will serve at least one, probably more, of these four motives and should accordingly be treated as an asset. These possessions include, in particular, equities in unconsumed durable goods. Saving and dissaving can thus be defined as the change in the net worth of an individual during a specified time period, and consumption is expenditure on nondurable goods and services plus current depreciation of consumer durable goods such as houses and their furnishings and equipment, and cars. A distinction is thus made between personal consumption, and personal consumption expenditures.

In consumption equation (iii) define average annual expected income as

$$y_t^{et} = \frac{1}{N - t} \sum_{i=t+1}^{N} \frac{y_i^t}{(1 + r)^{i-t}}, \tag{v}$$

and rewrite (iii) as

$$c_t^t = k_t^t a_t^t + k_t^t y_t^t + k_t^t (N - t) y_t^{et}, \tag{vi}$$

which says that consumption at t of a t year old individual is proportional to assets, current non-property income and expected non-property income. Assume that we can aggregate over ages and over individuals to obtain reasonably stable parameters (see Ando and Modigliani [1963] and their reference to Theil)[1] and hence our aggregate consumption function is

$$c_t = \alpha_1 y_t + \alpha_2 y_t^e + \beta_1 a_t \tag{vii}$$

where c_t, y_t, y_t^e and a_t are respectively aggregate consumption, current non-property income, expected annual non-property income, and net worth.

Note on permanent income

Friedman presented a version of this theory, similar in basic respects to that outlined above, but leading to alternative econometric inquiries.[2] He derives the relationship between consumption and wealth as in (iii) above, but expresses it in terms of permanent income, y_p, which is the income derived from existing wealth given the rate of interest r. It is thus equal to the sum of average expected labour income and average expected property income. Friedman's basic function is thus

$$c_t = k_p y_p \tag{iiia}$$

[1] H. Theil, *Linear Aggregation of Economic Relations*, Amsterdam: North Holland, Amsterdam, 1954.

[2] M. Friedman, *A Theory of the Consumption Function*, a study of NBER, N.Y., Princeton University Press, 1957.

where k_p depends on the shape of the utility function, the rate of interest and, according to Friedman, factors reflecting the influence of uncertainty.

Permanent income can be measured by a weighted average of past incomes, e.g. with geometric weights

$$y_{pt} = (1 - q)(y_t + qy_{t-1} + q^2y_{t-2} + \ldots), \qquad \text{(iiib)}$$

where $o < q \leqslant 1$ and y_t is total disposable income. This definition of y_p leads to the consumption function

$$c_t = k_p(1 - q)y_t + qc_{t-1}. \qquad \text{(iiic)}$$

The meaning of the introduction of lagged consumption into the function can be better seen if (iiic) is rewritten as

$$c_t - c_{t-1} = (1 - q)(k_py_t - c_{t-1}), \qquad \text{(iiid)}$$

which says that the change in consumption is a fraction of the difference between k_py_t, which can be called 'desired' consumption, and c_{t-1}, consumption in the last period.

Friedman suggests alternative measures of permanent income based on weighted averages of current income and recent peak income which lead to functions similar to those used by Duesenberry and Modigliani in their exploration of the relative income theory.[1] This theory assumes that an individual's consumption is determined at least in part by emulation. A family's spending will be guided by what its neighbours spend, and if income falls people will be reluctant to reduce their standard of living. From this argument Duesenberry suggested that the savings rate can be expressed as a function of the ratio of current income to the highest level previously reached.

Long and short run consumption behaviour

Let y_t grow at a constant rate and y_t^e either equal y_t or be proportional to it. Then write

$$c_t = \alpha y_t + \beta_1 a_t \qquad \text{(viii)}$$

If the return on assets, r, is constant, it follows that the income–asset ratio is constant, as are also the consumption–income and

[1] J. S. Duesenberry, *Income, Savings and the Theory of Consumer Behaviour*, Harvard University, Cambridge, Mass, 1949, and F. Modigliani, 'Fluctuations in the saving-income ratio: a problem in economic forecasting', in *Studies in Income and Wealth*, XI, NBER, New York, 1959.

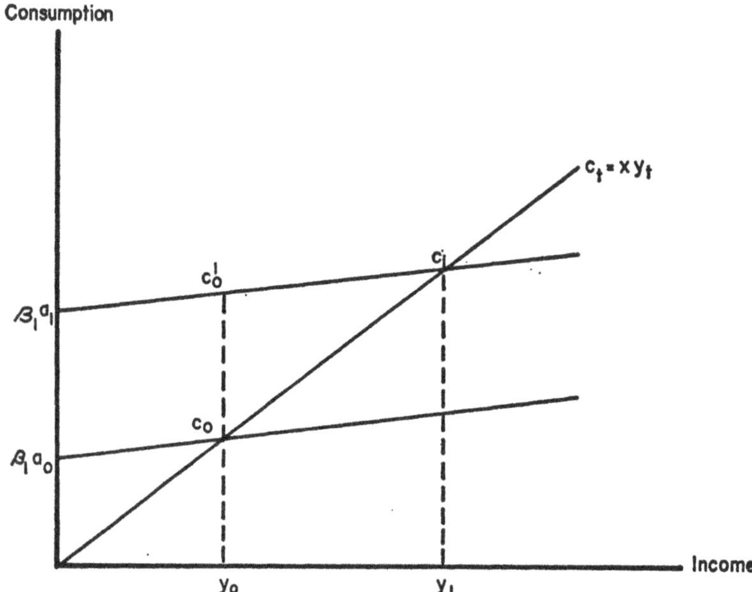

Fig. B.1: Long and short run consumption functions.

savings–income ratios. I shall interpret the situation when y_t grows at a constant rate as long run behaviour, or as trend behaviour.

In Fig. B.1 consumption and non-property income are measured on the axes. The straight line through the origin

$$c_t = \gamma y_t \tag{ix}$$

is the long run consumption function. The lines with positive intercepts are short run (annual) functions, as in equation (viii) above. Over time, saving (or dissaving) alters the value of assets and hence raises or lowers the short run function. This is shown graphically by alterations in the size of the intercept which measures the influence of assets. Short run changes in income will lead to levels of consumption different from those shown by the long run function. For example, if income fell from y_1 to y_0, consumption would decline from c_1y_1 to $c_0^1y_0$, and would not fall to c_0y_0 until dissaving reduced assets from a_1 to a_0. The general short run phenomenon is a sluggishness of response in the short run of consumption to changes in income, a tendency to remain at past levels for some time after incomes fall, and a delay in raising consumption when incomes rise. This is clearly related to the earlier empirical findings of Duesenberry [1949] and Modigliani [1949] who expressed consumption as a function of highest previous peak income (the ratchet effect).

The long run-short run distinction can be introduced into this analysis in a slightly different form. Let r^e be the expected average rate of return on assets, and p^e be the expected income from assets. Then

$$p_t^e = r_t^e a_t, \tag{x}$$

and substituting in (vii) we get,

$$c_t = \alpha_1 y_t + \alpha_2 y_t^e + \beta_2 p_t^e \tag{xi}$$

In the long run, and if the distribution of income between property and nonproperty is approximately constant, we can write

$$c_t = \delta(y_t + p_t), \tag{xii}$$

which is equivalent to the long run relationship in eq. (ix). On the other hand in the short run current property income may differ considerably from average expected income (consider the case of farmers) with consumption levels being maintained in periods of falling income by dissaving. Only if the decumulation of assets goes far enough will consumption be reduced. It is unlikely that any simple, close relationship will exist between current consumption and current property income.

Empirical results using annual time series

Ando and Modigliani [1963] have fitted equation (vii) in various forms to time series data obtaining good fits and results which agree with *a priori* considerations. In one version they approximate expected nonproperty income by current income multiplied by a scale factor. In another they approximate it by current income corrected for the degree of unemployment. The following equation is typical of their better results, op. cit., Table 2, eq. (6), and Fig. 1, pp. 407–9:

Eq. 1
$$\Delta c = \underset{(0{\cdot}116)}{0{\cdot}550}\Delta y + \underset{(0{\cdot}021)}{0{\cdot}079}\Delta a$$
$$R^2 = 0{\cdot}921 \quad S_e = 2{\cdot}335 \quad DW = 2{\cdot}01$$

Calculated by least squares from first differences of U.S. data 1929–59 excluding 1941–46. The constant term was suppressed. Data and their derivation given in Ando and Brown.[1]

c is expenditures on nondurable goods and services, plus depreciation of consumer durables; billions of current dollars.

y is labour income net of taxes; billions of current dollars.

a is net worth of consumers, i.e. households, institutions, non-corporate business and agriculture, billions of current dollars, end of preceding year. Net worth is tangible *plus* intangible assets, *minus* liabilities.

A similar equation in ratio form, with a higher level of serial correlation, is (Ando and Modigliani [1963], eq. (ii))

Eq.2 $$\frac{c_t}{y_t} = 0{\cdot}634 + \underset{(0{\cdot}020)}{0{\cdot}080}\frac{a_{t-1}}{y_t}$$

$$R^2 = 0{\cdot}962 \quad S_e = 0{\cdot}018 \quad DW = 1{\cdot}00$$

In these consumption functions net worth plays the part of a filter: it has a smoothing or averaging role, derived from both its relative insensitivity to short term fluctuations in property (and hence total personal) income, and its statistical definition as the sum of past savings, i.e. the sum of lagged income and lagged consumption. It was suggested above that this filtering function could be simulated by an expression for expected property income. Alternatively, it could be simulated by expressions containing lagged consumption and income.

The possibility that not all of the adjustment to changes in income and assets may take place within one year can be considered by introducing lagged consumption in the following form. Let

$$c_t - c_{t-1} = \varepsilon(\alpha y_t + \beta_1 a_t - c_{t-1})$$

or $$c_t = (1 - \varepsilon)c_{t-1} + \varepsilon\alpha y_t + \varepsilon\beta_1 a_t \qquad \text{(xiii)}$$

where ε measures the speed of adjustment of consumption. (The use of the adjustment hypothesis will be recognized as formally equivalent to the introduction of Friedman's permanent income concept in the specific form of the geometrically distributed lagged sum of $\alpha y_t + \beta_1 a_t$, i.e. consumption depends on the *trend* of $\alpha y_t + \beta_1 a_t$ as determined by their past values. See pp. 220–1 above.) Ando and

[1] A. Ando, and E. C. Brown, 'Lags in fiscal and monetary policy', in *Stabilisation Policies*, a series of research studies prepared for the Commission on Money and Credit, Prentice-Hall, Englewood Cliffs, N.J., 1963.

Modigliani [1963], p. 414, n. 21 tested this hypothesis in ratio form with the result

Eq.3
$$\frac{c_t}{y_t} = 0{\cdot}46 + \underset{(0{\cdot}077)}{0{\cdot}177}\frac{c_{t-1}}{y_t} + \underset{(0{\cdot}016)}{0{\cdot}072}\frac{a_{t-1}}{y_t}$$

so that $\varepsilon = 0{\cdot}82$, $\alpha = 0{\cdot}56$ and $\beta_1 = 0{\cdot}087$. The results suggest that most of the adjustment takes place within a year.

Quarterly aggregate consumption functions

Ando and Brown [1963] have fitted the above model to quarterly data. A typical result, comparable to Eq. 3 above, is eq. 14′, p. 127,

Eq. 4
$$c_t = \underset{(0{\cdot}067)}{0{\cdot}229y_t} + \underset{(0{\cdot}012)}{0{\cdot}044a_{t-1}} + \underset{(0{\cdot}095)}{0{\cdot}56c_{t-1}}$$
$$+ \text{ seasonal adjustment factor} + 16{\cdot}4$$
$$R^2 = 0{\cdot}998 \quad S_e = 1{\cdot}84$$

Fitted by least squares to data in current dollars not seasonally adjusted, 1947 I to 1958 IV. Definitions of variables as above; data in source.

If we suppose the consumption adjustment is incorporated as in Eq. 3, $\varepsilon = 0{\cdot}44$ indicates that less than half the adjustment takes place during one quarter.

Duesenberry, Eckstein and Fromm have developed a consumption function (the DEF function) which, while basically similar to the above, has some different features.[1] First, c_t is defined as personal consumption expenditures at constant prices per head (expenditures on consumer goods and services including durables, excluding purchases of houses). y_t is deflated total personal disposable income per head, i.e. property and non-property incomes are not separated. (Statistically this may not be important as property income in 1958 in the U.S. was only 14 per cent of total personal income.) Second, the net worth factor is replaced by a measure of the previous highest income y^0. Previous highest income may be regarded as a statistical substitute for net worth. Alternatively the combination of previous highest peak income and lagged consumption is equivalent to the

[1] J. S. Duesenberry, O. Eckstein and G. Fromm, 'A simulation of the U.S. economy in recession', *Econometrica*, XXVIII, October 1960, pp. 749–809, reprinted in *Readings in Business Cycles*, the American Economic Association's series of republished articles on economics, X, Irwin, Homewood, Ill., 1965.

introduction of Friedman's permanent income in the form of a distributed lagged function of previous peak income (see p. 221 above and Duesenberry *et al.*, op. cit., p. 275). Third, to improve the reliability of the results the function is cast in ratio form as follows[1]

$$\frac{c_t}{y_{t-1}} = \varepsilon\alpha + \varepsilon\beta\frac{y_{t-1}}{y^0_{t-1}} + (1-\varepsilon)\frac{c_{t-1}}{y_{t-2}} \qquad \text{(xiv)}$$

Duesenberry *et al.* give the following equation for 1948–57, op. cit., Table VII, p. 276,

Eq.5 $$\frac{c_t}{y_{t-1}} = 0{\cdot}8218 - \underset{(0{\cdot}0819)}{0{\cdot}6250}\frac{y_{t-1}}{y^0_{t-1}} + \underset{(0{\cdot}0526)}{0{\cdot}7843}\frac{c_{t-1}}{y_{t-2}}$$

$$R^2 = 0{\cdot}866 \quad S_e = 0{\cdot}0069 \quad d^2/S^2 = 1{\cdot}84$$

Calculated by least squares from quarterly seasonally adjusted data, per head, 1947–49 prices, 1948 I to 1957 IV. c_t is personal consumption expenditures per head. y_t is personal disposable income per head. y^0_t is highest value of y prior to y_t. $\varepsilon = 0{\cdot}22$, suggesting that less than one quarter of the adjustment takes place during one quarter of a year.

The same equation fitted to comparable data for 1930–38 produced a similar good fit but lower values of all the coefficients (and higher ε). Griliches *et al.* recalculated Equation 5 extending the data to 1960 IV with the result[2]

Eq.6 $$\frac{c_t}{y_{t-1}} = 0{\cdot}839 - \underset{(0{\cdot}134)}{0{\cdot}565}\frac{y_{t-1}}{y^0_{t-1}} + \underset{(0{\cdot}099)}{0{\cdot}705}\frac{c_{t-1}}{y_{t-2}}$$

$R^2 = 0{\cdot}533$ Data as in Eq. 5.

Griliches' results suggest that the coefficients are stable although the explanatory power of the equation declines with time. This is confirmed by re-estimation with data extended to 1964 IV:

Eq.7 $$\frac{c_t}{y_{t-1}} = 0{\cdot}7907 - \underset{(0{\cdot}1009)}{0{\cdot}4706}\frac{y_{t-1}}{y^0_{t-1}} + \underset{(0{\cdot}0963)}{0{\cdot}6529}\frac{c_{t-1}}{y_{t-2}}$$

$R^2 = 0{\cdot}451$ $S_e = 0{\cdot}0104$. Data from *SCB*, seasonally adjusted at 1958 prices.

[1] In the original source the coefficients are not interpreted to include the adjustment factor ε.

[2] Z. Griliches *et al.*, 'Notes on estimated aggregate quarterly consumption functions', *Econometrica*, XXX, July, 1962, pp. 491–500.

Estimation of the equation for periods within the 1948–64 span suggests that the original Duesenberry *et al.* result was influenced by the exceptional nature of the period 1953–57. The equation for this period, which experienced a steady rise in c_t, shows that previous peak income contributed little to the equation's explanatory power, and the high coefficient for lagged consumption suggests that virtually none of the adjustment occurred in the current quarter. The partial correlation of lagged consumption with current consumption is very high, and explains the high R^2 for the equation as a whole. The periods before 1953 and after 1957 both give relatively more importance to previous peak income, and allow more of the consumption adjustment to take place in the current quarter. The partial correlation of lagged consumption is much lower and R^2 is consequently lower. Hence it appears that the high R^2 of Eq. 5 should be regarded as due to the heavy weight given to the 1953–57 upswing in the data. The result of Eq. 7 with a moderate R^2 seems less surprising, and there is no real reason to think that the explanatory power of the equation has altered over the period as a whole. The difference between the high R^2 of Eq. 4 and the moderate R^2 of Eq. 7 is thus likely to be due at least in part to the exclusion of net purchases of consumer durables in one, and the inclusion of them in the other.[1]

From the formula $\alpha + \beta$ a long run (no growth) marginal propensity to consume can be estimated from the DEF function (xiv). Using the results of Eq. 7 it is 0·922, which compares with 0·91 based on annual data from a different period and a disaggregated model described in Note C below.

Disaggregated quarterly consumption functions

The most recent investigations are represented by the work of Suits and Sparks[2] which is part of the Brookings–SSRC econometric project. Their results will be considered in the light of the previous discussion. The period of the data is 1948 I to 1960 IV, and the data are seasonally adjusted at 1954 prices.

[1] In Note G below the DEF equation is used to interpret quarterly changes in consumption, 1948–50.

[2] D. B. Suits and G. R. Sparks, 'Consumption regressions with quarterly data', in *The Brookings Quarterly Econometric Model of the United States*, ed. J. S. Duesenberry *et al.*, North Holland, Amsterdam, 1965.

Durable goods

If there is a fixed relationship between consumption (depreciation) and stock of consumer durables (e.g. a fixed relationship such as proportionality implying a constant rate of depreciation), then if we disregard the question of ownership (purchasing or hiring) and assume that all durables are purchased for owners' use, the consumption function for durables can be expressed in terms of stocks (as in Note D below which is concerned with automobiles and housing). If desired stocks depend on income and assets, and if expenditures are a proportion of the difference between desired and actual stock, then expenditures will be a function of income, stock of durables and (other) assets.

Consumer expenditure on automobiles depends for the period 1953 III to 1960 IV significantly on personal disposable income (defined to exclude all transfers but servicemen's insurance dividend) and on the stock of cars. Neither relative prices nor liquid assets enter the regressions significantly. However the most important explanation of expenditure is an index of consumer attitudes and buying intentions, and this index appears to be related to short term deviations of income from its trend. The period before 1953, according to Suits and Sparks, was dominated by postwar and Korean War shortages and controls and was omitted from the regressions.

The demand for other durables behaves in the expected fashion, expenditures depending on income, stock of durables and liquid assets. The influence of the attitude index is insignificant. These results tend to agree with those of Klein and Popkin who have a single equation for all durables containing income, the ratio of non labour to labour income, lagged expenditures and the attitude index, and Liu whose durable equation contains income, lagged expenditures, stock of durables and housing expenditures.[1] It is likely that in these cases lagged consumption has the same filtering effect as liquid assets. The significance of residential housing may be explained by a high correlation of purchases of new houses with

[1] L. R. Klein and J. Popkin, 'An econometric analysis of the postwar relationship between inventory fluctuations and changes in aggregate economic activity', in *Inventory Fluctuations and Economic Stabilization, Part III* (papers prepared for the Joint Economic Committee), U.S. Congress, 87th Cong., 1st Sess., Joint Committee Print, Washington, 1961. Ta-Chung Liu, 'An exploratory quarterly econometric model of effective demand in the postwar U.S. economy', *Econometrica*, XXXI, July, 1963, pp. 301–48.

expenditures on household equipment and furnishings, or possibly by a more fundamental correlation of new household formation and expenditures on all durable goods. The relation between this association and the life cycle–expected income theory has not been explored.

Nondurable goods

Food expenditures are satisfactorily explained by income, relative price of food and population. Income appears to have two distinct effects: the effect of past mean income, and the effect of deviation of current income from the past mean. Other nondurables depend on income (with the distinction between trend and deviation), and liquid assets. Klein and Popkin's nondurable equation includes income, nonlabour–labour income ratio, lagged expenditures and liquid assets. Liu's equation is identical except for the income ratio.

Services

Service expenditures (excluding imputed expenditures) depend on income (again with the distinction between trend and deviation), relative price, liquid assets and lagged expenditures. The lagged expenditures imply that only one-fifth of the expenditure adjustment to a change in income occurs in the current quarter. Klein and Popkin's results are again similar, expenditures depending on income, income ratio, lagged consumption and liquid assets. Liu's result depends only on liquid assets and lagged consumption.

These disaggregated results appear to be in agreement with the aggregate equations considered above. The fundamental roles of income, assets (liquid assets in the case of the disaggregated data) and lagged consumption (representing the delay in adjustment to changes in income and assets) are common to both sets of results. The difference in explanatory power of consumption and expenditure equations is clearly due to the difficulty of explaining short period changes in expenditures on automobiles. There is more than a suggestion that short period deviations from the trend of income play a large part in explaining changes in expenditures on cars but this still remains an open question.[1]

[1] A. Zellner *et al.*, 'Further analysis of the short run consumption function with emphasis on the role of liquid assets', *Econometrica*, XXXIII, July, 1965, pp. 571–81, incorporate in the quarterly consumption function an adjustment to a difference between desired and actual liquid assets. In so far as this difference arises because of short run deviations from trend of income, it may be significantly linked to changes in attitudes and purchases of automobiles.

NOTE C

Consumption Expenditures and Savings During The War

Estimates of the amount by which consumer expenditures were curtailed during the war, and hence estimates of 'excess' savings, can be made by comparing actual expenditures with those expenditures which would have been made if prewar or postwar expenditure–income relationships had determined behaviour. The equations below express annual PCE at constant 1958 prices as a simple linear function of real DPI (Y). There is an equation for each of expenditures on durables (C_{Dur}), nondurables (C_{Nondur}) and services (C_{Ser}).[1] The data have been fitted to the years 1939–64, and in all cases the years 1941–46 are omitted. For nondurables, 1947, and for durables 1950 and 1955, were also omitted on the grounds that it was not desirable that the abnormally high expenditures on these goods during these years should influence the determination of normal relationships.[2]

Eq. 1 $\quad C_{\text{Dur}\ t} = -11{\cdot}4 + 0{\cdot}166\,Y_t \quad R^2 = 0{\cdot}984 \quad S_e = 2{\cdot}4$

Eq. 2 $\quad C_{\text{Nondur}}\ t = 25{\cdot}5 + 0{\cdot}360\,Y_t \quad R^2 = 0{\cdot}998 \quad S_e = 1{\cdot}3$

Eq. 3 $\quad C_{\text{Ser}}\ t = -11{\cdot}2 + 0{\cdot}383\,Y_t \quad R^2 = 0{\cdot}993 \quad S_e = 5{\cdot}2$

The equations are calculated by least squares. Data is at 1958 prices, $ billions, from *SCB*.

Added, the three equations give the aggregate simple consumption function

$$C_t = 2{\cdot}9 + 0{\cdot}909\,Y_t$$

[1] The special case of automobiles is treated in more detail in Note D below.

[2] This follows earlier more detailed results of E. J. Paradiso and M. A. Smith, 'Consumer purchasing and income patterns', *SCB*, March, 1959, pp. 18–28.

and if this equation is interpreted as a long run consumption function as in eq. (ix), of Note B, p. 222, then the intercept 2·9 is near enough to zero to be neglected, and the marginal propensity to consume, 0·91, equals the average propensity. This estimate of the marginal propensity compares with that of 0·92 from the re-calculated DEF function, Eq. 7 of Note B, p. 226. As is well known (see Suits [1963]) such results are heavily dependent on the existence of trends in C and Y. Correlations of first differences give greatly worsened fits:

Eq. 4 $\Delta C_{\mathrm{Dur}}\, t = 0{\cdot}3 + 0{\cdot}140 \Delta Y_t \; R^2 = 0{\cdot}121 \; S_e = 8{\cdot}1$

Eq. 5 $\Delta C_{\mathrm{Nondur}}\, t = 1{\cdot}0 + 0{\cdot}236 \Delta Y_t \; R^2 = 0{\cdot}599 \; S_e = 1{\cdot}5$

Eq. 6 $\Delta C_{\mathrm{Ser}}\, t = 2{\cdot}4 + 0{\cdot}132 \Delta Y_t \; R^2 = 0{\cdot}422 \; S_e = 1{\cdot}4$

The coefficient of ΔY_t in the aggregate function is 0·508, similar to Suits' conclusions ([1963] pp. 33–35).

Using Eqs. 1–3 above, the difference between estimated consumption, $\hat{C}$, and actual consumption, C, is:

$\hat{C} - C$, $ billions, 1958 prices

	Nondurables and Services	*Durables*	*Total*
1942	22·9	12·4	35·3
1943	24·2	15·3	39·5
1944	24·2	17·7	41·9
1945	12·5	16·1	28·6
1946	−0·1	5·7	5·6
1947	−5·5	0·2	−5·3

At 1945 PCE prices, total 'excess' savings during 1942–45 are thus $95·0 billion.

As an alternative an equation of the type developed by Ando and Modigliani [1963] can be used to estimate normal consumption (p. 408, Table 2, eq. (3)):

Eq. 7

$$C = \underset{(0{\cdot}039)}{0{\cdot}640\,Y} + \underset{(0{\cdot}008)}{0{\cdot}077A}$$

$$R^2 = 0{\cdot}999 \quad S_e = 2{\cdot}86 \quad DW = 0{\cdot}89$$

Estimated by least squares from data 1929–59 excluding 1941–46. Current prices.

C is expenditures on nondurables and services plus depreciation on consumer durables;

Y is disposable labour income;

A is net worth of households (including farms and noncorporate business).

This is the undifferenced form of Eq. 1 of Note B discussed above on p. 223. From Eq. 7, under-consumption during the years 1942–45 at 1945 prices is \$35·5 billions, to which net purchases of consumer durables must be added to make the estimate comparable to the above estimate of excess savings. Assuming that normal net expenditures on durables during 1942–45 would not have totalled more than \$25 billion[1] the estimate of excess savings from Eq. 7 could be of the order of \$60 billion, two-thirds of the previous estimate.

The evidence from income–expenditure relationships can be supplemented by the evidence from income–wealth relationships. The latter appear to have been stable in the decade following 1948, and by extrapolating the post-1948 relationship back to 1945 it is possible to estimate the extent to which asset holdings of households in 1945 were in excess of normal holdings. The Federal Reserve Board provides estimates of total financial assets of households (demand deposits and currency, savings accounts, life insurance and pension reserves, securities and mortgages). The following equation uses these estimates:

Eq. 8 $\quad \text{Log } A_F = 0{\cdot}1915 + 1{\cdot}4238 \text{ Log } Y \quad R^2 = 0{\cdot}956$

Estimated by least squares with annual data 1948–58 from *Federal Reserve Bulletin.*

A_F is total financial assets of households

Y is DPI, current prices, billions of dollars.

The estimate of total financial assets at end-1945 from Eq. 8 is \$255·3 billions, which is \$109·8 billions less than the actual *FRB* figure of \$365·1 billions. This excess holding of assets is slightly higher than the higher estimate of excess savings based on Eqs. 1–3, but of a similar order of magnitude.

[1] Compare R. W. Goldsmith, *The National Wealth of the United States in the Postwar Period,* studies in capital formation and financing No. 10 for NBER, N.Y., Princeton University Press, 1962, Table B-24, p. 246.

Goldsmith *et al.* have also provided estimates of household wealth under the comprehensive balance sheet headings of tangibles, intangibles (including financial assets) liabilities and equity—the latter being assets less liabilities—together with a reconciliation of their estimates of financial assets with those of the *FRB*.[1] The main differences arise from the difficulty of separating households from noncorporate business and farms, although there are differences arising from different methods of estimation as well.[2] From Goldsmith's data for nonfarm households the following equations were estimated:

Eq. 9 $\text{Log } A_I = -0{\cdot}9501 + 1{\cdot}2741 \text{ Log } Y \quad R^2 = 0{\cdot}971$
Eq. 10 $\text{Log } A_T = -1{\cdot}0561 + 1{\cdot}2327 \text{ Log } Y \quad R^2 = 0{\cdot}995$
Eq. 11 $\text{Log } E = -0{\cdot}6086 + 1{\cdot}1617 \text{ Log } Y \quad R^2 = 0{\cdot}984$

Estimates by least squares with annual data 1948–58 from op. cit., Table III-1, p. 118.

A_I is intangible assets, i.e. cash, pension and insurance funds, mortgages, securities and equity in business.
A_T is tangible assets, i.e. residential and non-residential structures, land, producer and consumer durables.
E equity or net worth.
Y DPI.

From the equations the following estimates of excess asset holdings at the end of 1945 were derived.

	(1) *Actual*	(2) *Estimated from equation $ billion*	(3) *Excess holding* (1) – (2)
Tangible assets	200·1	248·1	−52·0
Intangible assets	422·6	354·2	68·4
Equity	592·2	573·4	18·8

These figures suggest that in the light of the income–wealth relation-

[1] R. W. Goldsmith and R. E. Lipsey, *Studies in the National Balance Sheet of the United States*, II, studies in capital formation and financing No. 11 for NBER, N.Y., Princeton University Press, 1963.
[2] Op. cit., pp. 17–21.

ships prevailing after 1948, the aggregate household balance sheet at the end of 1945 was characterized by a slight excess of equity (3 per cent) over what would have been normal at existing levels of income, and a large deficit of tangible assets offset by a large excess of intangibles. The excess of intangible assets of the order of $70 billion is less than either the higher estimate of excess personal savings, $95 billion, or the estimate of excess financial assets of $110 billions.

NOTE D

Demand For Automobiles and Housing at the End of The War

Chow [1960] has used a model of the demand for cars consisting of a demand function of the desired stock of cars, and an adjustment relation showing the proportion of the difference between desired and actual stock purchased as new cars in a given period. Suppose desired stock S'_t, depends on price, P_t, and income I_t. For example,

$$S'_t = a + bP_t + cI_t \qquad \text{(i)}$$

New purchases, C_t, are

$$C_t = d(S'_t - S_{t-1}) + (1 - k)S_{t-1}, \qquad \text{(ii)}$$

where $d(S'_t - S_{t-1})$ is the fraction of the desired change in the stock made during the unit period, and (1-k) S_{t-1} is the replacement demand. Chow estimates both of these equations, the first by approximating desired stock (which is not observable) by actual stock, the second by substituting (i) in (ii) to eliminate S'_t.

Chow supposes desired stock depends on the ratio of the price of cars to the general level of prices, and on real disposable income. Out of a number of alternative versions of the stock equation given by Chow two appear to fit the data best, op. cit., pp. 158–69. The first is Chow's equation $X1e'$:

Eq. 1 $X_t = -0{\cdot}7482 - 0{\cdot}048800\,P_t + 0{\cdot}025526\,I_{et}$
$\qquad\qquad\qquad\qquad (0{\cdot}003553) \qquad (0{\cdot}001171)$

$R^2 = 0{\cdot}943$ $S = 0{\cdot}591$ Calculated by least squares for 1920–57 excluding 1942–46.

X_t is actual stock of cars per head (representing desired stock per head) expressed as new car units, i.e. as a sum of weighted numbers in each age group, the weights being the average prices of the cars in the age groups. (The rate of depreciation plus scrappage varies little from year to year, being approximately 0·25, and the stock measure can be regarded as an index of the consumption of car services.)

P_t is deflated average price of cars.

I_{et} is expected disposable personal income per head in 1937 dollars, calculated as a weighted average of current and the last seven years income.

The second equation, 1*e*′, is

$$\text{Eq. 2} \quad \text{Log}\, P_t = -6{\cdot}4988 - \underset{(0{\cdot}0544)}{1{\cdot}0600}\, \text{Log}\, X_t + \underset{(0{\cdot}0965)}{2{\cdot}1187}\, \text{Log}\, I_{et}$$

$R^2 = 0{\cdot}947$ $S = 0{\cdot}0988$ Calculated by least squares for 1920–57 from natural logarithms of the data.

The price and income elasticities implied by these equations are

	Price elasticity	*Income elasticity*
Eq. 1 (from means)	−0·74	1·83
Eq. 2	−0·94	2·00

Substitution of the 1942–46 values of P_t and I_{et} in Eq. 1 gives estimated values of X_t considerably below the actual values (in some cases negative) suggesting that the wartime behaviour pattern of demand and price formation differed significantly from the pre- and postwar pattern. Eq. 1 has been used to estimate the postwar demand for car stocks, although Eq. 2 gives roughly similar results.[1]

Chow's best equation explaining new car purchases, 4*S*′, is

$$\text{Eq.3}\ X_t' = -0.07391 - \underset{(0{\cdot}002603)}{0{\cdot}020218}\, P_t + \underset{(0{\cdot}001050)}{0{\cdot}011875}\, I_{dt} - \underset{(0{\cdot}04216)}{0{\cdot}22130}\, X_{t-1}$$

[1] Both Eqs. 1 and 2 present problems of identification and an explicit treatment in the model of price formation would be desirable. The absence of serial correlation is doubtful, according to Chow, p. 163.

$R^2 = 0{\cdot}880$ $S = 0{\cdot}307$ Calculated by least squares for 1920–57 excluding 1942–46.

X_t' is new cars purchased per head

I_{dt} is disposable personal income in 1937 dollars.

Expected income did not give as good a fit. At the means the price elasticity is $-0{\cdot}63$ and the income elasticity $1{\cdot}70$. The proportion of the difference between desired and actual stock purchased in one year is 0·48.

Suits' explorations tend to confirm Chow's results, although their models differ in details and as they stand cannot be compared precisely.[1] Suits' best comparable equation ([1961], p. 67, eq. (2)) is

Eq.4
$$\text{Log}\,\frac{R}{H} = \underset{(\cdot 173)}{1{\cdot}704}\left(\text{Log}\,\frac{Y}{H} - 1500\right) - \underset{(\cdot 195)}{\cdot 657}\,\text{Log}\,\frac{P}{M} - \underset{(\cdot\ 38)}{1{\cdot}156}\,\text{Log}\,\frac{S}{H} + \text{const.}$$

$R^2 = 0{\cdot}89$. Calculated by least squares for 1929–56, excluding 1942–48.

R is retail sales

H is population

Y is disposable personal income in 1947–49 dollars.

$\frac{Y}{H} - 1500$ 'supernumery income' after allowance for expenditures on 'essentials' has been made, the figure of 1500 being determined experimentally to give the best fit.

P/M is ratio of retail price to number of months duration of average credit contract.

S is the unweighted stock of cars.

The income elasticity implied in this equation is 2·88, higher than any estimated by Chow. Suits also found there was a significant difference between prewar and postwar behaviour, and that the error

[1] D. B. Suits, 'The demand for new automobiles in the United States 1929–1956', *R. econ. Statist.*, XL, August, 1958, pp. 273–80, and Suits, 'Exploring alternative formulations of automobile demand', *R. Econ. Statist.*, XLIII, February, 1961, pp. 66–69.

of failing to take account of the age distribution of the stock of cars was relatively minor.

Eq. 3 above (by Chow) gives a good estimate of new purchases in 1947 (the difference between estimated and actual values is less than one standard error) and an even better estimate for 1946 (of which year the data were not included in the regression). The results are:

New car purchases per 100 *persons*

	Estimate of Eq. 3	*Actual*
1946	1·128	1·283*
1947	1·973	2·198†

* New registrations, *SCB.*
† Chow, [1960].

Muth applies a similar stock adjustment model to the housing market.[1] He distinguishes the short run level of house prices and rents, determined by the current demand for accommodation and the stock of houses, relatively fixed, from the long run equilibrium level necessary to induce owners of structures to maintain the stock given level of incomes, cost of construction and interest rates. As in the automobile model, the discrepancy between desired and actual stock determines the rate of construction.[2] Muth's most useful equation, op. cit. (10) p. 49, similar to Eq. 3 above is

Eq. 5
$$h'g = \underset{(0{\cdot}589)}{-2{\cdot}49p} + \underset{(0{\cdot}0919)}{0{\cdot}438y_p} \underset{(4{\cdot}47)}{-8{\cdot}34r} - \underset{(0{\cdot}0695)}{0{\cdot}282h_{-1}} + \text{const.}$$

$R^2 = 0{\cdot}621$. Calculated by least squares from 1915–41, omitting 1917 and 1918.

$h'g$ is gross rate of nonfarm residential construction in 1935–39 construction in 1935–39 construction dollars per head of non-farm population.

p is ratio of construction cost index to consumer price index.

[1] R. F. Muth, 'The demand for non-farm housing', in *The Demand for Durable Goods*, ed. A. Harberger, University of Chicago Press, 1960.

[2] The short run determinants of housing starts are discussed in Note J.

y_p is expected disposable personal income (defined as for Chow) in 1935–39 dollars per head of nonfarm population.

r is the yield on ten year old bonds.

h is the end of year stock of housing at 1935–39 construction prices per head of nonfarm population. These housing stock estimates are based on Grebler, Blank and Winnick [1956] who provide estimates through 1953, but the postwar estimates were considered too unreliable to be used.

Muth also attempts to estimate the short run demand for accommodation in the form of an explanation of changes in rents, op. cit. (26) p. 64. His equation is

$$\text{Eq. 6} \quad R = \underset{(0{\cdot}0414)}{-0{\cdot}0875h} + \underset{(0{\cdot}0426)}{0{\cdot}121y_p} + \text{const.}$$

$R^2 = 0{\cdot}302$. Calculated by least squares from 1915–41, excluding 1917 and 1918.

R is the NICB rent index.

Neither Eqs. 5 nor 6 are very good forecasting equations. Eq. 5 explains only 62 per cent of the variation in the new construction series, while Eq. 6 explains only 30 per cent of the variation in rents. Furthermore, in each equation the residuals are probably serially correlated. There is, however, a general consistency about Muth's various price and income elasticity estimates. These are summarized in the table below (taken from Muth's Table 4, p. 72).

Summary of housing demand elasticities

Model	*Price*	*Income*	*Interest rate*
Demand for stock,			
Eq. 4	−0·904	0·879	−0·131
95% confidence limits	(−0·421; −1·80)	(0·538; 1·42)	
limits from alternative regressions	(−0·669; −1·60)	(0·652; 1·17)	
Demand for accommodation			
Eq. 5	−1·47	0·935	

The case for assuming the price and income elasticities are in the region of unity is strong. The elasticities derived from Eq. 5 have been used to estimate the desired stock of housing per head in 1946. The estimate and the data are as follows:

	h	y_p	p	r
1941	727	594	113·7	1·88
1945	616			
1946	798	687	120·4	1·61
% change 1941 to 1946	9·8	14·7	5·9	−14·1

Source: Muth, [1960], Tables B1 and B4

except: h 1945: Grebler *et al.*, [1956], Table 360, with non-farm population interpolated from Table 23, adjusted to 1935–39 prices.
y_p 1946: 1941 value extrapolated by Chow, [1960], Table 1, I_{et}.
r 1946: 1941 extrapolated by Moody's corporate average bond yield, *SCB*.

NOTE E

The Stock of Business Plant and Equipment

This note explains the method of estimating the desired capital stock figures given above in Table 2.5, p. 74. The method is based on the work of Hickman [1965] who uses a relatively simple model of annual fixed investment, similar in essentials to the more sophisticated quarterly models described in Note I. The quarterly models are useful in analyzing changes in the rate of investment in the years 1948 to 1950 (and later in the 1950s and 1960s), but for the immediate postwar years Hickman's annual model seems preferable largely because its treatment of the lag structure is simpler.

The desired stock of capital depends on expected long term or normal levels of output and relative prices, and on the state of the industrial arts which can be represented by a point on a time trend, i.e., in logarithmic linear form

$$\text{Log}\, K'_t = \text{Log}\, a_1 + a_2\, \text{Log}\, Y'_t + a_3\, \text{Log}\, P'_t + a_4 T \qquad \text{(i)}$$

where K' is desired capital stock, Y' and P' are expected output and relative prices, and T is a time trend. Log a_1 is a constant term depending on the units of measurement of the variables. a_2 and a_3 are the constant elasticity of desired capital with respect to output and price. a_4 measures the effect of the average rate of technical progress upon the desired stock of capital.

The short run (annual) demand for plant and equipment, which is the response to a discrepancy between desired capital, K'_t, and actual stock, K_{t-1}, depends on an adjustment equation

$$\frac{K_t}{K_{t-1}} = \left(\frac{K'_t}{K_{t-1}}\right)^b ; o < b \leqslant 1 \qquad \text{(ii)}$$

A.B.C—16

where the adjustment constant, b, represents the proportion of the percentage discrepancy eliminated during year t.

The values of the coefficients Log a_1, a_2, a_3 a_4 and b can be estimated from the equation obtained by substituting (i) in (ii):

$$\text{Log } K_t = b \text{ Log } a_1 + ba_2 \text{ Log } Y'_t + ba_3 \text{ Log } P'_t + ba_4 T + (1 - b) \text{ Log } K_{t-1} \quad \text{(iii)}$$

Equation (iii) is the form Hickman uses in studying business plant and equipment. In his aggregate version P'_t is omitted (relative prices do not have a significant influence in the regressions) and expected output is measured as a weighted geometric average of current and past output, i.e.

$$a_2 \text{ Log } Y'_t = a_{21} \text{ Log } Y_t + a_{22} \text{ Log } Y_{t-1} \quad \text{(iv)}$$

Preliminary regressions suggested that the fit of equation (iii) would be improved if a value of unity were imposed on a_2 (implying constant returns to scale). This is done in the equation which Hickman presents as his best for aggregate business investment, op. cit., Table 5, p. 56, All Industries:

$$\begin{aligned} \text{Eq. 1 Log } K_t - \text{Log } K_{t-1} = \; & \underset{(0{\cdot}0018)}{0{\cdot}0337} + \underset{(0{\cdot}0142)}{0{\cdot}1236} (\text{Log } Y_t - \text{Log } K_{t-1}) \\ & + \underset{(0{\cdot}0157)}{0{\cdot}1141} (\text{Log } Y_{t-1} - \text{Log } K_{t-1}) \\ & - \underset{(0{\cdot}0001)}{0{\cdot}0018T} \end{aligned}$$

$R^2 = 0{\cdot}919$. Durbin-Watson statistic is 2·48. All coefficients significant at 0·01 level. Calculated by least squares for 1949–60.

The equation and data refer to all industries included in the GNP definition of the business sector, excluding mining (but not petroleum extraction) and real estate. Government enterprises are included.

K_t is net depreciated value of stock of plant and equipment, end of year, 1954 prices.

Y_t is gross output, 1954 prices; i.e. GNP less gross output of general government, households and institutions, rest of world and industries listed above.

T is time in units of a year; 1949 = 1.

From Eq. 1, we find the equation for desired stock of capital is

$$\text{Log } K'_t = 0{\cdot}1418 + 0{\cdot}5200 \text{ Log } Y_t + 0{\cdot}4800 \text{ Log } Y_{t-1} - 0{\cdot}0076\, T \quad \text{(v)}$$

and $b = 0{\cdot}2377$. Thus the influence of current and lagged output on desired stock are nearly equal, about one-quarter of the difference, $K'_t - K_{t-1}$, is repaired during year t, and the trend rate of decline in desired rate of stock is 1·8 per cent per annum.

Hickman presents similar results for the individual industries. That for total manufacturing, op. cit., Table 5, p. 56, is:

$$\text{Log } K'_t = -0{\cdot}0716 + 0{\cdot}4130 \text{ Log } Y_t + 0{\cdot}5870 \text{ Log } Y_{t-1} + 0{\cdot}0019\, T - 0{\cdot}0005\, T^2 \quad \text{(vi)}$$

and $b = 0{\cdot}3702$. The basic regression from which this equation is derived has $R^2 = 0{\cdot}954$ and all coefficients except that of T are significant at the 0·01 level. Note that the term with T^2 implies that the rate of technical progress accelerates.

The estimates of desired stock in Table 2.5 above (p. 74) are derived directly from equations (v) and (vi). In estimating desired stock for 1946 it is assumed that $Y_t = Y_{t-1}$. In both equations the trend terms are neglected. The 1946 gross output (all Industries \$220·1 billion; Manufacturing \$79·4 billion) was derived from *SCB* August 1965, Table 12, deflated by Business GNP price index from *SCB* February 1966, pp. 18–19. The estimates of desired short run change in capital,

$b\,(\text{Log } K'_t - \text{Log } K_{t-1})$, and actual change in capital, $\text{Log } K_t - \text{Log } K_{t-1}$, agree as follows (the changes are converted to percentages):

Per cent Increase in Capital

	All Industries		*Manufacturing*	
	Desired Shortrun	*Actual*	*Desired Shortrun*	*Actual*
1946	6·4	6·1	10·6	14·4
1947	5·3	6·6	6·7	11·1
1948	4·5	5·3	5·4	8·1
1949	3·4	3·0	2·4	2·7

Assets of non-financial corporations

The asset–income relationships referred to on p. 75 are

Eq. 2 $A_T = -60{\cdot}072 + 2{\cdot}657X \quad R^2 = 0{\cdot}963$

Eq. 3 $A_I = -61{\cdot}243 + 1{\cdot}583X \quad R^2 = 0{\cdot}922$

Eq. 4 $E = -69{\cdot}583 + 2{\cdot}760X \quad R^2 = 0.953$

Estimated by least squares from annual data 1947–58

A_T is tangible assets, A_I is intangible assets and E is equity or net worth, from Goldsmith *et al.* [1963] II, Table III-4.

X is non-financial corporate income from *SCB*, September 1963, p. 53, Table 3, line 20. 1945 figure is $78·4 billion estimated from total corporate income.

NOTE F

Inventory Investment in Durable and Nondurable Goods, 1945 and 1946

Official constant price quarterly estimates of inventory investment for durable and nondurable goods industries are available only from 1947. Estimates for farm and nonfarm investment in 1945 and 1946 are given in Table A.1 of Note A. To get a rough estimate of quarterly changes divided between durable and nondurable goods industries I have deflated the book value of inventories at the end of each quarter with indexes of prices at the end of the quarter, and have used the resulting quarter to quarter changes. This simple process does not of course remove all the effects on inventory valuation of price changes, and to form an idea of the reliability of the results, they have been compared with the official estimates for 1947.[1]

Estimates based on deflated book values are given in Table F.1 and are compared with the official figures in Fig. F.1.

TABLE F.I: *Nonfarm Inventory Investment 1945 and 1946 $ billion, 1958 prices. Seasonally adjusted at annual rates*

	Durable	*Nondurable*
1945 II	−0·1	2·2
III	−4·9	2·0
IV	−4·7	−0·2
1946 I	6·7	11·8
II	6·0	2·2
III	5·3	8·8
IV	−0·2	−3·7

[1] My rough estimates include only manufacturing and trade, while the official estimates include also mining.

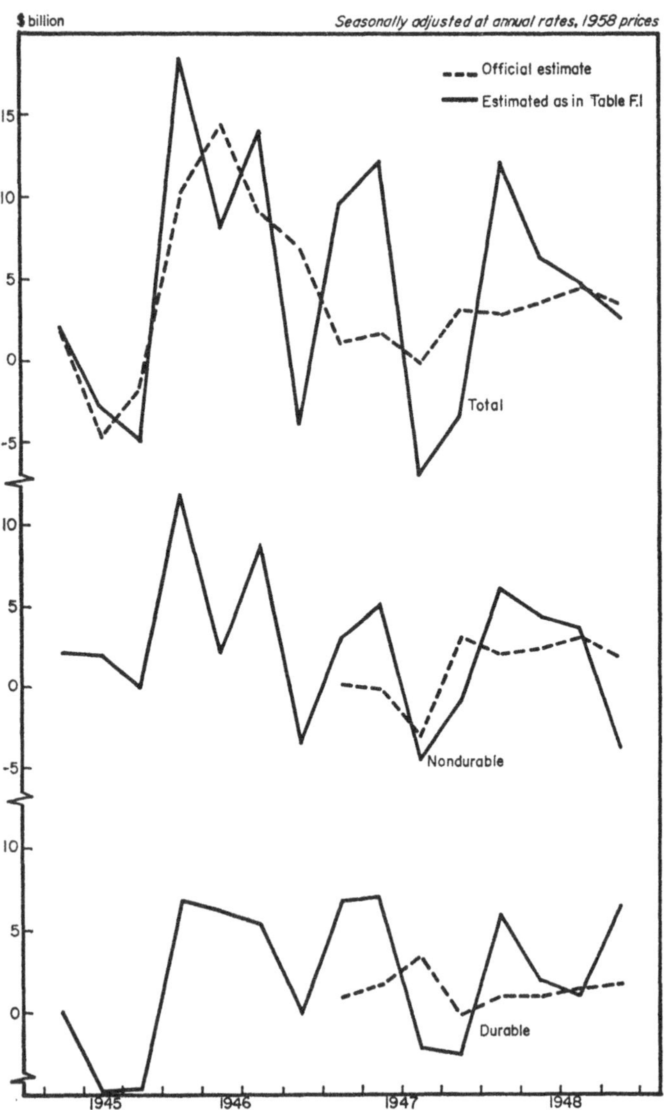

Fig. F.1: Change in nonfarm inventories, 1945–48.
Source: SCB and Table F.1.

The former give a \$9·2 billion change in nonfarm inventories for 1946 as a whole, compared to the official estimate of \$10·2 billion. The nondurable goods estimates give a good correspondence in 1947–48, but that for durable goods is poor. The fit for total nonfarm appears good for 1945–46 but poor in 1947–48. On the evidence there seems no reason to doubt that both durables and nondurables experienced a restocking boom in mid-1946 which for nondurables tended to decline later that year and early 1947. It appears that the sharp fall in investment in the book value series in 1946 IV is spurious. If the nondurable book value series with an interpolated value of zero for 1946 IV is subtracted from the nonfarm series, the resulting 'durable' series looks plausible, being

	\$ *billion*
1946 I	1·4
II	12·5
III	6·5
IV	10·2

The details of estimation are as follows. Official seasonally adjusted book values of manufacturing and trade inventories, classified into durable and nondurable goods, are published from January 1946. 1945 unadjusted book values were adjusted using 1946 seasonal factors. The two groups were deflated with the BLS wholesale price indexes for durable and nondurable goods. The figures in Table F.1 are quarterly changes at annual rates.

NOTE G

A Quarterly Consumption Function, 1948-50

In Chapter 4, pp. 116–17, the Modigliani-Ando model using long run and short run consumption functions was used to explain changes in consumption per head from 1948 to 1950. In this note the changes are interpreted econometrically, using the DEF function which is shown in Note B to describe the same ideas as lie behind the Modigliani–Ando model. The function used is

$$\frac{c_t}{y_{t-1}} = \alpha + \beta\frac{y_{t-1}}{y^0_{t-1}} + \gamma\frac{c_{t-1}}{y_{t-2}} + \delta\frac{c_{t-2}}{y_{t-3}}$$

where c is PCE per head

y is DPI per head

y^0 is previous highest DPI per head, regarded as a proxy variable for wealth or permanent expected income.

When income changes at a constant rate, r (which may be zero), the marginal—and average—propensity to consume out of last quarter's income, $\frac{c_t}{y_{t-1}}$, will tend towards a long term level, $\frac{\alpha + \beta(1 + r)}{1 - \gamma - \delta}$, and any initial displacement from this level or temporary alteration in the change in income will be followed by fluctuations about the long term level the nature of which will depend on the values of γ and δ.

At any point in time the value of the marginal propensity depends on two factors: the first is slow response, and it is measured by:

$$\gamma\frac{c_{t-1}}{y_{t-2}} + \delta\frac{c_{t-2}}{y_{t-3}}$$

which is a weighted average of recent propensities; the second I call resistance and measure it by

$$\alpha + \beta \frac{y_{t-1}}{y^0_{t-1}} \qquad (\beta < o)$$

which implies that if income falls the marginal propensity will rise, and will remain at a higher level as long as income is below its previous peak level. As income rises again the propensity will decline and once the previous peak level is reached remains unchanged for constant rate of growth of income.

That is to say, if we consider only income and the resistance factor, when income grows at a constant rate the marginal propensity will be constant and consumption will rise. Any acceleration in the growth of income will result in an offsetting fall in the propensity, while any reduction in the rate of growth or decline in income will lead to offsetting increases in the propensity. In terms of the Modigliani–Ando model, the constant proportionality between income and consumption for a constant rate of growth of income represents the long run consumption function, while the offsetting changes in the marginal propensity in response to fluctuations in the rate of change of income represent the short run function.

The equation fitted to quarterly data 1948 I to 1952 I gave the result

$$\alpha = 1{\cdot}0629 \qquad \bar{R}^2 = 0{\cdot}786$$
$$\beta = -0{\cdot}9470\ (0{\cdot}1400)$$
$$\gamma = 0{\cdot}2968\ (0{\cdot}1253)$$
$$\delta = 0{\cdot}5695\ (0{\cdot}1284)$$

Standard errors are in brackets. The values of γ and δ show that a change in income will be followed by a damped, but oscillating, movement of $\frac{c_t}{y_{t-1}}$ converging on the value determined by the resistance factor. The movement would be lengthy, not much more than one-tenth of the change taking place in the first quarter. β is negative as expected. The long run marginal propensity is 0·867, which is lower, but considering the sampling errors is not significantly lower, than the long term estimate of 0·91 based on period 1948 I to 1964 IV (see note B, p. 227).

In Fig. G.1 the analysis using the econometric results is illustrated in terms of changes in the marginal propensity, $\frac{c_t}{y_{t-1}}$. It can be compared with Fig. 4.2, p. 116, which explains the same data using explicit shifts in a short period function. *oo'* represents the normal consumption function of 1947–50. The rise in income between 1948 I to 1948 III resulted in the function falling to *op*. The following fall in income to 1949 I caused the function to rise. The slowness of consumers' responses to change in income allowed the function to rise only to *oq* by the time income stopped falling but during the following year to 1949 IV while income remained unchanged the function gradually returned to the original position *oo'*. The NSLI dividend in 1950 I resulted in a temporary decline in the function to *or* followed in the next quarter by a return to normal. By this time the Korean War had broken out.

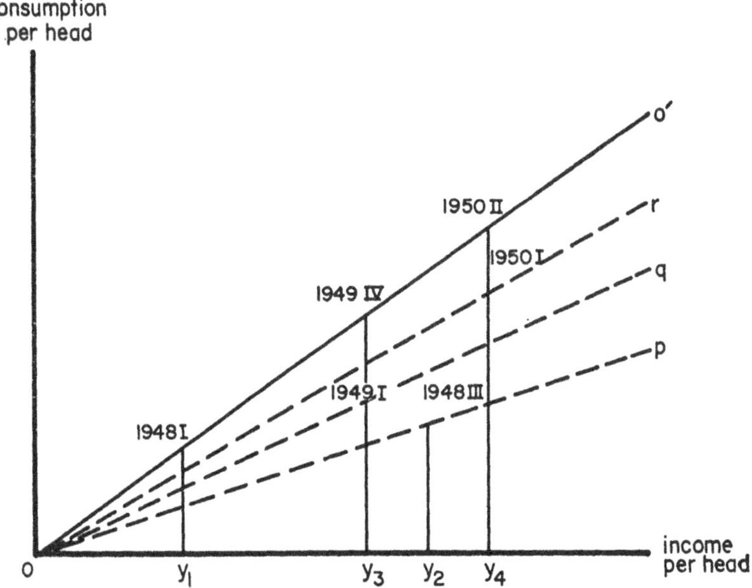

Fig. G.1: Changes in short run consumption, 1948–50.

These changes are analysed quantitatively in Fig. G.2. Line *a* is income per head (lagged a quarter), line *b* is the resistance factor,

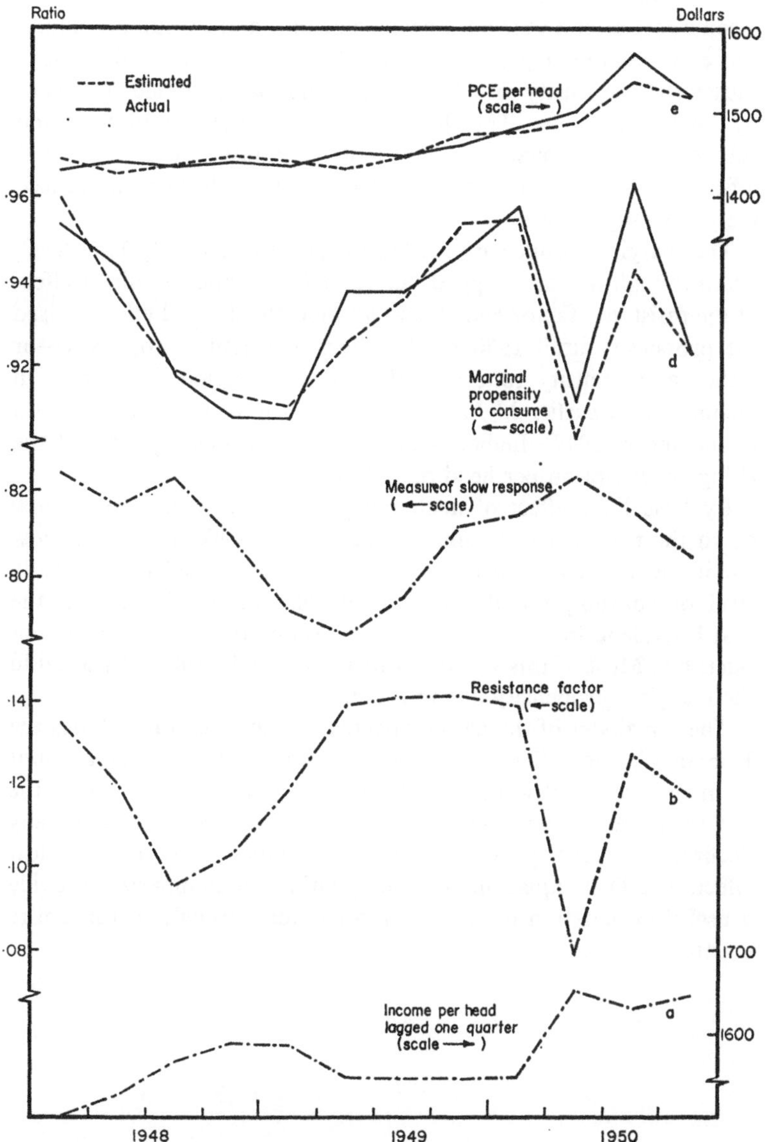

Fig. G.2: Explanation of estimated changes in consumption, 1948–50.

line *c* is the measure of slow response. From 1948 I to 1948 III income rose after a year during which income and consumption (and hence the marginal propensity) had been fairly stable. Resistance caused the propensity to fall, delayed at first but prolonged to 1949 I by the slow response. The check to the income rise in 1948 IV and subsequent fall reversed the effect of resistance, which in 1949 II offset the continued slow response to the earlier changes and caused the propensity to rise.

The marginal propensity started to return to its early 1948 level, and although income stopped falling in 1949 I and the direct effect of the resistance factor ended next quarter, the delayed effects raised the propensity until 1950 I. The effect of a rising propensity—or rather a propensity returning after a short period fluctuation in income to its earlier higher level—combined with the steady level of income in 1949—higher than that of early 1948—produced the rising consumption per head of 1949 II to 1950 I.

By 1950 I the effect of unchanging income was starting to slow down the rise in the marginal propensity. It is likely that the slow rise in incomes commencing at that time would have led to a steady level of consumption if no accidents had occurred. Instead, the NSLI dividend in the first half of 1950 raised income per head considerably. Most of this was offset in 1950 II and 1950 III by a fall in the marginal propensity due to resistance.

The remainder of the period covered by the equation includes the Korean War and effects on household behaviour not taken account of in the econometric model. However it is useful to note that the rise in incomes after 1949 led, as we would expect, to a gradually declining marginal propensity as the resistance factor had its slow effect. The DEF equation and the hypothesis it summarizes provide a useful explanation of consumer behaviour throughout this entire eventful period.

NOTE H

The Automobile Market, 1945-50

At the end of the war in August 1945 it has been estimated that to get car prices back to a prewar relationship with other prices and incomes would have required 9½ million new cars, about three times the annual output of 1940–41. This demand would have been inflated by any post 1945 growth in incomes as well as replacement demand (which on prewar experience would be about one-quarter of the stock a year or some 3 million cars in 1946). Any failure of prices to return to prewar relationships due to for example a rise in manufacturing costs would reduce the demand.[1] The events of the five years after the end of the war can be summarized as follows. By the end of 1950 20·4 million cars had been produced for the domestic market:

	Factory sales: domestic *millions*
1946	2·005
1947	3·297
1948	3·676
1949	4·951
1950	6·512

The relative price of automobiles (price index of cars divided by general price index) with 1937 = 100, was 449 in 1945. It fell rapidly at first to 339 in 1946 and 263 in 1947, then a slower fall to 236 in 1948. In 1949 however when output rose to nearly 5 million cars the index declined to 160 at which level it stayed in 1950 and 1951.

[1] The wartime conditions and the demand for cars at the end of 1945 are discussed above on pp. 70–2 and Note D.

In view of the fact that the relative price of cars dropped only slightly after 1952,[1] and in the light of other evidence referred to below, it seems that the car market by the end of 1950 had returned to a state of equilibrium where the level of prices prevailing equated long term demand and supply as these were regarded at that time. Of course the Korean War led to a period of further shortages in 1951 and 1952, but all the evidence suggests that in the absence of the war the market would have been in equilibrium at the end of 1950 or in early 1951 at the latest. The long period of time before equilibrium was reached was due to production difficulties: partly labour problems and severe strikes, but more importantly material shortages in which steel was dominant. The big increase in output in 1949 and 1950 came only when the level of activity in other parts of the economy receded and steel supplies became plentiful. Between the end of 1945 and end 1948 the capacity of the industry, as measured by capital invested, rose by 50 per cent, but capacity is not in general regarded as a factor limiting output over the period. Capacity was not increased in 1949, and rose only slightly in 1950.[2]

Although automobile manufacturers had started to prepare for car production early in 1945, less than 70,000 cars were produced in 1945, and for nearly a year after the actual end of the war strikes and shortages severely frustrated attempts to expand output. It was not until the beginning of July 1946 that all car manufacturers were producing at the same time and in that month output was 209,000 cars (average monthly output in 1941 had been 315,000). There was a strike against General Motors which lasted from November 21, 1945 to the end of March 1946, and a steel strike which started on January 21st and dragged on until April when production was hampered by coal strikes. Strikes in component industries—like plate glass in May and nuts, bolts and screws in July—continued through 1946. The upshot of the labour difficulties was that the industry produced in the first half of 1946 less than one-third of what it had intended.

After July output increased and in 1946 IV over 800 thousand cars were made. But by now material and component capacity shortages were becoming apparent. Not only was sheet steel in short supply but lead, copper, leather and burlap were needed. Furthermore it

[1] See Table 2.4, p. 71.

[2] See B. G. Hickman, [1965], Table B4, p. 230.

became apparent that these shortages were not going to be removed in 1947. Output of cars rose to over 300,000 in April but declined in mid-year as steel shortages forced plants to close down. In August 1947 General Motors halted production for lack of steel and the situation was serious enough for some car makers—including Ford—to start making their own steel. Production rose again at the end of the year, reaching particularly high rates from November to January.

The state of the market was such that dealers were able to sell 1946 and 1947 model cars for several hundred dollars above the manufacturers' list prices for new vehicles. There were reports in late 1947 of buyer resistance to high prices, which we can take to indicate that the price mechanism was performing its rationing function. The ending of controls over consumer credit on November 1, 1947, was expected by dealers to cause an increase in sales which did rise substantially in 1947 IV and again in 1948 I. It is likely however that the major influence was the large increase in supplies of new cars which rose by 20 per cent between 1947 III and 1948 I.[1]

In early 1948 there was considerable uncertainty amongst used car dealers and financial commentators about the future of the market. However despite some gloomy predictions that the bottom would drop out of the used car market, prices did not fall very greatly and demand continued unchecked. Shortages of steel persisted and output of cars fell in May as a consequence of a strike against Chrysler. In August the Automobile Dealers Association estimated that there were 7·3 million unfilled orders and that it would take 26 months to catch up on current rates of production.[2] In the prevailing concern about inflation the state of the car market loomed large. Criticisms of exorbitant profiteering by dealers were widespread and Congressional investigations of the situation were begun. In September controls were reimposed over instalment buying as part of the anti-inflation measures passed by Congress. The opinion of dealers was that downpayments were already so high that the regulations would have little effect. There is no sign in the registration or sales figures of any check to buying, although there

[1] There was a fall in new registrations in November and a rise in December which may have represented buyers delaying purchases in expectation of reduced down-payments, but as Rendigs Fels has pointed out to me the effect of the ending of controls was probably to raise dealers' margins.

[2] *NYT* August 31, 1948 (26:3).

were reports of a fall in prices. Insofar as this was true it was probably due to the great rise in output that now commenced and went on into 1950.

Between 1948 II and 1948 IV output of cars rose by over 25 per cent, partly due to recovery from strikes, partly to larger supplies of steel. Between 1948 IV and 1949 III—before the effect of the steel strike in October—output rose another 25 per cent. Behind this 1949 jump lay a complete reversal of the sheet steel situation. Demand by other users eased off in November and December 1948 and scrap prices started to fall. With this big increase in supplies prices in all parts of the automobile market started to fall: prices of new and used cars, and dealers' margins. Not once during 1949 was there any flagging in the volume of sales as long as prices were falling. The easing supply situation did however cause changes in the trade. By October it was reported that 30 per cent of the 40,000 used car dealers in 1948 were no longer in business.[1] As early as January 1949 there were complaints from manufacturers that the consumer credit controls were affecting sales. In March and April the Federal Reserve Board extended the repayment period and in June the restrictions were completely removed. Again there is no firm evidence that the succeeding rise in sales was due to the removal of controls—sales maintained the growth begun earlier.

By the middle of 1949 it was becoming apparent that a strike was in prospect in the steel industry due to failures to reach agreement over wage increases. After several months of negotiation the steel workers' union struck on October 1st, and steel production ceased for six weeks. Business had been forewarned by the lengthy negotiations and inventories of steel had been accumulated by most users, including automobile manufacturers. Car production was consequently maintained in October, but fell substantially in November and December. In 1949 III 1·5 million cars were made; in 1949 IV only 1·1 million. By December, however, steel output was flowing again, and car production rose in January. Full production by all manufacturers was delayed in 1950 I by strikes in the industry: nevertheless 1·3 million cars were made. The biggest increase, however, came in 1950 II and in June alone the industry made 721,000 cars for the domestic market.

Opinion in the industry in February, 1950, was that at last a

[1] *Fortune*, October 1949, p. 15.

buyers' market had reappeared and there was vigorous competition for the first time since 1941. Used car prices had fallen substantially and dealers were attempting to trim their new car inventories. A General Motors economist was reported to have said that by mid-year the war deferred demand for automobiles would be met.[1]

The first effect of the outbreak of the Korean War was to increase demand for cars. Consumer purchases in 1950 III rose to the record level of \$15·8 billions—a rise of 22 per cent above the previous quarter. Business purchases rose similarly. Output in the third quarter also broke all records—1·9 million cars for the domestic market compared with 1·7 million the quarter before (although the June month rate of output was not surpassed). At the end of July, despite this huge volume of production, signs were on hand of a shortage of cars as prices and unfilled orders rose. By August the effect of growing industrial demand and rearmament in particular was causing material shortages to appear. Copper, aluminium and tin were causing concern, but not sheet steel as yet. Controls over instalment credit were once again reimposed on September 18th, and were tightened again at the end of October. There was a general complaint that these controls were effective. The fall in sales in the final quarter of the year bears out the complaint, although some part of the fall must have been caused by the premature satisfying of demand the previous quarter. From July until November the rate of output maintained a high and steady level, starting its year long fall in December. By this final quarter of the year the automobile industry was back once again into the mesh of war production and controls, but not before it had restored—or had come very close to restoring—equilibrium in the car market for the first time in nearly a decade.[2]

[1] *Newsweek*, February 27, 1950, p. 58.

[2] The statements made in this Note have been based on a wide variety of sources, including in particular the *New York Times*, *Newsweek* and *Fortune*.

NOTE I

Determinants of Quarterly Business Fixed Investment

The most useful and reliable econometric models of business investment behaviour are based on one or other versions of the acceleration principle for which Jorgenson has given a derivation from neo-classical production theory.[1] Briefly, Jorgenson's procedure is to maximize the net worth of a firm, subject to a standard neo-classical production function, obtaining the condition among others that the marginal product of capital equals the ratio of user cost of capital to price of output.[2]

In general this will imply that the desired stock of capital depends on the expected level of output, the price of output and user cost, amongst other factors. In the special case of a Cobb–Douglas function used by Jorgenson, capital is proportional to the value of output deflated by user cost, i.e.

$$K' = a\frac{pX}{c} \tag{i}$$

where K' is desired stock of capital

[1] D. W. Jorgenson, 'Anticipations and investment behaviour', in *The Brookings Quarterly Econometric Model of the United States*, ed. J. S. Duesenberry *et al.*, North Holland, Amsterdam, 1965, pp. 35–92.

[2] User cost, the rental of a unit of capital service per period of time, depends on the price of capital goods (q), the rate of interest (r), the rate of depreciation (d), the rate of tax on net income (u), the rate of capital loss ($-\dot{q}/q$), and the proportions chargeable for tax purposes against income of depreciation (v), cost of capital (w) and capital loss (x) according to the formula

$$c = q\left\{\left[\frac{1-uv}{1-u}\right]d + \left[\frac{1-uw}{1-u}\right]r - \left[\frac{1-ux}{1-u}\right]\frac{\dot{q}}{q}\right\}$$

X is output
p is price of output
c is user cost of capital
and a is the elasticity of output with respect to capital.

The ratio of capital to output is thus $a\frac{p}{c}$ i.e. the product of the output elasticity and the 'real' price of output. This model is essentially an accelerator model, with explicit allowance for price changes incorporating changes in tax rates, interest rates, etc., through their effect on user cost.

The next step in Jorgenson's analysis is common to most theories of investment. Time elapses between the initiation of an investment project and its completion—there is the planning, the appropriation of funds, the letting of contracts, the issuing of orders as well as the actual investment. Suppose that the distribution of times to completion of new projects is fixed, so that the proportion of new projects commenced now completed in an interval of time is given. Then investment now in new projects is a weighted average of past starts, and if it is assumed that starts are made as long as the actual stock is less than the desired stock, then investment in new projects is a weighted average of past desired stocks of capital. If, furthermore, it is assumed that replacement investment is proportional to the capital stock, gross investment at time t, I_t, can be written as

$$I_t = \frac{[1 - \tau]w(\tau)}{1 - \tau w(\tau)}[K' - K_{t-1}] + dK_{t-1} \qquad \text{(ii)}$$

or,

$$I_t = w(\tau)[K'_t - K'_{t-1}] + dK_{t-1} \qquad \text{(iii)}$$

where d is the replacement proportion (or rate of depreciation), K_t is the actual stock of capital at t, and $w(\tau)$ is a power series in the lag operator τ. Substituting (i) in (iii) we have

$$I_t = w(\tau)\left[a\frac{p_t X_t}{c_t} - a\frac{p_{t-1}X_{t-1}}{c_{t-1}}\right] + dK_{t-1} \qquad \text{(iv)}$$

or, more concisely,

$$I_t = aw(\tau)\Delta\overline{X}_t + dK_{t-1}$$

where

$$\Delta\overline{X}_t = \frac{p_t X_t}{c_t} - \frac{p_{t-1}X_{t-1}}{c_{t-1}} \qquad \text{(v)}$$

One important special case arises when the lag function is distributed geometrically (the sequence of weights declines geometrically) so that

$$w(\tau) = \frac{1 - s}{1 - s\tau}. \qquad \text{Then}$$

$$I_t = (1 - s)[a\bar{X}_t - K_{t-1}] + dK_{t-1} \qquad \text{(vi)}$$

which is the flexible accelerator or capacity model of Chenery.[1] As is explained in Note E, I used this model in the version developed by Hickman [1965] to explain annual business fixed investment in 1946 and 1947. Note C describes how the model can explain investment in consumer durable goods.

This geometrically distributed lag function is a special case of general Pascal distributed lag functions, whose power series is rational, i.e. a ratio of polynomials in the lag operator τ, implying that the function can be written with finite lags in both independent and dependent variables. Investment equations of the type of equation (v) with Pascal lag functions have been explored by Jorgenson. A general interpretation is as follows: let

$$w(\tau) = \frac{\gamma(\tau)}{\mu(\tau)}$$

Then

$$\mu(\tau)[I_t - dK_{t-1}] = a\gamma(\tau)\Delta\bar{X}_t \qquad \text{(vii)}$$

which is a difference equation[2] with a solution of the form

$$[I_t - dK_{t-1}] = Y(t) + \sum A_i\lambda_i^t \qquad \text{(viii)}$$

where the λs are the roots of the auxiliary equation, the A's are constants depending upon the μ's, and $Y(t)$ is the particular solution, giving the trend of net investment, and determined by a $\gamma(\tau)\Delta\bar{X}_t$. Thus net investment will fluctuate about a path determined by the changes in deflated output, the precise nature of the fluctuations depending upon the exact form of eq. (viii) which in turn depends on the values of the sequences of μs and γs. Jorgenson's model is essentially the mechanism by which the investment backlog, new

[1] H. B. Chenery, 'Overcapacity and the acceleration principle', *Econometrica*, XX, January, 1952, pp. 1–28.

[2] See, for example R. G. D. Allen, [1959], pp. 192–3.

starts and investment expenditures respond to changes in the demand for capital as measured by deflated output.

Other theories explicitly introduce profits, interest rates and utilization of capacity as determinants of the rate of investment, either in place of or alongside the factors in (v) above. While these determinants could be derived from models of business behaviour different from the neo-classical model on which Jorgenson's theory is based, they can also be regarded as arising from alternative versions of the neo-classical model. For instance, in eq. (iv) a rate of interest is included in the formula for calculating user cost, the effect being that a rise in the rate of interest (*ceteris paribus*) will reduce the rate of investment. This effect could be approximated by introducing the rate of interest separately as a term in a linear model, e.g.

$$I_t = aw(\tau)\Delta \overline{X}_t + dK_{t-1} + br_t \qquad \text{(ix)}$$

Of the other factors not explicitly considered in Jorgenson's theory, profits are in a special role. The marginal condition on which the theory depends springs from the maximization of net worth, which is the stream of discounted net receipts of the enterprise, net receipts measured as gross receipts less all current and capital payments. With the exception of short-period liquidity considerations arising from particular methods of finance, eq. (v) incorporates all of the influences acting on profits, expressed *via* price of output, output and user cost. The model is thus to some extent an alternative to a simple theory relating the level of investment to the level of profits: the model expresses the ways in which particular determinants of profits affect investment decisions. It is also an alternative to theories such as those which separate desired capital changes (based on expected levels of output) from levels of profits, and regard the investment decision as the outcome of a balancing of the two influences: e.g. despite high levels of output, low levels of profits might cause investment to be reduced. This type of behaviour is embraced by Jorgenson's model but described and analyzed differently.

I shall now survey Jorgenson's empirical results and also consider a similar type of model which introduces profits and an interest rate explicitly. The general Pascal version of eq. (v) is fitted by Jorgenson [1965] to quarterly data of business investment in plant and equipment from the OBE–SEC Investment Survey for four groups

total durables
total nondurables
total regulated (transport, communications, utilities)
all other (trade and commerce).

The model is applied also to anticipations data but this use is not considered here. For each industry group the form of the distributed lag function giving the best fit was chosen, e.g. for durables the form is

$$w(\tau) = \frac{\gamma(\tau)}{\mu(\tau)}$$

where

$$\gamma(\tau) = \gamma_3\tau^3 + \gamma_4\tau^4 + \gamma_5\tau^5,$$
$$\mu(\tau) = 1 + \mu_1\tau + \mu_2\tau^2$$

so that

$$I_t = a\gamma_3\Delta\bar{X}_{t-3} + a\gamma_4\Delta\bar{X}_{t-4} + a\gamma_5\Delta\bar{X}_{t-5} - \mu_1(I_{t-1} - dK_{t-2}) - \mu_2(I_{t-2} - dK_{t-3}) + dK_{t-1} \quad \text{(x)}$$

Equation (x) will be recognized as a second degree version of the difference equation in net investment (eq. vii).

Initial values of the rate of depreciation (or replacement), d, were obtained from the calculation of the capital stock, K, the values being:

total durables	0·02790
total nondurables	0·02648
total regulated	0·01147
all other	0·02460

In all cases there was close agreement between these initial values and the estimates of d obtained from the regression equations similar to (x). Consequently by restricting the parameter d to its initial value, the efficiency of the estimates of the remaining parameters is improved. Total durables and nondurables were fitted to data for 1952–62; the others to 1949–62.

In the following table the results of the restricted version are summarized. Jorgenson gives a full review of his results, and applies several tests including a reconciliation of the actual and anticipated investment results. The results discussed here are chosen for the light they throw on explanations of quarter to quarter changes in investment. The first and most important result is that the level of net investment in any quarter is determined by decisions taken on average about two years previously. Second, as far as an explanation of changes in the current level of investment is concerned, the most important immediate determinants are the levels of investment in the two preceding quarters. For instance, the determinants for total durables could be approximated by

$$I_t - dK_{t-1} = 0{\cdot}8(I_{t-1} - dK_{t-2}) + 0{\cdot}5\Delta(I_{t-1} - dK_{t-2})$$
$$+ \text{(terms in change in deflated output)}$$

which says that net investment in t equals something less than the level in $t - 1$, plus a proportion of the increase between $t - 2$ and $t - 1$ (or less a proportion of the decrease).[1] This approximation applies to total nondurables and total regulated as well. In general these results mean that changes in investment from 1949–62 can be explained tolerably well by a model which says that given an initial change in the demand for capital, the rate of investment will, after a delay associated with the planning of the investment, rise to a peak subsequently falling off as the project is completed, the average lag ranging from seven quarters in the case of durables to 2½ years in the case of nondurables. The change in demand depends upon changes in output (or sales), in price of output and in user cost.

Changes in user cost reflect changes in prices and tax structure, and are felt after the lags. Jorgenson tabulates the various responses of demand for capital to these influences, op. cit., Table 2.8, p. 88. For instance, the long term response of investment of all groups to a reduction in the tax rate by ten percentage points would be a rise in the rate of investment of \$0·033 billion per quarter.[2] The long term response of a one percentage point fall in the interest rate would raise the investment of all groups by \$0·003 billions. The response in the short run would of course be greater, e.g. in the sixth quarter after the initial change in the tax rate, investment would rise by \$0·206 billions.

De Leeuw's model [1962] takes as its basic hypothesis that the backlog of investment projects, decided on and existing at a point in time, depends on capital requirements (C), internal funds (F) and

[1] The auxiliary equation for durables is $\lambda^2 - 1{\cdot}295\lambda + 0{\cdot}428$. $(1{\cdot}295)^2$ is sufficiently close to four times 0·428 for the roots to be treated as equal. In this case the solution is dominated by a term $0{\cdot}65^t$, and hence is damped. Thus an initial change in the demand for capital will initiate an increase in the rate of investment which eventually will fall. Jorgenson, op. cit., pp. 81–83, gives tables of the time form of the lagged responses to changes in the demand for capital.

[2] The estimate assumes 1962 IV values of variables.

TABLE I.1: *Summary of Jorgenson's results*

	$a\gamma_3$	$a\gamma_4$	$a\gamma_5$	$a\gamma_6$	$a\gamma_7$	μ_1	μ_2	$\bar{R}^2$	*Lag*[1]
Total durables	0·00096	0·00080	0·00034	—	—	−1·29501	0·42764	0·94004	7·02
	(0·00036)	(0·00037)	(0·00040)	—	—	(0·14392)	(0·13700)	(0·91324)	—
Total nondurables	—	—	—	0·00009	—	−1·19735	0·33170	0·83970	9·97
	—	—	—	(0·00033)	—	(0·14940)	(0·14799)	(0·76686)	—
Total regulated	—	—	0·00197	0·00111	0·00118	−1·00559	0·27369	0·69146	7·52
	—	—	(0·00135)	(0·00133)	(0·00134)	(0·13705)	(0·13744)	(0·83927)	—
All other	0·00033	0·00021	—	—	—	0·84109	—	0·79045	8·68
	(0·00014)	(0·00013)	—	—	—	(0·06137)	—	(0·78094)	—

[1] Average lag between changes in demand for capital and actual investment expenditure.

Source: Jorgenson [1965] Tables 2.1–2.6.

industrial bond yields (R). Capital requirements are the volume of projects at t which will bring capacity into an optimum relationship to output at $t + n$, assuming that capital projects decided on in t are not completed until $t + n$. C includes projects needed to bring capacity into an optimum relationship with present output, projects needed to take account of expected changes in output, and projects needed to offset the continual wearing-out of the present capital stock. De Leeuw prepared special estimates of quarterly capital requirements (see Fig. 4.4, p. 121 above) based on measures of manufacturers' utilization of capacity and explicit assumptions of expected rate of growth of output (see de Leeuw, op, cit., p. 412 for details). Internal funds are retained earnings plus depreciation allowances. The bond yield is Moody's series for industrial bonds.

It is assumed that new projects take n quarters to complete. Investment at t, I_t, is thus a weighted average of past starts and hence

$$I_t - \sum_{i=1}^{n} k_i I_{t-1} = \sum_{i=1}^{n} k_i(b_c \Delta C_{t-i} + b_f \Delta F_{t-i} + b_r \Delta R_{t-i}), \qquad \text{(xi)}$$

where the k_i are the lag coefficients, k_j being the proportion of projects started in $t - j$.[1]

De Leeuw's approach was to select three distributions of lag coefficients which were consistent with previous studies, fit the distributions and choose that which gave the best fit. The distributions selected were a declining geometric series, a rectangular distribution (all ks equal) and an 'inverted V' distribution (the last for various values of n). The equation was fitted to quarterly manufacturing data from 1947 to 1959. The best fit was obtained for an 'inverted V' distribution with $n = 12$, where $\bar{R}^2 = 0{\cdot}872$. The b-coefficients and their standard errors were:

Capital requirements	0·347
	(0·035)
Internal funds	1·266
	(0·594)
Bond yield	−4·892
	(0·943)

[1] Eq. (xi) is given in de Leeuw's notation. It is identical in form to the Jorgenson equation (ii) above (excepting that replacement investment is included in capital requirements) with the expression in the brackets equalling $\Delta[K'_t - K_{t-1}]$ i.e. the change in the backlog of uncompleted projects, and the sequence (k_i) equivalent to the sequence (w_i).

These coefficients imply that a rise in capital requirements of $1 billion would result in a rise in the backlog of projects of $0·347 billion. De Leeuw comments that '[the] fact that the coefficient is well below unity may be taken to suggest that current changes in the output–capacity ratio are in the first instance discounted rather heavily in planning for new investment' (p. 419). Slightly more than the full effect of a rise in profits is felt in the backlog; while a fall of one percentage point in the bond yield results in a decline of about $5 billion in the backlog. The 'inverted *V*' distribution with $n = 12$ implies that the average lag between changes in demand and investment expenditure is 6·5 quarters.

The implication and meaning of de Leeuw's results can be best appreciated by comparing them with those of Jorgenson. The one clear point of agreement is the importance of distributed lags—delays between a change in demand and the actual expenditure—and the fact that the average lag in manufacturing is greater than eighteen months, possibly nearer two years. The main difference stems from Jorgenson's assumption that a difference between desired and actual capital stock $[K_t' - K_{t-1}]$, is fully—after a delay—reflected in an increase in the rate of investment, and de Leeuw's assumption that a rise in capital requirements is not necessarily fully reflected—from the estimate of b_c he concludes it is only partly reflected. Jorgenson's $[K_t' - K_{t-1}]$ represents the backlog; de Leeuw's C_t is a factor which influences the backlog. C_t is based on expected increases in output in relation to current capacity; Jorgenson's measure is based on current and past changes in output and also on current and past prices and user costs. While current and past changes in output may be used in some circumstances to forecast future output, there are sufficient differences between Jorgenson's and de Leeuw's measures to make the different results not surprising.

One interpretation of the differences is that investment decisions are not greatly influenced by long term forecasts of the future; that business normally has sufficient spare capacity or inventory to allow it to plan capacity increases only after an increase in sales or change in costs has occurred (this conclusion springs from the low value of de Leeuw's b_c and the general acceptableness of Jorgenson's results). Furthermore the role of changes in current and recent prices, costs and sales, played by the X's in Jorgenson's theory, is played in de Leeuw's theory by profits (retained earnings plus depreciation allowances). Changes in profits reflect all of the factors in changes in user cost and in value of sales, and it seems reasonable to think that in some circumstances change in profits are a proxy for desired change in capital. The fact that all of change in profits in de Leeuw's results are reflected in the change in the backlog is strong support for this interpretation. The final difference between the two models lies in the effect of changes in the rate of interest upon the backlog: de Leeuw's result means that the effect is substantially greater than that given by Jorgenson's results—in fact, it is so large that we must suspect that de Leeuw's bond rate is a substitute for other factors.

Studies by Resek and Evans subsequent to those of de Leeuw and Jorgenson, while using different methods (such as differently distributed lags) and providing new details, do not conflict with the results outlined above.[1] Evans confirms the importance of the cash flow in manufacturing (but not non-manufacturing), and both find the interest rate important and the average lag a long one.

The conclusions to be drawn from the investigations described above are that there is a lag of from one to two years on average between change in the desired stock of capital and actual expenditure; that the major determinant of change in the desired stock (or in the backlog of investment projects) is the level of output, but that the effect of this is modified by changes in prices and user cost, the latter being influenced by tax and interest rates and tax structure; and that the combined effect of changes in output, prices and user cost can be approximated by changes in the level of internal funds.

[1] R. N. Resek, 'Investment by manufacturing firms: a quarterly time series analysis of industry data', *R. Econ. Statist.*, XLVIII, August, 1966, pp. 322–33, and M. K. Evans, 'A study of industry investment decisions', *R. Econ. Statist.*, XLIX, May, 1967, pp. 151–64.

NOTE J

Short Run Determinants of Housing Starts

The following is an outline of a model to explain quarterly changes in housing starts. It is based primarily on Muth's stock adjustment model for annual data [1960], and Guttentag's empirical study of postwar quarterly data [1961].[1] The analyses of Alberts, Grebler and Maisel have also been taken into account.[2] No distinction is drawn between owner-occupiers and owners of rental units, and hence between houses started on the order of owner-occupiers, on the order of owners intending to rent, or by speculative builders. No distinction is made between houses of different types, sizes, locations and (hence) values. It is assumed that the stock of houses and starts can be adequately defined in terms of a standard, measurable unit which we call a housing unit.

At any point of time, t, homeowners and owners of rental units wish to hold a stock of housing units depending first on the demographic structure—size of population, age and sex distributions, marital structure, etc.—which is collectively called D. D is not the expected net change in households: instead it is intended to represent the demographic factors determining the net change. Second, the desired stock depends upon expected real income, Y, and the

[1] Muth's model was used above to estimate the demand for houses at the end of the war. See Note D.

[2] W. W. Alberts, 'Business cycles, residential construction cycles, and the mortgage market', *J. polit. Econ.*, LXX, June, 1962, pp. 263–81, L. Grebler and S. J. Maisel, 'Determinants of residential construction: a review of present knowledge', in *Impacts of Monetary Policy*, a study prepared for the commission on money and credit; Prentice-Hall, Englewood Cliffs, N.J., 1963, pp. 475–620, and S. J. Maisel, 'Nonbusiness construction', in *The Brookings Quarterly Econometric Model of the United States*, ed. J. S. Duesenberry *et al.*, North Holland, Amsterdam, 1965, pp. 179–202.

expected real user cost of home ownership, C. Thus desired stock, h_{dt}, is

$$h_{dt} = h_d(D_t, Y_t, C_t) \tag{i}$$

The desired stock will be a relatively stable variable unless expected income changes substantially due to, say, severe unemployment, or the demographic structure alters substantially due to, say, the end of a war. The potential demand for new units at t is thus the difference between desired stock and the actual stock, h_{t-1}, plus losses from stock (demolitions, conversions, mergers, etc.), h_{rt}, plus normal vacancies, h_{vt}, minus units under construction, h_{ct}, i.e.

$$h_{dt} - h_{t-1} + h_{rt} + h_{vt} - h_{ct}.$$

Both losses and normal vacancies could, as a first approximation, be regarded as proportional to the size of the existing stock, i.e.

$$h_{rt} + h_{vt} - h_{t-1} = -\beta h_{t-1}.$$

Units under construction are fractions of the starts of the last two quarters, S_{t-1} and S_{t-2}, i.e.

$$h_{ct} = \gamma_1 S_{t-1} + \gamma_2 S_{t-2}.$$

Only a fraction of potential demand for new units at t is started at t, i.e.

$$S_t = \alpha[h_{dt} - \beta h_{t-1} - \gamma_1 S_{t-1} - \gamma_2 S_{t-2}] \tag{ii}$$

Where α, the delay factor, has a value lying between 0 and 1. α is not constant as a general rule: the proportion of potential demand translated into starts depends upon the conditions of supply of credit for housing at t, of which the most important are the rate of interest (yield on mortgages in the first instance) and the proportion of the value of the work required as a cash downpayment. Call these conditions collectively r so that

$$\alpha_t = \alpha(r_t).$$

r, the conditions of supply of housing credit, are expected to vary substantially in the short run and to be a major factor in quarter to quarter changes in starts.

Alberts in his cited study of postwar data, similar in some respects to Guttentag's study, provides a model of the short term links between the credit markets and the housing markets. He argues that the postwar period is characterized by four conditions: (a) a high cross-elasticity of demand for mortgages with respect to yields on competing investments on the part of lenders (e.g. insurance companies, mutual savings banks, commercial banks, savings and loan associations); (b) a demand schedule for mortgage funds that has been relatively stable over the period; (c) an elastic supply schedule of new houses (this would not apply in 1946); and (d) an elastic demand schedule for mortgage funds. The supply of mortgage funds and hence the rate of housing starts is closely related to the change in the difference in yields between mortgages and other securities such as bonds. Typically, in a business upswing, yields on other securities rise faster than on mortgages and the supply of mortgage credit is reduced; in the downswing the process is reversed.

It appears to be implicit in this hypothesis that mortgage yields respond—with a lag—to conditions in other parts of the credit market. Alberts' thesis is offered as an alternative to the argument that the supply of mortgage credit is regulated by the difference between the (fixed) interest rate charged on mortgage loans insured by the FHA or guaranteed by the VA, and the yield on other securities.

The model in equations (i) and (ii) allows for three sources of fluctuations in housing starts. In the first place the 'long term' factors of demography, income and costs can fluctuate. Second, the conditions of supply of credit can fluctuate. Third, given changes in either 'long term' factors or credit supply, starts could fluctuate because of the lags in the completion of houses. If the existing stock is described as a weighted sum of past starts, i.e.

$$\beta h_{t-1} - \gamma_1 S_{t-1} - \gamma_2 S_{t-2} = \sum_{i=1}^{n} \delta_i S_{t-i}$$

so that

$$S_t = a[h_{dt} - \sum_{i=1}^{n} \delta_i S_{t-i}] \qquad \text{(iii)}$$

the history of housing starts from a point in time can be regarded as a fluctuation about a moving equilibrium, the moving equilibrium being determined by the changes in demographic structure, income and costs, the fluctuations being determined by the past history of starts (or the age distribution of housing) and the changes in credit conditions.

Maisel has one equation (op. cit., p. 195, eq. 6.4) which can be regarded as a rough approximation to (ii) above. Private starts are explained as depending upon change in households, real rents, interest rates, houses under construction, losses and normal vacancies. The fit is good and the parameter values are not implausible.

NOTE K

Foreign Trade Elasticities

Rhomberg and Boissonneault have estimated U.S. foreign trade elasticities from aggregate import and export equations using quarterly data.[1] The typical import equation has as independent (explanatory) variables real disposable income or manufacturing production, deflated price index, and imports lagged one quarter. The lagged imports imply a difference between the impact (short run) elasticity and the long run elasticity. For imports of unfinished goods the change in nonfarm business inventories was included as an additional explanatory variable. For exports the independent variables were world exports excluding U.S., deflated export price and lagged exports. A summary of the elasticities is given in Table K.1.

The elasticities given are short run: they show the effects of changes in the explanatory variables in the quarter during which the changes occur. The long run elasticities are likely to be from two to three times the values of the respective short run elasticities, but such calculations are much less reliable than those shown in the table.

The price elasticity for exports is relatively high and reliable: that from the 1948–53 period was used. A reliable import price elasticity for finished goods was not obtained, and the figure of −0·3 used above is a weighted average of the 1948–53 estimates. The relatively high import elasticities with respect to income and output in the early period and their decline in the later period is interesting, but the figures are not reliable. It is possible that the high values before 1954 arise from the special features of the pre-1949 and Korean War periods, when U.S. import demand was abnormally high because of domestic shortages and little excess industrial capacity,

[1] R. R. Rhomberg and L. Boissonneault, 'The foreign sector', in *The Brookings Quarterly Econometric Model of the United States*, ed. J. S. Duesenberry *et al.*, North Holland, Amsterdam, 1965, pp. 375–408.

TABLE K.I: *Short run Foreign Trade Elasticities*

	Fitting Period		
	1948–61	*1948–53*	*1954–61*
Imports of finished goods and services (including food)			
Disposable income	0·80	1·11‡	0·37§
Deflated price*	−0·19§	−0·21§	−1·20‡
Imports of unfinished goods			
Manufacturing production	0·41	0·66‡	0·27§
Deflated price*	−0·32	−0·49	−0·34‡
Exports of goods and services			
World trade excluding U.S.	0·33	0·30	0·40
Deflated price†	−0·57	−0·64	−1·20‡

Source: Rhomberg and Boissonneault [1965], Table 11.7, p. 388.

Notes: Evaluated at sample means 1948–61 of respective variables.
* deflator: implicit GNP goods price index.
† deflator: world export unit value (excluding U.S.).
‡ Not significant at 1 per cent level.
§ Not significant at 5 per cent level.

and consequently declined abnormally sharply when activity fell in 1949 and 1954. The decline in the high postwar income elasticity is thus due to the disappearance of the transiently marginal U.S. import demand especially for finished goods. Along with the decline in the income elasticity is the rise in the price elasticities of both finished imports and exports. The former is the counterpart of the fall in the income elasticity; both reflect the changing trends in world trade and are acceptable for that reason; neither however are statistically reliable.

For a summary of earlier studies of long term elasticities, see MacDougall [1957].

NOTE L

Inventories, Sales and Unfilled Orders

This note examines the theory of inventory investment, and in particular the econometric evidence of the relationships between inventories, sales and unfilled orders. Table L.1 classifies business inventories according to holding sector (and for manufacturers according to stage of fabrication). For durable goods manufacturers work in progress is considerably more important than it is in the nondurable goods industries, reflecting the longer periods of fabrication for durable goods. Lengthy periods of fabrication partly account for the importance of the stock of unfilled orders for durable goods manufacturers, although this is large because of the amount of production to order in these industries.

The fluctuations in inventory investment by durable goods manufacturers have tended to dominate non-farm inventory investment changes ever since the end of the war, while in the period up to 1952 investment by durable goods traders (excluding autos) experienced large changes. The prominence of durable goods manufacturers in investment explains to some extent why most econometric work has been concerned with this sector.

Most modern study of inventories has centred on the 'flexible accelerator' concept which is a version of the capital stock adjustment principle used in inquiries into the demand for durable goods.[1] The version presented here is based on the recent work of Darling

[1] See above, Notes C, D, E and I. I am not concerned here with micro-economic theories of inventory holding, although of course the 'flexible accelerator' model can be derived from micro-economic assumptions. The model described here is to be regarded as an approximation to micro-economic behaviour considered in the aggregate.

TABLE L.1: *Inventories, Sales and Unfilled Orders of Manufacturers and Traders, 1948*

		$ million	
	Inventories	*Sales (Shipments)*	*Unfilled Orders*
Manufacturers of durable goods	14,662	90,945	26,619
Materials and supplies	(5,408)	—	—
Work in progress	(4,942)	—	—
Finished goods	(4,289)	—	—
Manufacturers of nondurable goods	13,881	116,852	4,117
Materials and supplies	(6,397)	—	—
Work in progress	(1,902)	—	—
Finished goods	(5,619)	—	—
Automotive dealers	1,992	20,726	—
Other durable goods traders	8,579	53,263	—
Nondurable goods traders	13,393	141,329	—

Source; SCB and Bureau of the Census.

Note; Inventories: year end, book value. State of fabrication estimated from Old Series.
Sales: annual total.
Unfilled orders: year end.

and Lovell.[1] The basic hypothesis is that the demand for inventory depends on the need to have goods in the production and distribution pipeline because of normal delays in ordering, fabrication and delivery. For firms producing or ordering for stock the level of inventory—finished goods, goods in process and materials—will depend on expected sales. For firms producing or delivering to order the level of inventory—predominantly goods in process and materials—will depend on the stock of unfilled orders. This causal relationship can be approximated by the simple equation:

$$\frac{I'}{S'} = a + b\frac{U}{S'} \qquad \text{(i)}$$

[1] P. G. Darling, 'Inventory fluctuations and economic instability', in *Inventory Fluctuations and Economic Stabilization*, part III (papers prepared for the Joint Economic Committee), U.S. Congress, 87th Cong., 1st Sess., Joint Committee Print, Washington, 1961; P. G. Darling and M. C. Lovell, 'Factors influencing investment in inventories', in *The Brookings Quarterly Econometric Model of the United States*, ed. J. S. Duesenberry *et al.*, North Holland, Amsterdam, 1965; M. C. Lovell, 'Factors determining manufacturing inventory investment', in *Inventory Fluctuations and Economic Stabilization, Part II*, causative factors in the movements of business inventories (papers prepared for the Joint Economic Committee), U.S. Congress, 87th Cong., 1st Sess., Joint Committee Print, Washington, 1961).

or $$I' = aS' + bU \qquad \text{(ii)}$$

where I' is desired inventory
S' is expected sales
U is unfilled orders

(i) expresses the desired inventory–sales ratio as a constant plus a variable parameter which depends on the unfilled orders–sales ratio; (ii) expresses desired inventories in the linear form used below. a and b are constants whose values reflect the normal needs of the pipeline and the choice of units.

This basic hypothesis can be elaborated and developed in a number of different ways. In the first place it is necessary to forecast expected sales, and make allowances for errors in forecasts and hence for unintended inventory investment or disinvestment. The simplest type of forecast is to assume that sales grow steadily at a rate r, so that

$$S'_t = (1 + r)S_{t-1} \qquad \text{(iii)}$$

and $$I'_t = a'S_{1-1} + bU_{t-1} \qquad \text{(iv)}$$

where $a' = a(1 + r)$

Forecast errors can be dealt with either by adding to the final expression for desired investment an expression for unintended investment $[(1 + r)S_{t-1} - S_t]$, to obtain total inventory investment, or by regarding the error as stochastic, distributed independently of the other variables, and hence contributing to the residuals in the regression equation. Other forecasting devices make use of distributed lags of sales (in effect projecting a trend) and sales anticipations data, although it has not yet been reported that the latter have been used in time series regressions. The second elaboration is to make allowance for changes in supply conditions. (i) and (ii) assume a pipeline demand in normal circumstances, where normal is defined in terms of production and delivery conditions. As these conditions alter so the inventory demand will change.

'When supply conditions are tight and deliveries subject to delays and uncertainties, firms find it advisable to carry larger inventories of purchased materials in order to forestall interruptions in the production process when difficulties arise in the procurement of key items.'[1]

[1] Darling and Lovell, op. cit., p. 136, summarizing the argument of Stanback [1962].

As a measure of the tightness of supply conditions several variables have been proposed: the level of unfilled orders (as in (i) and (ii) above), the change in unfilled orders and an index of manufacturing capacity. To incorporate this influence we can write (iv) as

$$I'_t = a'S_{t-1} + b'U_{t-1} + c\Delta U_{t-1} \qquad \text{(v)}$$

where the use of b' indicates the twofold influence of unfilled orders.[1]

The final relationship is a description of the way in which business responds to a difference between desired and actual inventories, i.e. repairs the discrepancy. The approach used in most inventory models (and in most models of durable goods demand) is to assume that because of delays in ordering, fabrication and delivery the discrepancy is only repaired over an interval of time. Then the simplest hypothesis about business behaviour is that inventory investment in period t is some fixed proportion, d, of the difference between desired and actual inventories at the end of $t - 1$,

i.e. $$\Delta I'_t = d[I'_t - I_{t-1}] \; o < d \leqslant 1 \qquad \text{(vi)}$$

ΔI_t can replace $\Delta I'_t$ if forecasting errors are disregarded or treated stochastically.

This adjustment mechanism is a special case of a distributed lag where the weights are a geometrical series, i.e.

$$I_t = d[I'_t + (1 - d)I'_{t-1} + (1 - d)^2 I'_{t-2} + \ldots] \qquad \text{(vii)}$$

The more general case places no restrictions on the weights, inventories at any date being a weighted average of past desired inventories, i.e.

$$I_t = w_o I'_t + w_1 I'_{t-1} + \ldots + w_n I'_{t-n} \qquad \text{(viii)}$$

where the weights w_i, $(i = o, \ldots, n)$, measure the lags in the adjustment of actual to desired inventories.

Substituting (v) in (vi) we have the standard equation to explain inventory behaviour:

$$\Delta I_t = da'S_{t-1} + db'U_{t-1} + dc\Delta U_{t-1} - dI_{t-1} \qquad \text{(ix)}$$

where the forecasting errors are assumed to be distributed stochasti-

[1] The motives summarized in (i) and (ii) can be regarded as transactions motives for holding inventories; the additions made in (v) represent the precautionary motive; the speculative motive could be incorporated by adding expressions measuring expected change in prices. See below, p. 281.

cally and to be included in the residuals of the regression. A constant is usually added to the equation.

Equation (ix) or modifications of it have been fitted by Lovell and Darling to quarterly data. Table L.2 illustrates their results. Equations (1) and (2) are variations on the basic theme: it appears that the different choice of lags in (2) improves the fit considerably. The inclusion of ΔI_{t-1} in (2) with a large, significant coefficient results in the introduction of a longer lag in the adjustment mechanism of (vi). We can write

$$-0{\cdot}265 I_{t-1} + 0{\cdot}383 \Delta I_{t-1} \sim -0{\cdot}383 I_{t-2}$$

so that $d = 0{\cdot}383$ and the lag in (vi) is two quarters. Paradiso used such a lag in one equation with good results.[1] With allowance for differences in lags, the results of eqs. (1) and (2) imply that the parameters of (ix) are

Equation	1	2
$d =$	0·165	0·265
$a' =$	0·739	0·151
$b' =$	0·084	0·132
$c =$	−0·022	0·340

It is clear that no firm conclusions about parameter values can be drawn from these results.

Lovell has suggested that the fit of the equation would be improved if military purchases and orders are introduced separately. In equation (3) this is done. O_t is Department of Defence obligations (new orders) for durable goods, and E_t is Department of Defence expenditures on durable goods. This move in the direction of a disaggregated treatment has the effect of substantially reducing the coefficient of I_{t-1}, viz. d, and also reducing the influence of unfilled orders, while the influence of current sales is increased slightly.[2] Otherwise the improvement in the fit leaves the structure of the model unchanged.

[1] L. J. Paradiso, Statement in hearings, *Inventory Fluctuation and Economic Stabilization*, subcommittee on economic stabilization, automation, and energy resources, Joint economic committee, U.S. Congress, 87th Cong., 1st Sess., Joint Committee Print, Washington, 1962, p. 51, for durable manufacturing, 1948–62, *current dollars*, gives the equation
$\Delta I_t = -0{\cdot}245 + 0{\cdot}119 \Delta U_{t-1} + 0{\cdot}335 S_{t-1} - 0{\cdot}142 I_{t-2}$ ($R^2 = 0{\cdot}72$)

[2] The implied inventory-sales ratio, a', becomes 2·7 which is surely too high and arises because d is so low. Allowance for the influence of E_t on a' does not alter the situation.

Military expenditures have a negative coefficient which Weidenbaum has explained by the fact that payment for defence hardware coincides approximately in timing with the delivery of the goods, and at this time inventories will be falling.[1]

The model is applied to durable goods manufacturing in equations (4) and (5). In (4) which corresponds to (1) the fit is poor, and the implied values of the parameters are

$$d = 0{\cdot}083,\ a' = 2{\cdot}63,\ b' = 0{\cdot}216,\ c = 1{\cdot}242$$

When in equation (5) the military influence is added the fit is again considerably improved. Darling and Lovell also introduce an alternative measure of supply conditions, K_t, which is defined as an index of capacity utilization multiplied by an index of sales.[2] The parameters in (5) are $d = 0{\cdot}117$ and $a' = 1{\cdot}346$ which appear to be more plausible values than those in (4). The influence of military orders is strong, although the coefficient of military expenditures is not significantly different from zero. The influence of supply conditions is significant. Darling and Lovell have considered other variations on this basic model without getting any improvement, and their conclusions are that neither unfilled orders nor change in unfilled orders add much when military orders (Defence obligations) are included, that the coefficient of Defence expenditures tends to be not significantly different from zero, that a time trend is useful, and that speculative and cost measures such as price changes and interest rates are not significant. The implied values of d range from 0·05 to 0·12, and of a' from 1·3 to over 2.

I have tested an alternative model based on the more general case of an unrestricted weighted average as in (viii) above. The equation used is

$$\Delta I_t = a_0 + b_0\Delta S_t + b_1\Delta S_{t-1} + c_1 + c_1\Delta U_{t-1} \qquad \text{(x)}$$

Equation (6) is an example of the results.[3] It refers to 1947–54, and the S refers to final sales not shipments. A longer period does not alter the conclusions. The fit is good. The coefficient of U_{t-1} is large and significant, and the influence of unfilled orders appears to

[1] M. L. Weidenbaum, 'The timing of the economic impact of government spending', *National Tax J.*, XII, March, 1959, pp. 79–85.

[2] This parameter arises because, if to (i) above, a term eC is added, C being an index of capacity utilization, multiplication through by S produces $K = CS$.

[3] The data differ from those in the other equations: the values are in 1958 prices and sales are measured exclusive of auto sales.

be much greater than is the case in the Lovell–Darling equations. The marginal inventory–sales ratio, a', which in this model is measured by $b_0 + b_1$, is considerably less than unity, and this result appears whatever the period taken, and also irrespective of whether inventories are defined as durable manufacturing, total manufacturing or total durable goods. Allowing for the fact that final sales of durables are about one-half shipments, this is about at the lower range of the Darling–Lovell results.

The Darling–Lovell model when applied to nondurable manufacturing inventories gives poor results (see equation (7)). The influence of I_{t-1} is not significantly different from zero, and the main explanatory force is given by unfilled orders. An application of a version of (x) by myself tends to confirm these conclusions, the coefficient of U_{t-1} being large and that of a' being in the region of 0·25.[1]

The model when applied to trade inventories is slightly more satisfactory than when applied to nondurable manufacturing.[2] Lovell and Darling's equation is

$$\Delta I_t = \underset{}{-0{\cdot}1896} + \underset{(\cdot 0165)}{0{\cdot}0732\ S_t} + \underset{(\cdot 0089)}{0{\cdot}0253\ C_t} + \underset{(7{\cdot}62)}{15{\cdot}44}\ \frac{P_{t+1} - P_t}{P_t} \underset{(\cdot 0653)}{-0{\cdot}2408\ I_{t-1}}$$

$R^2 = 0{\cdot}466$ $S_e = 0{\cdot}273$. Darling and Lovell [1965], p. 151.

where C_t is an index of capacity utilization in manufacturing industry and P_t is the wholesale price index for consumer nondurable goods. Both inventories and sales are defined exclusive of automobiles. The period is 1951–60. The fit is not good (this is typical of trade inventory regressions) but the coefficients are all significant and the parameters implied accord with a priori ideas: $d = 0{\cdot}24$ and $a' = 0{\cdot}304$.

[1] The equation for 1947–54 is

$$\Delta I_t = -2{\cdot}397 + \underset{(0{\cdot}124)}{0{\cdot}603U_{t-1}} + \underset{(0{\cdot}076)}{0{\cdot}092\Delta S_t} + \underset{(0{\cdot}077)}{0{\cdot}135\Delta S_{t-1}} + \underset{(0{\cdot}077)}{0{\cdot}050\Delta S_{t-2}}$$

$R^2 = 0{\cdot}447$ $S_e = 0{\cdot}912$. S is final sales.

[2] As mentioned above, the version in (x) when applied to total durables, both manufacturing and trade, gives results similar to those in (6). For example, for 1947–64

$$\Delta I_t = 1{\cdot}110 + \underset{(0{\cdot}076)}{0{\cdot}705\Delta U_{t-1}} + \underset{(0{\cdot}098)}{0{\cdot}222\Delta S_t} + \underset{(0{\cdot}102)}{0{\cdot}284\Delta S_{t-1}}$$

$R^2 = 0{\cdot}677$. $S_e = 1{\cdot}168$. S is final sales.

Explicit account is taken of the speculative motive for holding inventories by using (so as to simulate expected price change) the change in the price index a quarter in advance of the inventory change. The effect of such a price change appears to be significantly large: for example, a 5 per cent change in the price index during $t + 1$ is associated with a \$0·75 billion inventory change during t which in 1958 would have been just over 2 per cent of traders' inventories (less autos). Disaggregation shows that this result applies to the wholesale and durable retail sectors: it is not found amongst nondurable retailers. The economic meaning of this result, however, would appear to be in doubt because it is possible that inventory change, representing an increased demand for both finished goods and materials, may itself cause a rise in prices. The device of correlating price change with lagged inventory changes does not settle the direction of cause.

The influence of supply conditions, measured in this case by an index of capacity utilization in manufacturing, is also significant, although the same doubt about what causes what arises. The capacity index does not enter the regression in a lagged form, hence it is possible and surely likely that an increase in planned inventory investment would cause a rise in the degree of utilization of capacity. This doubt arises of course in the interpretation of the influence of any of the measures of supply conditions when they are included in an inventory regression in an unlagged form. (The relationship between goods in process and unfilled orders was referred to above). In particular the strongly marked relation between durable manufacturers' inventory change and the measure of supply conditions used in equation (5) above is suspect, although the particular measure used—the product of a capacity index and a sales index—may remove some of the doubts.

When the rate of interest is used in the regression the coefficient is not significantly different from zero. Disaggregation does not alter the picture.

The conclusion of this survey of recent econometric work is that some version of the flexible accelerator does appear to operate as a determinant of business investment in inventories. The relation is perhaps strongest and most pervasive amongst manufacturers of durable goods. To the influence of sales has to be added the influence of orders, either in the form of the stock of unfilled orders or as orders for military hardware. For durable goods manufacturers the effect of a given change in unfilled orders is nearly as important as a similar change in sales.

Minor influences upon inventory investment appear to be supply conditions and—in the case of traders—price changes. However the statistical evidence is not clear about the direction of cause, and the significance of these influences cannot be regarded as well established as is the influence of sales and orders.

The work described above does not lead to any precise quantitative results, but can be summarized in terms of upper or lower limits of a marginal non-farm inventory–GNP ratio. For manufacturers of durable goods, the most plausible values of the ratio to shipments given by Lovell and Darling are between 1·0 and 3·0. As a ratio to final sales they are 0·5 and 1·5. My estimate from equation (6) lies within this range. To these figures have to be added the ratio to unfilled orders, the estimates of which vary considerably. A range of from 0·5 to 1·0 is suggested, with my estimate near the lower limit. The value of quarterly final sales is approximately one-half of unfilled orders, and thus the total inventory to final sales ratio for manufacturers of durable goods lies between the limits of 1·5 and 3·5. For nondurable goods manufacturers the estimate of the ratio to final sales is 0·25, which appears low compared to that of durables. (The coefficient of unfilled orders is large, but the value of unfilled orders is negligible in relation to sales.) A range from 0·25 to 0·75 seems possible. In the absence of any other information for traders I take Lovell and Darling's estimate of their combined ratio to sales, 0·3, as within a range 0·25 to 0·75, and add these estimates to both the durable and nondurable manufacturing estimates. Assuming that the ratio in the service and other sectors is zero, the aggregate marginal inventory–GNP ratio lies between the limits 0·49 and 1·28.[1]

[1] The ratios and weights are:

Sector	*Upper limit*	*Lower limit*	*Weight (final sales in 1962 $ billion)*
Durable goods	4·25	1·75	106
Nondurable goods	1·50	0·50	172
Other	0	0	276
			554

These calculations suggest that as a working hypothesis we can assume the marginal inventory–GNP ratio is close to unity for quarterly data, and close to 0·25 for annual data. The hypothesis is not in conflict with calculations of the ratio of non farm CBI to change in GNP over lengthy periods since 1945. For instance, the ratio of such changes from 1948 to 1964, and also 1953 to 1960, is exactly 0·2. The significance of the hypothesis is that in a simple dynamic multiplier-accelerator model with a long run marginal propensity to consume out of GNP of, say, 0·04, with the change in consumption following a change in output lagged and spread out over at least two quarters, an inventory accelerator coefficient of unity results in either damped oscillations in GNP in response to outside shocks, or steady transitions from one equilibrium to another.

TABLE L.2: *Manufacturing Inventory Investment Equations*

Equation	1	2	3	4	5	6	7
Data	*Total Manufacturing 1948–60*	*Total Manufacturing 1948–60*	*Total Manufacturing 1948–60*	*Durable Manufacturing 1950–61*	*Durable Manufacturing 1950–61*	*Durable Manufacturing 1947–54*	*Nondurable Manufacturing 1950–61*
Source	*Lovell [1961]*	*Darling [1961]*	*Lovell [1961]*	*Darling & Lovell [1965] p. 139*	*Darling & Lovell [1965] p. 139*	*Blyth*	*Darling & Lovell [1965] p. 141*
R^2	0·53	0.811	0·636	0·567	0·740	0·793	0·582
S_e	—	0·373	—	0·460	0·370	1·502	0·176
DW ratio	—	2·105	—	1·38	1·78	—	1·87
Constant	−1·47 (0·12)	6·297	−4·01 (1·36)	−3·102	−2·445	0·4815 (0·2950)	−1·169
Regression of ΔI_t on:							
S_t sales	0·122 (0·024)	— —	0·184 (0·46)	0·2174 (0·0464)	0·1574 (0·0532)	— —	0·0424 (0·0203)
S_{t-1}	— —	0·040 (0·020)	— —	— —	— —	— —	— —
ΔS_t	−0·0118 (0·0376)	— —	0·0298 (0·0534)	— —	— —	0·2797 (0·1295)	— —
ΔS_{t-1}	— —	— —	— —	— —	— —	0·2379 (0·1371)	— —
I_{t-1} inventories	−0·165 (0·035)	−0·265 (0·076)	−0·0683 (0·0450)	−0·827 (0·355)	−0·1169 (0·0465)	— —	0·0500 (0·0487)
ΔI_{t-1}	— —	0·383 (0·086)	— —	— —	— —	— —	— —
U_t unfilled orders	0·0138 (0·0054)	— —	0·0112 (0·0092)	0·0179 (0·0089)	— —	— —	0·3286 (0·0742)
U_{t-1}	— —	0·035 (0·011)	— —	— —	— —	— —	— —
ΔU_t	−0·0021 (0·0240)	— —	−0·0158 (0·0413)	0·1095 (0·0381)	— —	— —	−0·4174 (0·0768)
ΔU_{t-1}	— —	0·055 (0·028)	— —	— —	— —	0·4323 (0·0728)	— —
T time	— —	0·062 (0·022)	— —	— —	0·00032 (0·00029)	— —	— —
O_t D of D obligations	— —	— —	0·124 (0·060)	— —	0·1710 (0·0459)	— —	— —
E_t D of D expenditures	— —	— —	−0·295 (0·166)	— —	−0·1482 (0·1551)	— —	— —
K_t supply conditions measure	— —	— —	— —	— —	0·0930 (0·0217)	— —	— —

Notes: 1. Data for all equations are quarterly, seasonally adjusted at annual rates.
2. For all equations except (6) data are in \$ 1954, and sales (S) are gross (i.e. shipments).
3. For equation (6) data are in \$ 1958 and sales are final sales.

Bibliographical Note

Business cycle theory

Theories of business fluctuations can be classified by their position on a spectrum at one end of which are endogenous theories which assert that the structure of the economy generates persisting oscillations (like Marx's theory of capitalistic crises); while at the other end are exogenous theories which assert that factors outside the structure of the economy influence it in such a way that expansions and recessions succeed one another (like Jevons' theory of the effect of periodic sunspots). In between these extremes exogenous and endogenous factors can interact with differing degrees of importance. Modern theories lie on all points of the spectrum. My view in this book lies on the exogenous side of the spectrum, but not at the far end: the structure of the economy, as described by the short-run multiplier-accelerator model is very stable, with a heavily damped response to a change in an exogenous variable (such as military expenditure) or a structural parameter (such as the marginal propensity to consume). Since the end of the Second World War in the United States at least, recessions and expansions can be identified with changes in particular exogenous variables or (less frequently) in structural parameters. In the absence of these changes, the economy would grow slowly at a fairly steady rate. The writer to whose views mine are closest in this respect and to whom I am probably most indebted is J. S. Duesenberry.[1]

Endogenous theories are represented by the non-linear models of N. Kaldor, J. R. Hicks [1950] and R. M. Goodwin.[2] Hicks of course has provided the expository device I have used in this book. These

[1] J. S. Duesenberry, *Business Cycles and Economic Growth*, McGraw-Hill, New York, 1958.

[2] N. Kaldor, 'A model of the trade cycle', *Econ. J.*, L, March, 1940, pp. 78–92. R. M. Goodwin, 'The nonlinear accelerator and the persistence of business cycles', *Econometrica*, XIX, January, 1951, pp. 1–17.

theories rely on systematic parameter changes at the peak and trough of the cycle—changes in the fixed investment accelerator—which arise from ceilings, floors and buffers. The buffer approach appears to have some relevance to the balance of payments cycle which some economies experience: as full employment is reached, imports rise so rapidly that payments and exchange crises force the authorities to reduce demand. The resulting recession improves the balance of payments and the authorities then increase demand. And so the cycle persists. It can be argued that the U.S. monetary and housing cycle is of this type, with fears of inflation taking the place of exchange crises up to the late 1950s. I prefer to regard the monetary and housebuilding changes not as an administrative cycle but as resulting from discretionary actions of the authorities which are by no means as predictable as the parameter changes of the true endogenous models are assumed to be.

An example of a mixed model is that of D. J. Coppock, who suggests in complete contrast to me that the post-1945 fluctuations can be explained by an unstable inventory accelerator, leading to only slightly damped oscellations with a period of 2 or 3 years.[1] Another mixed model, nearer the exogenous end of the spectrum, is suggested by I. and F. L. Adelman, who attempt to test the suggestion of Slutzky and Frisch that cycles may be caused by the effect of random stocks on stable systems.[2] They conclude that a large-scale econometric model of the U.S. economy, that of Klein and Goldberger, is basically very stable, and that it absorbs isolated large exogenous shocks without producing a persisting oscillation. When subjected to a succession of random shocks it produces cycles similar to those observed in real life. The Adelmans' ideas are close to mine, and if this book needed a motto I would take Mrs Adelman's statement that 'the primary task of the business cycle analyst is to investigate the reaction patterns of an economic system to various shocks, for it is in this sphere of activity that his efforts are likely to be most significant' [1960], p. 795.

[1] D. J. Coppock, 'The postwar short cycle in the U.S.A.', *Manchester Sch.*, XXXIII, January, 1965, pp. 17–44.

[2] I. Adelman, 'Business cycles-endogenous or stochastic?', *Econ. J.*, LXX, December, 1960, pp. 783–90; F. L. Adelman and I. Adelman, 'The dynamic properties of the Klein–Goldberger model', *Econometrica*, XXVII, October, 1959, pp. 592–625.

A general review of these theories, covering most modern problems, is provided by R. C. O. Matthews.[1]

1948–49 recession

The literature on the postwar boom and recession is slight. General works on business cycles such as R. A. Gordon and A. H. Hansen contain brief descriptions and analyses.[2] A more detailed account is contained in B. G. Hickman [1960]. Earlier analytical studies of the recession were by D. Hamberg, E. P. Bratt and J. P. Ondrechen, B. Caplin and myself.[3] The only recent published study is that of R. Fels [1965] who also contributed to the earlier debate.[4] Although I believe Professor Fels unduly emphasises the effect of the end of excess demand upon inventory policy in 1948, his approach and general conclusions are close to mine.

Published official analyses of the recession written at the time are disappointing except as a guide to official actions. The Economic Reports of the President of mid-1948 and January 1949 are coloured by fear of inflation. In mid-1949 and January 1950 the return to normal in most markets was recognized, and it was emphasized that the fall in private investment was mainly in inventories. In the report for mid-1950 there is evidence of analysis: it is asserted that the description of the events of 1949 as an inventory recession 'confuses a description of what happened with an explanation of events (p. 33)', a statement with which I agree wholeheartedly, but upon which many business cycle analysts and historians do not appear to have pondered. However, this report also adopts an under-consumptionist

[1] R. C. O. Matthews, *The Trade Cycle* (Digswell Place: Nisbet and Co.) Cambridge University Press, 1959.

[2] R. A. Gordon, *Business Fluctuations*, 2nd. ed., Harper and Row, New York, 1961. A. H. Hansen, *Business Cycles and National Income*, expanded edition, Allen and Unwin, London, 1964.

[3] D. Hamberg, 'The recession of 1948–49 in the United States,' *Econ. J.*, LXII (March, 1952), pp. 1–14; and '1948–49 recession re-examined: a rejoinder', *Econ. J.*, LXIII, March, 1953, pp. 104–10. E. C. Bratt and J. P. Ondrechen, '1948–49 recession re-examined', *Econ. J.*, LXIII, March, 1953, pp. 98–104. B. Caplin, 'A case study: the 1948–49 recession', in *Policies to Combat Recession*, NBER special conference series No. 7, Princeton University Press, 1956, pp. 27–58. C. A. Blyth, 'The United States cycle in private fixed investment, 1946–50', *R. Econ. Statist.*, XXXVIII, February, 1956, pp. 41–9; and 'The 1948–49 American recession,' *Econ. J.*, LXIV, September, 1954, pp. 486–510.

[4] R. Fels, 'Theoretical significance of the 1949 recession,' *Amer. econ. R.*, XLV, May, 1955, pp. 358–66.

line which seems to me to confuse description and analysis also: 'The central cause of the recession was to be found in the unwillingness or inability of buyers of all types to absorb at current high prices the full product at full employment of a highly productive industry and a flourishing agriculture (p. 31)'. The explanation given of the rapid recovery (p. 35) relies heavily on business confidence, which appears to be a case of an official body congratulating itself for not rocking the boat. In general, in the documents of the time one misses the detailed and often acute analysis contained in the President's Economic Report under later Administrations. The reports of the Congressional Joint Economic Committee on its hearings on the President's Reports contain useful testimony from witnesses (see particularly *Senate Reports* 88, 81st Congress 1949, and 1843, 81st Congress 1950).

List of References

ADELMAN, I. 'Business cycles-endogenous or stochastic?' *Economic Journal*, LXX, December, 1960, pp. 783–96.

ADELMAN, F. L. and I. 'The dynamic properties of the Klein-Goldberger model', *Econometrica*, XXVII, October, 1959, pp. 592–625.

ALBERTS, W. W. 'Business cycles, residential construction cycles, and the mortgage market', *Journal of Political Economy*, LXX, June, 1962, pp. 263–81.

ALLEN, R. G. D. *Mathematical Economics*, 2nd ed., Macmillan, London, 1959.

ANDO, A. and BROWN, E. C. 'Lags in fiscal and monetary policy', in *Stabilization Policies*, a series of research studies prepared for the Commission on Money and Credit, Prentice-Hall, Englewood Cliffs, N.J., 1963, pp. 97–163.

ANDO, A. and MODIGLIANI, F. 'The life cycle hypothesis of saving: aggregate implications and tests', *American Economic Review*, LIII, March, 1963, pp. 55–84, reprinted in *Readings in Business Cycles*, the American Economic Association's series of republished articles on economics, X, Irwin, Homewood, Ill., 1965, pp. 398–426.

BIRD, R. C. 'Consumption, savings and windfall gains: comment', *American Economic Review*, LIII, June, 1963, pp. 443–4.

BLYTH, C. A. 'The 1948–49 American recession', *Economic Journal*, LXIV, September, 1954, pp. 486–510.

BLYTH, C. A. 'The United States cycle in private fixed investment, 1946–50', *Review of Economics and Statistics*, XXXVIII, February, 1956, pp. 41–9.

BODKIN, R. 'Windfall income and consumption', *American Economic Review*, XLIX, September, 1959, pp. 602–14.

BRATT, E. C. and ONDRECHEN, J. P. '1948–49 recession re-examined', *Economic Journal*, LXIII, March, 1953, pp. 98–104.

CAPLIN, B. 'A case study: the 1948–49 recession', in *Policies to Combat Recession*, NBER special conference series No. 7, Princeton University Press, 1956, pp. 27–58.

CHENERY, H. B. 'Overcapacity and the acceleration principle', *Econometrica*, XX, January, 1952, pp. 1–28.

CHOW, G. C. 'Statistical demand functions for automobiles and their use for forecasting', in *Demand for Durable Goods*, ed. A. C. Harberger, University of Chicago Press, 1960, pp. 147–78.

COPPOCK, D. J. 'The postwar short cycle in the U.S.A.', *Manchester School*, XXXIII, January, 1965, pp. 17–44.

DARLING, P. G. 'Inventory fluctuations and economic instability', in *Inventory Fluctuations and Economic Stabilization*, part III (papers prepared for the Joint Economic Committee), U.S. Congress, 87th Cong., 1st Sess., Joint Committee Print, Washington, 1961.

DARLING, P. G. and LOVELL, M. C. 'Factors influencing investment in inventories', in *The Brookings Quarterly Econometric Model of the United States*, ed. J. S. Duesenberry *et al.*, North Holland, Amsterdam, 1965, pp. 131–61.

DE LEEUW, F. 'The demand for capital goods by manufacturers: a study of quarterly time series', *Econometrica*, XXX, July, 1962, pp. 407–23.

DUESENBERRY, J. S. *Income, Savings and the Theory of Consumer Behaviour*, Harvard University Press, Cambridge, Mass., 1949.

DUESENBERRY, J. S. *Business Cycles and Economic Growth*, McGraw-Hill, New York, 1958.

DUESENBERRY, J. S., ECKSTEIN, O. and FROMM, G. 'A simulation of the U.S. economy in recession', *Econometrica*, XXVIII, October, 1960, pp. 749–809, reprinted in *Readings in Business Cycles*, the American Economic Association's series of republished articles on economics, X, Irwin, Homewood, Ill., 1965, pp. 237–77.

EVANS, M. K. 'A study of industry investment decisions', *Review of Economics and Statistics*, XLIX, May, 1967, pp. 151–64.

EVANS, W. D. and HOFFENBERG, M. 'The interindustry study for 1947', *Review of Economics and Statistics*, XXXIV, May, 1952, pp. 97–142.

FELS, R. 'Theoretical significance of the 1949 recession', *American Economic Review*, XLV, May, 1955, pp. 358–66.

FELS, R. 'The U.S. downturn of 1948', *American Economic Review*, LV, December, 1965, pp. 1059–76.

FERBER, R. 'Research on household behaviour', in the American Economic Association and the Royal Economic Society *Surveys of Economic Theory*, III, Macmillan, London, 1966, pp. 114–54.

FRIEDMAN, M. *A Theory of the Consumption Function*, a study of NBER, N.Y., Princeton University Press, 1957.

FRIEDMAN, M. and SCHWARTZ, A. J. *A Monetary History of the United States 1867–1960*, NBER Studies in Business Cycles No. 12, Princeton University Press, 1963.

FRIEND, I. and BRONFENBRENNER, J. 'Plant and equipment programs and their realisation', in *Short Term Economic Forecasting*. NBER Studies in Income and Wealth 17, Princeton University Press, 1955, pp. 53–111.

FRISCH, R. and PARIKH, A. K. 'Parametric solution and programming of the Hicksian model', in *Essays on Econometrics and Planning*, ed. C. R. Rao, Pergamon Press, Oxford, 1965, pp. 45–82.

GALBRAITH, J. K. 'The disequilibrium system', *American Economic Review*, XXXVIII, June, 1947, pp. 287–302.

GOLDSMITH, R. *The National Wealth of the United States in the Post-war Period*, studies in capital formation and financing No. 10 for NBER, N.Y., Princeton University Press, 1962.

GOLDSMITH, R. and LIPSEY, R. E. *Studies in the National Balance Sheet of the United States*, II, studies in capital formation and financing No. 11 for NBER, N.Y., Princeton University Press, 1963.

GOODWIN, R. M. 'The nonlinear accelerator and the persistence of business cycles', *Econometrica*, XIX, January, 1951, pp. 1–17.

GORDON, R. A. *Business Fluctuations*, 2nd. ed., Harper and Row, New York, 1961.

GREBLER, L. *Housing Issues in Economic Stabilization Policy*. Occasional paper No. 72, NBER, New York, 1960.

GREBLER, L., BLANK, D. M. and WINNICK, L. *Capital Formation in Residential Real Estates: Trends and Prospects*, studies in capital formation and financing No. 1 for NBER, N.Y., Princeton University Press, 1956.

GREBLER, L. and MAISEL, S. J. 'Determinants of residential construction: a review of present knowledge', in *Impacts of Monetary*

Policy, a study prepared for the commission on money and credit, Prentice-Hall, Englewood Cliffs, N.J., 1963, pp. 475–620.

GRILICHES, Z. *et al.* 'Notes on estimated aggregate quarterly consumption functions', *Econometrica*, XXX, July, 1962, pp. 491–500.

GUTTENTAG, J. M. 'The short cycle in residential construction, 1946–59', *American Economic Review*, LI, June, 1961, pp. 275–98.

HAMBERG, D. 'The recession of 1948–49 in the United States', *Economic Journal*, LXII, March, 1952, pp. 1–14.

HAMBERG, D. '1948–49 recession re-examined: a rejoinder', *Economic Journal*, LXIII, March, 1953, pp. 104–10.

HANSEN, A. H. *Business Cycles and National Income*, expanded edition, Allen and Unwin, London, 1964.

HICKMAN, B. G. *Growth and Stability of the Postwar Economy*, Brookings, Washington, 1960.

HICKMAN, B. G. *Investment Demand and U.S. Economic Growth*, Brookings, Washington, 1965.

HICKS, J. R. *A Contribution to the Theory of the Trade Cycle*, Clarendon Press, Oxford, 1950.

HOLMANS, A. E. *United States Fiscal Policy 1945–1959*, Oxford University Press, 1961.

JOHNSON, H. G. *Essays in Monetary Economics*, Allen and Unwin, London, 1967.

JONES, R. C. 'Transitory income and expenditures on consumption categories', *American Economic Review*, L, May, 1960, pp. 584–92.

JORGENSON, D. W. 'Anticipations and investment behaviour', in *The Brookings Quarterly Econometric Model of the United States*, ed. J. S. Duesenberry *et al.*, North Holland, Amsterdam, 1965, pp. 35–92.

KALDOR, N. 'A model of the trade cycle', *Economic Journal*, L, March, 1940, pp. 78–92.

KLEIN, L. R. *Economic Fluctuations in the U.S., 1921–41*, Wiley, New York, 1950.

KLEIN, L. R. and POPKIN, J. 'An econometric analysis of the postwar relationship between inventory fluctuations and changes in aggregated economic activity', in *Inventory Fluctuations and*

Economic Stabilization, Part III (papers prepared for the Joint Economic Committee), U.S. Congress, 87th Cong., 1st Sess., Joint Committee Print, Washington, 1961.

LERNER, A. P. 'Rising prices', *Review of Economics and Statistics*, XXX, February, 1948, pp. 24–7.

LERNER, A. P. 'The inflationary process: some theoretical aspects', *Review of Economics and Statistics*, XXXI, August, 1949, pp. 193–200.

LEWIS, W. *Federal Fiscal Policy in the Postwar Recessions*, Brookings, Washington, 1962.

LIU, Ta-Chung. 'An exploratory quarterly econometric model of effective demand in the postwar U.S. economy', *Econometrica*, XXXI, July, 1963, pp. 301–48.

LOVELL, M. C. 'Factors determining manufacturing inventory investment', in *Inventory Fluctuations and Economic Stabilization, Part II*, causative factors in the movements of business inventories; papers prepared for the joint economic committee, U.S. Congress 87th Cong., 1st Sess., Joint Committee Print, Washington, 1961.

MACDOUGALL, D. *The World Dollar Problem*, Macmillan, London, 1957.

MAISEL, S. J. 'Nonbusiness construction', in *The Brookings Quarterly Econometric Model of the United States*, ed. J. S. Duesenberry *et al.*, North Holland, Amsterdam, 1965, pp. 179–201.

MATTHEWS, R. C. O. *The Trade Cycle* (Digswell Place: Nisbet and Co.), Cambridge University Press, 1959.

METZLER, L. A. 'The nature and stability of inventory cycles', *Review of Economics and Statistics*, XXIII, August, 1941, pp. 113–29, reprinted in *Readings in Business Cycles*, the American Economic Association series of republished articles on economics, X, Irwin, Homewood, Ill., 1965, pp. 100–29.

MINTZ, I. *Cyclical Fluctuations in the Exports of the United States Since 1879*, NBER Studies in Business Cycles No. 15, NBER, New York, 1967.

MODIGLIANI, F. 'Fluctuations in the saving–income ratio: a problem in economic forecasting', in *Studies in Income and Wealth*, XI, NBER, New York, 1959, pp. 369–441.

MODIGLIANI, F. and BRUMBERG, R. 'Utility analysis and the consumption function: an interpretation of cross-section data', in

Post-Keynesian Economics, ed. K. K. Kurihara, Rutgers University Press, New Brunswick, N.J., 1954, pp. 388–436.

Moore, G. H. ed. *Business Cycle Indicators*. NBER Studies in Business Cycles No. 10, Princeton University Press, 1961.

Moore, G. H. and Shiskin, J. *Indicators of Business Expansions and Contractions*, NBER Occasional paper No. 103, NBER, New York, 1967.

Muth, R. F. 'The demand for non-farm housing', in *The Demand for Durable Goods*, ed. A. Harberger, University of Chicago Press, 1960, pp. 27–96.

Paradiso, L. J. Statement in hearings, *Inventory Fluctuation and Economic Stabilization*, subcommittee on economic stabilization automation, and energy resources, Joint economic committee, U.S. Congress, 87th Cong., 1st Sess., Joint Committee Print, Washington, 1962.

Paradiso, L. J. and Smith, M. A. 'Consumer purchasing and income patterns', *Survey of Current Business*, March, 1959, pp. 18–28.

Polak, J. J. 'Contribution of the September 1949 devaluations to the solution of Europe's dollar problem', *IMF Staff Papers*, II, September, 1951, pp. 1–32.

Reid, M. G. 'Consumption, savings and windfall gains', *American Economic Review*, LII, September, 1962, pp. 728–37.

Reid, M. G. 'Consumption, savings and windfall gains: reply', *American Economic Review*, LIII, June, 1963, pp. 444–5.

Resek, R. N. 'Investment by manufacturing firms: a quarterly time series analysis of industry data', *Review of Economics and Statistics*, XLVIII, August, 1966, pp. 322–33.

Rhomberg, R. R. and Boissonneault, L. 'The foreign sector', in *The Brookings Quarterly Econometric Model of the United States*, ed. J. S. Duesenberry *et al.*, North Holland, Amsterdam, 1965, pp. 375–406.

Samuelson, P. A. 'Interactions between the multiplier analysis and the principle of acceleration', *Review of Economics and Statistics*, XXI, May, 1939, pp. 75–8.

Sapir, M. 'Review of economic forecasts for the transition period', *Studies in Income and Wealth*, XI, NBER, New York, 1949, pp. 271–351.

Scherer, J. 'The report of the President's Commission on Budget concepts: a review', *Federal Reserve Bank of New York Monthly Review*, XLIX, December, 1967, pp. 231–8.

SHACKLE, G. L. S. *A Scheme of Economic Theory*, Cambridge University Press, 1965.

STANBACK, T. M. *Postwar Cycles in Manufacturers' Inventories*. NBER Studies in Business Cycles No. 11, NBER, New York, 1962.

SUITS, D. B. 'The demand for new automobiles in the United States 1939–1956', *Review of Economics and Statistics*, XL, August, 1958, pp. 273–80.

SUITS, D. B. 'Exploring alternative formulations of automobile demand', *Review of Economics and Statistics*, XLIII, February, 1961, pp. 66–9.

SUITS, D. B. 'The determinants of consumer expenditure: a review of present knowledge', in *Impacts of Monetary Policy*, a research study prepared for the commission on money and credit, Prentice-Hall, Englewood Cliffs, N.J., 1963, pp. 1–57.

SUITS, D. B. and SPARKS, G. R. 'Consumption regressions with quarterly data', in *The Brookings Quarterly Econometric Model of the United States*, ed. J. S. Duesenberry *et al.*, North Holland, Amsterdam, 1965, pp. 203–23.

THEIL, H. *Linear Aggregation of Economic Relations*, North Holland, Amsterdam, 1954.

U.S. Bureau of the Census, *Historical Statistics of the United States, Colonial Times to 1957*, Washington, D.C., 1960.

WEIDENBAUM, M. L. 'The timing of the economic impact of government spending', *National Tax Journal*, XII, March, 1959, pp. 79–85.

ZELLNER, A. *et al.* 'Further analysis of the short run consumption function with emphasis on the role of liquid assets', *Econometrica*, XXXIII, July, 1965, pp. 571–81.

INDEX

For Product Safety Concerns and Information please contact our EU representative GPSR@taylorandfrancis.com Taylor & Francis Verlag GmbH, Kaufingerstraße 24, 80331 München, Germany

Printed and bound by CPI Group (UK) Ltd, Croydon, CR0 4YY
08/05/2025
01864467-0001